Applying the Good Lives and Self-Regulation Models to Sex Offender Treatment:

A Practical Guide for Clinicians

Applying the Good Lives and Self-Regulation Models to Sex Offender Treatment:
A Practical Guide for Clinicians

Pamela M. Yates, Ph.D., R.D. Psych
David Prescott, LICSW
Tony Ward, Ph.D., DipClinPsyc

Brandon, Vermont

Copyright © 2010 by the Safer Society Press, Brandon, Vermont

First Edition

All rights reserved. No part of this book may be reproduced in any form or by any electronic or mechanical means, including information storage and retrieval systems, without permission in writing from the publisher, except by a reviewer, who may quote brief passages.

Printed in the United States of America
10 9 8 7 6 5 4 3

Library of Congress Cataloging-in-Publication Data
Yates, Pamela M.
Applying the good lives and self-regulation models to sex offender treatment : a practical guide for clinicians / Pamela M. Yates, David Prescott, Tony Ward.
   p. cm.
Includes bibliographical references.
ISBN 978-1-884444-87-6
1. Sex offenders--Rehabilitation. 2. Cognitive therapy. I. Prescott, David (David Francesca) II. Ward, Tony, 1954 Mar. 17- III. Title.
RC560.S47Y38 2010
616.85'83--dc22
                          2010040447

P.O. Box 340
Brandon, Vermont 05733
www.safersociety.org
(802) 247-3132

Safer Society Press is a program of the Safer Society Foundation, a 501(c)3 nonprofit dedicated to the prevention and treatment of sexual abuse.
For more information, visit our Web site at www.safersociety.org

Applying the Good Lives and Self-Regulation Models to Sex Offender Treatment:
A Practical Guide for Clinicians
$45 plus shipping and handling
Order # WP145

*This book is dedicated to
the clinicians, therapists, community supervision officers,
and others working in the difficult field of sexual offender intervention.
Through their efforts and dedication, they strive to help their clients
and to make the world a safer, better place.*

Contents

Introduction ix

Part I–Foundations of Sexual Offender Treatment
Chapter 1: Fundamentals of Sexual Offender Treatment 3
Chapter 2: Motivation and Effective Client Engagement 23
Chapter 3: Fundamentals of the Good Lives, Self-Regulation, and Integrated Models .. 37

Part II–Assessment And Treatment Planning
Chapter 4: Assessment of the Components of Good Lives 65
Chapter 5: Assessment of Self-Regulation Determination of Offense Pathway 87
Chapter 6: Integrating Assessment 105
Chapter 7: Developing a Case Formulation and Treatment Plan 125

Part III–Treatment
Chapter 8: Treatment Using the Integrated Good Lives/Self-Regulation-Revised Model .. 149
Chapter 9: Offense Progression I: Personal History............................. 181
Chapter 10: Offense Progression II: Offense Disclosure 195
Chapter 11: Self-Regulation Pathway Treatment Methods 221
Chapter 12: Developing an Integrated Good Lives/Self-Regulation Plan............ 245

Part IV–Post-Treatment Follow-Up and Community Reintegration
Chapter 13: Post-Treatment Maintenance and Supervision 277

About the Authors... 293
References 295

Introduction

The aim of this book is to provide clinicians, parole and probation supervisors, and others involved in the treatment and supervision of sexual offenders with a working understanding of how to utilize the Good Lives and Self-Regulation-Revised models in practice. Since their initial development, the Good Lives Model (GLM) of offender rehabilitation (Ward and Gannon, 2006; Ward and Stewart, 2003) and the Self-Regulation Model (SRM) of the offense process (Ward and Hudson, 1998) have been combined into a comprehensive, integrated approach to the treatment and supervision of sexual offenders (Yates and Ward, 2008). The GLM approach is intended to augment and enhance intervention delivered within the framework of the Risk/Need/Responsivity Model (Andrews and Bonta, 2007; Ward, Melser, and Yates, 2007) and using a cognitive-behavioral orientation, both of which have been found to be effective in reducing re-offending (Andrews and Bonta, 2007; Dowden and Andrews, 2000; Hanson, Bourgon, Helmus, and Hodgson, 2009; Hanson et al., 2002; Hanson and Yates, 2004; Lösel and Schmucker, 2005; Yates, 2002, 2003).

Treatment of sexual offenders has traditionally followed adaptations of the Relapse Prevention Model (RPM) (Marques, Day, and Nelson, 1992; Pithers, 1990; 1991); however, the RP approach is problematic when applied to sexual offenders, for numerous reasons (Hanson, 2006; Laws, 2003; Laws and Ward, 2006; Ward and Hudson, 1998; Yates, 2003, 2005, 2007; Yates and Kingston, 2005; Yates and Ward, 2007). As a result of problems with the RP approach, the Self-Regulation Model (SRM), specifically developed with sexual offenders, was proposed as an alternative approach (Ward and Hudson, 1998; Ward, Hudson, and Marshall, 1995). Self-regulation is a complex set of goal-setting and decision-making processes that direct action through the control and integration of cognition, affect, and behavior (Baumeister and Heatherton, 1996; Baumeister and Vohs, 2004; Karoly, 1993). As compared to the RPM, the SRM is better suited to address the heterogeneity of, and motivation for, sexual offending. For example, the SRM proposes four distinct pathways in the offense process, whereas the RPM elucidates only a single pathway to offending.

Subsequent to the development of the SRM, the Good Lives Model (GLM) was proposed as an overarching approach to the rehabilitation of offenders (Ward and Gannon, 2006; Ward and Stewart, 2003). The GLM is based on the assumption that risk-based and avoidance-oriented approaches, such as the RNR and RP models, are necessary but insufficient to address the treatment of sexual offenders. Instead, the GLM proposes that sexual offenders, like all human beings, seek to attain important goals in life (termed *primary human goods* or *primary goods*), as part of an overall good lives plan or roadmap to achieving a fulfilling and well-balanced life. What differs with this clientele from non-offenders, however, is that sexual offenders often attempt to meet these personal needs via harmful behavior toward others. That is, while their goals are important and valued, the problem lies in the means they use to obtain primary goods and to achieve their goals in life. In following the GLM, treatment is explicitly framed and presented to clients as a positive, approach-oriented activity designed to assist them to achieve a better life. Treatment activities are conducted directly in service of this goal in addition to managing risk to re-offend.

The Good Lives and Self-Regulation models have recently been integrated into a comprehensive approach to guide the treatment of sexual offenders (Ward, Yates, and Long, 2006; Yates and Ward, 2008). This combined model explicitly addresses both the promotion of a good life and the management of risk. It is based on an understanding of the relationships between risk, sexual offending, and clients' attempts to implement a good lives plan. The GLM/SRM-R approach also includes assessment of primary and secondary goods, offense-related goals, strategies, and pathways, and their interrelationships (Yates, Kingston, and Ward, 2009). The GLM/SRM-R utilizes the full range of cognitive-behavioral treatment methods in practice in order to maximize the effectiveness of intervention in assisting clients to manage risk and attain good lives.

This book was designed for clinicians and community supervisors responsible for intervention with sexual offenders who are well versed, experienced, and trained in effective practices with sexual offenders (i.e., the RNR Model and cognitive-behavioral treatment approaches, among others). It is assumed that users have experience and specialized training in assessment and treatment. While elements of these models are reviewed, it is important to note that this book does not provide a comprehensive guide to using these approaches. The focus is instead on assisting users to integrate the Good Lives and Self-Regulation-Revised models into existing practice using the risk/need/responsivity approach and cognitive-behavioral methods. It is also noted that this book is not designed to provide explicit "how-to" instructions for delivering treatment to sexual offenders, as effective treatment and supervision are therapeutic exercises rather than scripted instructional activities (although a framework for treatment targets and interventions is required).

In addition to the above, the reader will note a change in language used within this book. Typically, texts and treatment itself use such terms as *deficit, deviance, distortion, risk,* and *prevention.* All such words are associated with negative evaluations or negative expectancies (Mann and Shingler, 2006). By contrast, the approach described herein is a positive model, based on the assumption that people are more likely to embrace positive change and personal development—and to be motivated to participate in treatment—when the language used is non-judgmental and when the approach to intervention is future-oriented, optimistic, and focused on what clients can personally gain from treatment.

This book is structured in four sections: (I) an introduction to basic constructs; (II) assessment and treatment planning; (III) treatment, and (IV) post-treatment maintenance and supervision.

In part I, chapters 1 and 2 describe the essential foundations of effective intervention with sexual offenders, including the Risk/Need/Responsivity Model, cognitive-behavioral approaches, empirically-based targets of treatment, and motivational approaches that increase engagement with treatment and the change process. Chapter 3, the concluding chapter in the first section, describes in detail the foundations and assumptions of the Good Lives Model, the Self-Regulation-Revised Model, and their integration into a comprehensive approach to intervention.

Part II (assessment and treatment planning) details assessment of the GLM constructs, such as primary goods, secondary goods, and their relationship to offending. These constructs are illustrated in chapter 4. Chapter 5 includes guidelines for evaluating offense-related goals, strategies, and the pathway followed in the progression to offending. Chapter 6 provides information pertaining to integrating GLM and SRM-R assessment into an overall evaluation of clients, including risk and other relevant assessment. Chapter 7 concludes part II with an analysis of case formulation and treatment planning.

In part III, chapter 8 describes using the Good Lives Model to guide treatment within a risk-management and cognitive-behavioral orientation and the integrated GLM/SRM-R approach. Chapters 9 and 10, respectively, provide specific treatment activities pertaining to the development of a relevant personal history and an analysis of the offense progression and patterns. The two chapters also address vulnerability factors for offending (i.e., an "autobiography"), and the offense progression, which provides an alternative to the concept of the offense "cycle" typically used in treatment.

Part III's chapter 11 addresses the variation in approaches to treatment for clients who have followed different pathways in offending, based on the different motivations and self-regulation styles associated with offending behavior within each pathway. Each of these chapters also concentrates on the elements of the GLM in all of these treatment activities. Lastly, in this section, chapter 12 describes the process of constructing an integrated good lives/self-regulation plan as an alternative to the relapse prevention plan that therapists and clients traditionally develop in treatment.

Finally, in part IV, chapter 13 addresses the use of the integrated GLM/SRM-R in post-treatment maintenance and community supervision. In addition to the standard elements of these activities, such as monitoring risk and entrenching skills learned in treatment, this chapter focuses on the additional need to assist clients with the implementation of their plans for achieving well-balanced and fulfilling lives, and looks at the contribution of these plans to reducing the risk to re-offend.

PART I

*Foundations of
Sexual Offender Treatment*

CHAPTER 1

Fundamentals of Sexual Offender Treatment

The ultimate goal of sexual offender treatment is to prevent a recurrence of re-offending. In order to achieve this objective, sexual offender programs use specific methods and procedures, and aim to change specific social and psychological factors known to be causally linked with sexual offending, both in empirical research and in individual clients' cases. Effective and comprehensive treatment adheres to the following specific criteria (see Hanson and Yates, 2004; Yates, 2002, 2003, in press, for reviews), including

- a cognitive-behavioral orientation to intervention;
- the use and application of the Risk/Need/Responsivity Model of offender intervention;
- the use of cognitive, behavioral, and social learning methods of intervention;
- a skills and competency-based approach; and
- the use of effective therapeutic methods to enhance clients' engagement with treatment and to increase their motivation.

COGNITIVE–BEHAVIORAL TREATMENT

Cognitive-behavioral treatment is presently the most widely accepted and effective type of intervention with sexual offenders (Hanson et al., 2002; Lösel and Schmucker, 2005). Cognitive-behavioral treatment is based on the premise that cognition, affect, and behavior are closely linked, with each influencing the other. Within this model, sexual offending is regarded as a pattern of behavior that has developed over time through modeling and learning. It also is behavior that has been maintained through reinforcement and an activity that results in entrenched habitual responses to certain specific situations that facilitate sexual offending. In treatment, cognitive-behavioral intervention aims to equip individuals with the skills and competencies necessary to effectively cope with their life problems and to handle any areas of difficulty they encounter. In implementing treatment, a skills-based approach—in which individuals develop, enhance, and reinforce specific skills to prevent re-offending—is considered an essential element of cognitive-behavioral treatment (Hanson, 1999; Hanson and Yates, 2004; Yates et al., 2000).

In addition to following a cognitive-behavioral orientation, effective treatment of offenders is guided by the principles of risk, need, and responsivity (RNR Model; Andrews and Bonta, 2007). The principles of this model represent a framework within which cognitive-behavioral techniques are used to change behavior. For example, problem-solving skills are imparted in sex offender treatment to help clients solve various problems in more adaptive ways, both in terms of life problems and risk management. Problem-solving training may result in reduced impulsivity—a dynamic risk factor or criminogenic need associated with offending (Andrews and Bonta, 2007). The principles of the RNR Model consider the conditions under which treatment is most likely to be effective and allow interventions to be tailored to individuals' risk, needs, and personal circumstances and conditions in order to be most effective in reducing risk. Significant limitations accompany taking a solely risk-based approach, however, and, therefore, this approach has been integrated within a broader framework (i.e., the integrated GLM/SRM-R; Ward et al., 2007; Yates and Ward, 2008).

Lastly, enhancing motivation through specific techniques and therapist characteristics is considered essential to the effective treatment of sexual offenders. The motivation factor focuses on the importance of the therapeutic relationship with offenders, and reminds practitioners that a responsive, motivational approach is essential to treatment success. Research has shown that sexual offender therapists whose styles are warm, empathic, rewarding, supportive, and directive are more effective than those who are harsh and confrontational (Marshall, 2005). Research shows this finding to be consistent in other treatment areas as well, such as depression, mental health interventions, and addictions. In all those arenas, research finds that a positive therapeutic relationship between the client and the therapist accounts for a significant proportion of the variance in treatment outcome (Duncan, Miller, Wampold, and Hubble 2009). With respect to sexual offenders, the establishment of a strong therapeutic alliance has been found to be associated with reduced recidivism rates (Wong, Witte, and Nicholaichuk, 2002), and a recent meta-analysis found significant treatment effects associated with positive therapist characteristics (Hanson, 2006). Aside from the pragmatic advantages of establishing a strong therapeutic alliance, powerful ethical reasons support it as well (Ward and Salmon, in press). These reasons center on the importance of treating offenders with respect and seeking to work collaboratively with them during therapy, as opposed to imposing therapy upon them. Unfortunately, many clinicians believe themselves to be more helpful than their clients find them to be (Beech and Fordham, 1997). This finding speaks to the importance of the clients' views of the therapeutic process and to their perceptions of therapists' styles and helpfulness.

Each of these principles and elements of treatment is reviewed below. It is to be noted that this chapter is not intended to provide a comprehensive overview or prescriptive guide to treatment, but rather to offer a review of the common principles and elements of effective treatment of sexual offenders.

PRINCIPLES OF RISK, NEED, AND RESPONSIVITY

The *risk principle* states that the intensity of treatment should be matched to the level of risk posed by each individual client, with the most intensive levels of intervention reserved for higher risk offenders, and lower intensity or no intervention applied to lower risk offenders. The level of risk is typically established via assessment of the client's static (unchangeable) and dynamic (changeable) re-offense factors. Static factors associated with sexual offense risk include such factors as young age, previous offense history, specific offense characteristics (e.g., male victims, stranger victims, non-contact offenses), and early onset of sexual offending (e.g., Hanson and Bussière 1998; Hanson and Morton-Bourgon, 2005; Hanson and Thornton, 1999).

The *need principle* states that the most effective interventions are those that target offenders' criminogenic needs or dynamic risk factors—those factors that are associated with risk for re-offending, but that can be changed through intervention, and that when changed, are associated with changes in risk and recidivism. Dynamic risk factors can also be conceptualized as psychological vulnerabilities or mechanisms that, in conjunction with situational triggers, culminate in sexually abusive actions (Beech and Ward, 2004). Dynamic risk factors are, therefore, clinically significant social and psychological features of offenders and their lives that can be modified in some way. These risk factors are legitimate and empirically-derived and represent specific targets in treatment. In practice, this means that the therapist needs to differentiate between treatment targets that may be clinically desirable to change but that are unrelated to recidivism risk, and treatment targets that have been empirically shown to be related to sexual offending (Gordon and Hover, 1998; Yates, 2009a). As discussed in chapter 2 and throughout this volume, however, addressing noncriminogenic needs can strengthen the therapeutic alliance and increase engagement with treatment (Ward and Maruna, 2007; Ward et al., 2006).

Presently, dynamic risk factors demonstrated to be associated with sexual offending include such factors as problems with sexual self-regulation (e.g., problems of deviant sexual interests or sexual preoccupations), negative social influences, intimacy deficits, emotional identification with children (among child molesters), and problems with general self-regulation (e.g., impulsivity, poor cognitive problem-solving skills; Hanson, Harris, Scott, and Helmus, 2007). In addition, some sexual offenders are at risk to re-offend with nonsexual offenses. Often, different risk factors, such as antisocial orientation and problems with general self-regulation, predict non-sexual re-offending, although some overlap exists among factors that predict sexual and non-sexual re-offending (Hanson and Morton-Bourgon, 2005). Dynamic risk factors have consistently received comparatively less research attention in comparison to static risk factors (Yates and Kingston, 2007).

The *responsivity principle* states that interventions should be delivered in a manner that is consistent with offenders' learning styles, abilities, and personal circumstances. Important considerations include language, culture, personality style or disorders, motivation, anxiety, mental disorder, cognitive abilities, and so forth. According to this principle, such factors influence the interaction between the client and the treatment process. This interaction, in turn, influences the effectiveness of the intervention for that individual. Thus, in order to be most effective, sexual offender treatment programs must tailor their services to match those individual characteristics. For example, clients who have literacy issues will fare less well in a treatment program that requires significant written work. Thus, it is incumbent on treatment providers to find alternative opportunities for these individuals to complete the required program work. Examples of creative methods a therapist can use include assigning another participant as a mentor to assist the client, reducing the requirement for written work, or allowing the client to produce pictorial rather than written work. Similarly, treatment providers must adapt their style and mode of service delivery so as to maximize effective participation in treatment. For example, as will be seen in chapter 2, clients who deny, minimize, or do not recognize problematic behavior will require additional work on motivational enhancement either prior to treatment or within the treatment context, in order that they may fully engage with the change process. Consider the following example:

Example: Responsivity Principle

Bill is a Native American man whose family lives on a reservation. He presents for treatment with a general deep distrust of authority and with a specific distrust of the Anglo-American culture. Because his offenses were committed against minors, the court has imposed limitations on his ability to visit his own children. Although this ruling appears to be a straightforward cautionary measure to his treatment providers, Bill experiences this restriction as a chilling reminder of the historical relocation of Native Americans by Anglo-Saxon authorities. Likewise, his family is less supportive of his treatment efforts in part because of their own concerns about unfair treatment by "the system." Bill's distrust of his treatment providers deepens as he comes to consider them agents of a police state rather than the therapists they believe themselves to be. Not surprisingly, Bill becomes resistant to engaging in treatment. A brief assessment shows that Bill very likely has an undiagnosed attention deficit hyperactivity disorder, creating further difficulty for his meaningful engagement in treatment.

As can be seen in the above example, it is highly unlikely that Bill can meaningfully engage in treatment until he is able to explore and resolve his concerns about participation and his therapist. Bill's therapist will want to ensure that she listens with empathic interest to his concerns. Bill will doubtless be ambivalent about engaging with an Anglo-American therapist and will have many questions about his own willingness to engage in treatment if it seems to him to be nothing more than a means of social control across cultures. The therapist will need to accept this perspective as central to Bill's existence and make sure that the treatment process is focused on relevant personal change rather than simply being about complying with orders of the court. This approach is likely so important in Bill's case that, if it is not taken, a working alliance with the therapist will not be established, and Bill will not benefit as much as possible from treatment, and could eventually drop out. It is also possible that treatment for Bill will be deemed unsuccessful by the therapist. The therapist will want to be diligent in monitoring the therapeutic relationship with Bill, and she must never take this relationship for granted. It can be easy to think of therapeutic rapport as something developed at the outset of treatment and that remains stable throughout treatment. The establishment of such rapport is seldom what happens early in sexual offender treatment, however, and it requires continual work to attain and maintain. Bill's therapist will want to check in with Bill frequently, solicit his feedback about how things are going, and work to refine and strengthen their working relationship throughout the course of treatment.

The therapist will also need to find ways to approach and frame treatment in Bill's own cultural terms. For example, if Bill's culture is one that holds a more collective than individualistic orientation, Bill will likely have difficulty with standard psychological constructs that focus on the individual. If that is the case, the therapist will need to ensure that these constructs are conveyed to Bill in such a way as to allow him to interpret them more collectively. For example, Bill may experience difficulty with developing empathy for the individual victim of his offense if his cultural belief is that his entire community was harmed by his behavior in addition to the victim. Thus, if Bill is to fully engage in this treatment exercise, the therapist will need to allow him to conduct victim empathy work that focuses both on the individual victim as well as on Bill's community.

Given that Bill very likely also has an undiagnosed attention deficit hyperactivity disorder (ADHD), the therapist will need to make appropriate referrals for an additional diagnosis and possible treatment for the ADHD, and she must do so very carefully due to the cultural and interpersonal reasons mentioned above. The therapist will further want to ensure that treatment sessions include a sufficient number of rest breaks and, depending on circumstances, access to skills training for Bill to focus himself (e.g., bio- or neuro-feedback) in order to improve Bill's participation in treatment as well as his overall functioning as he attempts to make changes to his life.

The therapist will also need to understand that Bill may not be able to focus on treatment as well as other clients who do not have ADHD, and so she will need to respond accordingly. For example, the therapist will need to monitor herself to ensure that she is not interpreting Bill's behavior as simply not paying attention or as disengagement. She will need to find strategies to assist Bill during times when he is unfocussed in treatment. Other group members should also be recruited to assist Bill. If the therapist simply threatens to enforce group rules and impose sanctions for "disruptive" behavior, such actions will be ineffective and can easily be perceived as dismissal of Bill's legitimate fears, suggesting those fears are irrelevant and without merit.

Finally, the therapist will need to be highly sensitive to Bill's family situation. After all, the therapist is only one small part of Bill's life, while his family members are undoubtedly more important to him. Bill will experience considerable stress about disclosing aspects of his life that could be harmful to them or that could place their relationships, or his relationship with them, in jeopardy. It is likely that his family members will be as distrustful as Bill of what they perceive to be an alien, unjust, and dominant culture.

In total, Bill's therapist will have no shortage of responsivity elements to attend to before Bill can consider and implement substantive changes to his life. Care must be taken by the therapist to adjust treatment to Bill's needs and expressed concerns, and to closely monitor his responses for any disengagement or negative reactions, at which point further adjustments to therapeutic methods may be needed. To do otherwise will reduce the potential effectiveness of treatment for Bill.

With respect to the risk, need, and responsivity principles overall, research indicates that correctional treatment in general is most effective and most cost-effective when it adheres to these principles (Andrews and Bonta, 2007; Correctional Service Canada, 2009; Gendreau and Goggin, 1996, 1997; Gendreau, Little, and Goggin, 1996; Gordon and Nicholaichuk, 1996; Hanson et al., 2009; Nicholaichuk, 1996; Prentky and Burgess, 1990). In addition, a recent meta-analytic study demonstrated that these principles also apply to sexual offender treatment specifically, and the study showed that treatment is most effective when programs adhere to all three principles as compared to adhering to only one or two of these (Hanson et al., 2009). As noted above, however, some problems have been identified with the Risk/Need/Responsivity Model—specifically that, because of its focus on problematic situations and risk management, the model is unlikely to sufficiently increase offender motivation and does not consider the influence of non-criminogenic needs on treatment progress and outcome (Ward et al., 2007). This potential failing is addressed more fully in the following two chapters, which sequentially address motivating clients to participate in treatment (chapter 2) and the Good Lives Model (chapter 3).

Components of Treatment

Specific problems have been identified in research as appropriate goals for intervention in sexual offender treatment. These factors have been found to be related to either the occurrence of offending and/or to re-offending. Other treatment targets have received less research support, but are viewed as clinically relevant and are, therefore, included in many treatment programs. Common treatment targets include the following.

Sexual Self-Regulation/Deviant Sexual Fantasy, Arousal, and Interests

Deviant sexual fantasy, arousal, and interests are hypothesized to develop as a result of early developmental and neurobiological factors, observational learning, modeling, reinforcement, pairing of deviant sexual stimuli with sexual arousal or aggression, and the interactions amongst these factors, each of which influences the development and maintenance of deviant sexual interest and behavior (Abel and Rouleau, 1986; Hanson, 1999; Laws and Marshall, 1990; Marshall, Anderson, and Fernandez, 1999; Ward and Beech, 2006; Wilson and Yates, 2005, Yates, 2002, 2003).

It is important to note that deviant sexual arousal alone does not explain sexual offending behavior. Such arousal occurs in conjunction with other variables that result in the actual expression of sexually aggressive behavior. Specifically, sexual aggression occurs as a function of numerous contextual, affective, neurobiological, and cognitive factors, such as negative mood, desire for power and control, sexual preference for nonconsensual sexual activities, self-regulation deficits, and excessive alcohol use (Barbaree, Marshall, Yates, and Lightfoot, 1983; Blader and Marshall, 1989; Groth, 1979; Johnston, Ward, and Hudson, 1997; Marshall et al., 1999; Marshall and Barbaree, 1988; Marshall and Darke, 1982; McKibben, Proulx, and Lusignan, 1994; Pithers, Beal, Armstrong, and Petty, 1989; Proulx, McKibben, and Lusignan, 1996; Ward and Beech, 2006; Ward, Keenan, and Hudson, 1998; Yates, 1996, 2002, 2003). Thus, while treatment can involve decreasing sexual arousal to inappropriate stimuli and increasing arousal to appropriate stimuli, such as age-appropriate and consenting partners (Abel, Becker, and Cunningham-Rathner, 1984; Lockhart, Sanders, and Cleveland, 1988), as well as pharmacological interventions as needed, research supports taking a broad approach to treatment, rather than targeting only deviant sexual preferences. In other words, individuals commit sexual offenses for a wide range of reasons (Ward, Polaschek, and Beech, 2006), each of which should be addressed in treatment when relevant to individual clients.

Cognition

Research indicates that all behavior—including sexual offending behavior—is influenced by attitudes, beliefs, cognitive processes, and information processing (Hanson and Scott, 1995; Johnston and Ward, 1996; Stangor and Ford, 1992; Ward, Hudson, Johnston, and Marshall, 1997).

Historically, sexual offender treatment has primarily targeted clients' cognitive distortions, based on findings that such distortions play an active role in sexual offending via clients' interactions with the environment (Abel et al., 1984; Barbaree, 1991; Johnston and Ward, 1996; Laws, 1989; Marshall and Pithers, 1994; Murphy, 1990; Stermac and Segal, 1989). Cognitive distortions are defined as assumptions, beliefs, thinking styles, or self-statements about deviant sexual behaviors that facilitate sexual offending (Abel and Rouleau, 1986; Plaud and Newberry, 1996; Ward et al., 2006). Examples of cognitive distortions include specific statements that serve to minimize, justify, or deny either the offending behavior or the harm caused to victims.

Recently, greater attention has been paid to cognitive schemas in treatment rather than, as done previously, focusing predominantly on cognitive distortions. Cognitive schemas are defined as broad cognitive structures whose function is to process, organize, interpret, and evaluate incoming information in order to direct cognitive activity and behavior (Beck, 1964, 1967, 1976). Based on an individual's previous experiences, schemas contain specific themes, attitudes, beliefs, stereotypes, attributions, and assumptions about such things as the self, the world, and others. Schemas provoke affective and behavioral responses, and influence the processing of information in specific circumstances. Within a social information processing model (Augoustinos and Walker, 1995; Fiske and Taylor, 1991; Gannon, 2009; Gannon, Ward, Beech, and Fisher, 2007), individuals are proposed to be *cognitive misers* who respond relatively automatically and unconsciously to incoming information in the context of pre-existing beliefs. That is, when confronted with ambiguous or threatening circumstances, individuals encode, interpret, and respond to incoming social information by filtering this information through existing cognitive schemas, attending to information that confirms beliefs and discounting information that is incongruent with the schemas (Barber, 1988; Fiske and Taylor, 1991; Welford, 1960).

For a brief example, let's return to Bill, the client mentioned earlier. Bill holds a number of beliefs about society, about sexual offender treatment, and about the therapists who provide treatment. His beliefs and attitudes will present a challenge to many therapists. For example, if he believes that the world is a dangerous place, Bill will likely respond quickly to overtures by professionals as evidence that he is being singled out by an uncaring state. Phrases such as, "I'm here to help," or, "I understand where you're coming from," will likely be perceived by Bill as false and will backfire. Bill already has a cognitive belief system in place regarding his world and his place within it. His beliefs are characterized by distrust and fear. It is much more likely that he will view these statements as confirmatory evidence of the therapist's disingenuousness than he will as attempts to be helpful. Bill, like other humans, is simply filtering the social information from the therapist through his schemas, and he is doing so automatically. This response is one reason why the therapist will have to build and re-build therapeutic rapport throughout the course of Bill's treatment, as well as be aware of, and responsive to, Bill's interpretation of the world.

Cognitive schemas are held by all individuals. They serve an evolutionary function and have survival value by providing a framework for making rapid decisions in challenging situations (Beck, Freeman, and Davis, 2004). For example, the ability to make rapid social judgments in uncertain situations based on past experiences (e.g., a stranger starting a conversation with an individual in a poorly monitored public area) can mean the difference between safety and serious harm. Similarly, schemas reflecting suspiciousness and the belief that the world is a dangerous place (see, for example, the case of Bill described above) may have served an adaptive function for individuals who, during their early development, were exposed to environments characterized by abuse and/or lack of safety. Products of cognitive schemas, such as cognitive distortions, attributions, and self-verbalizations, are manifestations of these broader schemas, and are activated in the presence of situational cues, particularly in ambiguous or threatening situations (Mann and Shingler, 2006).

In interpreting social and other cues, individuals do so in such a manner as to match pre-existing beliefs. People search for confirmatory evidence of their own beliefs, and they discount evidence that does not confirm their beliefs (Harris, 1991; Williams, Watts, Macleod, and Mathews, 1997). For example, a client who views sexual offender treatment providers as agents of a cruel and punitive system can easily interpret references to legal impositions by the therapist as further evidence of this belief. In such a situation, clients are likely to dismiss statements and behavior that suggest other motivations by the therapist. Similarly, clients with a strong belief that women are not trustworthy may easily disregard situations in which women are in fact straightforward and honest, ignoring evidence that contradicts these beliefs and paying attention to information that supports this schema.

Cognitive schemas related to aggression—including sexual aggression—include such client attitudes as hostility, deceit, suspicion, or sexual entitlement. Researchers hypothesize that these attitudes result from developmental experiences and reinforcement and are extremely influential in leading to adverse modes of perceiving and responding to the world, as well as to dysfunctional interpersonal relationships (e.g., Beck, 1999; Beck et al., 2004; Hanson, Gizzarelli, and Scott, 1994; Huesmann, 1988; Malamuth and Brown, 1994; Malamuth, Heavey, and Linz, 1993; McFall, 1990). Such schemas increase the likelihood of sexually aggressive behavior being selected as an appropriate course of action in a given situation (Mann and Beech, 2003).

Example: Influence of Cognitive Schemas

Ramos believes that when women say no to sex, they actually mean yes, and that they are being consciously deceptive more often than not. Ramos also believes that having a desire for sex entitles him to seek it out by whatever means are available to him. Ramos's chaotic family of origin helped to instill adversarial schemas in him from a very young age. Although many who grow up in adversity learn to challenge their dysfunctional beliefs, Ramos has consistently viewed perceived and real wrongdoing by women as further evidence that they cannot be trusted. Likewise, he views evidence of wrongdoing as further justification to behave as he pleases, and he quickly dismisses any argument to the contrary.

Similarly, the notion of implicit theories has recently been put forward as a refinement of the schema theory of cognitive distortions among sexual offenders. Among sexual offenders, specific schemas have been identified, such as grievance, control, and entitlement, as well as regarding oneself as a victim, having disrespect for particular women, and viewing children as sexual beings (Keenan and Ward, 2003; Mann and Hollin, 2001; Neidigh and Krop, 1992; Polaschek and Gannon, 2004; Polaschek and Ward, 2002; Ward, 2000; Ward and Keenan, 1999). These implicit theories are concerned both with general assumptions about people and the world, as well as with specific assumptions regarding women, children, and/or specific victims.

Specific schemas or implicit theories (Ward and Keenan, 1999) have been identified among sexual offenders and include the following:

- Children are viewed as sexual objects, capable of making decisions with respect to sexual behavior and consenting to sexual activity.

- The offender feels a sense of entitlement, in that he has the right to take whatever course of action he selects, regardless of its impact on others.

- The offender believes that the world is a dangerous place and that others will act against him or his interests; as a result, the offender may act out against others before they have the opportunity to harm him first.

- The offender believes that his personality and sexuality are uncontrollable and, as a result, he does not attempt to control harmful or deviant sexual urges, and believes that he cannot change.

- The offender believes that sexual activity, even if nonconsensual, is not harmful if he does not use other, non-sexual violence, resulting in the belief that his behavior does not constitute a sexual offense.

Although a client's ability to change cognitive distortions still forms an important part of treatment, it is more effective to view such distortions as the *products* of cognitive schemas, with schemas representing larger and broader belief structures. These structures provide the foundation from which very specific beliefs manifest as cognitive distortions. For example, an individual may believe that children are sexual beings capable of consenting to sexual activity (the cognitive schema). In a specific situation in the presence of a child against whom he offends, the individual may state that the child was sexually provocative in her behavior and that she was willing to engage in sexual activity (the cognitive distortion). In this example, the schemas provide the framework or implicit theory through which the individual interprets a child's innocuous behavior as sexual, and the offending behavior is subsequently justified to oneself and to others via cognitive distortions. An appropriate analogy might be to a river, where cognitions and schemas interact as a confluence "upstream" from the cognitive distortions that take place further along the river's path. Without the underlying schemas, no related cognitive distortions would exist. As such, both schemas and individual cognitions are important targets for change in treatment (Gannon and Polaschek, 2006; Mann and Beech, 2003; Ward and Keenan, 1999; Yates, 2009b).

Social Functioning, Attachment, Intimacy, and Relationships

The literature on sexual offenders indicates that they often experience considerable social functioning and relationship problems, intimacy deficits, difficulties forming and maintaining relationships, self-esteem problems, and loneliness. However, not all those characteristics are supported by research with respect to their association with recidivism (Garlick, Marshall, and Thorton, 1996; Hanson and Bussière, 1998; Hanson et al., 2007; Hanson and Morton-Bourgon, 2005; Keenan and Ward, 2000; Marshall, 1996; Marshall and Barbaree, 1990; Marshall, Bryce, Hudson, Ward, and Moth, 1996; Marshall, Champagne, Brown, and Miller, 1997; Marshall and Hambley, 1996; Marshall et al., 1999; Seidman, Marshall, Hudson, and Robertson, 1994; Smallbone and Dadds, 2000; Ward, Hudson, Marshall, and Siegert, 1995). For example, difficulties with problem-solving and intimacy deficits are directly or indirectly associated with sexual offending (Hanson et al., 2009), whereas self-esteem and loneliness are not (Hanson and Bussière 1998; Hanson and Morton-Bourgon, 2005). However, sexual offenders themselves report that such factors as low self-esteem, loneliness, depression, and the like, underlie or trigger their offending behavior. Thus, many of these non-criminogenic factors may have as much, or more, to do with motivation and the capacity to change as they do with a specific re-offense process. For example, although low self-esteem does not appear in research to be directly related to re-offending, it can be difficult to make progress in treatment without the offender gaining some sense of positive belief in himself. Enhancing self-esteem can also create a positive sense of expectancy and the belief for the client that he can make meaningful changes in his life. In addition, as discussed in chapter 3, these factors are also integral to the Good Lives Model of intervention.

As a result of early adverse developmental and learning experiences, sexual offenders may develop problematic attachments to others, which in turn can cause them to have difficulty relating effectively to others. These early experiences can also result in apprehension about relationships, lack of satisfaction in relationships, lack of intimacy, and sexual aggression (Marshall et al., 1999; Ward et al., 1995; Ward et al., 1999). In addition, child molesters frequently describe their motivation to offend as driven by a need for affection, intimacy, and closeness (Finkelhor, 1986; Hudson, Wales, and Ward, 1998; Ward, Hudson, and France, 1993). Intimacy deficits among both child molesters and rapists appear to be related to a general lack of intimacy in all relationships (Bumby and Hansen, 1997), and negative social influences have been identified as a dynamic risk factor in re-offending (Hanson et al., 2007).

Research has also shown that self-esteem is significantly lower in sexual offenders than in matched controls (Marshall, 1996; Marshall and Mazucco, 1995), and that improved self-esteem following treatment is significantly correlated with changes in other treatment targets, such as empathy, intimacy, loneliness, and deviant sexual preferences (Marshall, 1997; Marshall et al., 1997). However, low self-esteem on its own is ultimately not directly related to re-offending, but it may moderate changes in other risk factors that are related to recidivism.

Treatment of sexual offenders typically involves understanding their attachment styles, relationship and intimacy deficits, experiences of loneliness, and feelings of low self-worth. The goal of treatment for these clients is the development and reinforcement of effective relationship skills and strategies, and the building of a sense of self-efficacy.

Emotion Regulation

Early treatment programs typically included a component that targeted the development of anger management skills. Researchers and therapists now acknowledge that treatment should focus on the regulation or management of emotions more broadly than solely focusing on anger. The regulation of emotions covers a wide range of related emotional competencies, including the identification, control, management, and effective communication of emotion in oneself and others (Ward et al., 2006; Yates et al., 2000). General self-regulation is a dynamic risk factor that has been found to be associated with both sexual and non-sexual re-offending (Hanson et al., 2007; Hanson and Morton-Bourgon, 2005).

Although little research has been done in the area of the regulation of emotions and its relationship to offending, researchers widely believe that many sexual offenders lack the skills that would allow them to effectively identify and manage their emotions (e.g., Miner, Day, and Nafpaktits, 1989). In addition, offenders report that negative emotional states such as anxiety, guilt, and loneliness are associated with deviant sexual arousal and fantasy (Hanson and Bussière, 1998; McKibben, Proulx, and Lusignan, 1994). Furthermore, a variety of both positive and negative emotional states and processes appear to be associated with sexual offending behavior at various stages during an offense (Hall and Hirschman, 1991; Johnston and Ward, 1996; Marshall, Hudson, Jones, and Fernandez, 1995; Pithers, 1990; Ward, Louden, Hudson, and Marshall, 1995). Importantly, individuals' ability to cope with negative affect also plays a major role in general psychological well-being when confronted with negative or stressful life events (Endler and Parker, 1990).

Individual clients will experience different affective states at different times during offending. For example, some offenders show consistently high levels of positive affect throughout their sexual offenses (Johnston and Ward, 1996; Ward and Hudson, 1998). For these offenders, it is suggested that sexual offending will occur more frequently because it is desirable and pleasurable and is, therefore, reinforced. Conversely, other individuals may offend as a result of attempting to escape negative emotional states (Ward et al., 1995) or due to a lack of emotional control. For example, some child molesters may lack confidence, experience loneliness, be fearful of relationships with adults, or may feel more comfortable in relationships with children than with adults. In escaping negative emotional states, sexual offending behavior may be reinforcing because it alleviates these negative affective states, at least temporarily.

Given the above, treatment in this area targets emotional deficits associated with sexual offending behavior and focuses on the development and reinforcement of emotion regulation skills for a variety of emotions evident in an individual's pattern of sexual offending (Yates et al., 2000). As with the other treatment components discussed thus far, cognitive-behavioral treatment with respect to emotion management begins with increasing clients' awareness of the range and breadth of human emotional states. Clients can then develop an understanding of their own difficulties in both experiencing and managing emotional states. Through treatment, clients can come to understand how these problems are linked to their sexually aggressive behavior, cognitive processes, cognitive distortions, relationships, empathy, and deviant sexual arousal. Specifically, clients learn to identify the emotions that contributed to their sexual offending behavior and that could contribute to future offending. Strategies to manage emotional arousal are then learned and rehearsed (Yates et al., 2000). The relationship between emotional experiences, attaining a satisfying life, and achieving one's goals is also an objective within the Good Lives Model (Ward and Maruna, 2007).

Treatment in this area aims to help clients to recognize, monitor, understand, and manage emotions effectively, and focuses on developing and reinforcing skills to manage emotional states that have influenced offending and life problems more generally. Individuals learn to understand and identify emotions and their impact on behavior, and learn physiological skills (e.g., relaxation techniques), cognitive skills (e.g., challenging or interrupting negative thoughts), and behavioral skills (e.g., communication skills for expressing emotions such as assertiveness, anger management, and conflict resolution) (Hudson et. al, 1998). It is also important to consider the close relationship between primary and secondary goods (see chapters 3 and 4), goals, and emotions. That is, goals are derived from clients' values and represent ways to achieve these values in particular contexts. Emotions organize actions and inform people as to whether or not they are making progress toward achieving their goals (Ward and Nees, 2009). Thus, affective states such as affection, anxiety, or disappointment can signal how well a person is progressing toward a particular goal (Ward and Maruna, 2007).

With respect to self-regulation more broadly, treatment assists in developing capacities such as effective problem-solving, managing impulsivity, and lack of concern for others, each of which has been found to be predictive of re-offending (Hanson et al., 2007). Self-regulation theory and its relationship to offending is discussed in greater detail in chapter 2.

Victim Awareness and Empathy

Developing empathy for the victims of one's sexual offenses has traditionally been viewed as an important target of treatment for sexual offenders. As a result, most treatment programs include a victim-empathy component (Schwartz, 1992; Wormith and Hanson, 1991). However, empathy has not been definitively found to be associated with re-offending (Hanson and Bussière 1998; Hanson and Morton-Bourgon, 2005). Some research suggests that individuals who commit sexual offenses may do so at least partially as a function of a lack of empathy and an inability to understand the victim's feelings and experience (Barbaree and Marshall, 1991; Hudson et al., 1993; Marshall et al., 1995, 1996; Mulloy, Smiley, and Mawson, 1997; Rice, Chaplain, Harris, and Coutts, 1994; Williams and Khanna, 1990). For example, child molesters have been found to experience problems with such things as recognizing emotions, feeling distress for victims, and identifying their feelings toward victims (Marshall et al., 1995, 1996; Williams and Khanna, 1990).

Research has also found that some sexual offenders have marked deficits in their empathy for others and that treatment can have a positive effect on their ability to relate to others empathically (Marshall, Hudson, and Hodkinson, 1993; Pithers, 1994; Williams and Khanna, 1990). Research has not consistently found differences in empathy deficits among sexual offenders, however, as compared to other offenders or to non-offenders, nor has the relationship between lack of empathy and re-offending in the long-term been demonstrated (Hanson and Bussière, 1998; Hanson and Morton-Bourgon, 2005; Hudson et al., 1993; Langevin, Wright, and Handy, 1988; Pithers, 1994; Rice et al., 1994).

Empathy is hypothesized to regulate behavior via its association with pro-social and altruistic behavior as well as by inhibiting aggression (Hildebran and Pithers, 1989; Miller and Eisenberg, 1988; Moore, 1990; Pithers, 1993; Prentky, 1995). Therefore, lack of empathy is presumed to facilitate offending by permitting cognitive distortions that allow or permit offending to occur despite clear indications of victim distress (Fernandez, Marshall, Lightbody, and O'Sullivan, 1999; Marshall, O'Sullivan, and Fernandez, 1996), thus being indirectly related to sexual offending (Barbaree and Marshall, 1991; Mulloy et al., 1997; Rice et al., 1994). Finally, empathy may also foster social control by encouraging self-regulation (Scully, 1988).

In treatment, empathy is typically targeted by increasing individuals' awareness and understanding of the victim's experience of sexual aggression and of harm caused, developing the capacity to take the perspective of the victim, developing the ability to identify and alleviate another person's distress, and understanding the influence of lack of empathy on cognition and behavior (Hanson, 1997; Hanson and Scott, 1995; Marshall et al., 1996; Pithers, 1991; Williams and Khanna, 1990; Yates et al., 2000). Treatment also aims to identify barriers or "blocks" to empathy and the cognitive distortions associated with these blocks, in order to develop strategies to challenge these and to be able to take another person's perspective, with respect to offending but also more generally. It is generally believed that empathy is best addressed in treatment as the development of cognitive perspective-taking skills (i.e., learning to take the perspective of the victim and others) rather than attempting to instill empathy as an enduring trait within the client.

Finally, some research, although not conclusive, has found that demonstrations of empathy by both therapists and clients can result in giving the client a sense of caring for others, improved relationships, a reduced likelihood of exploiting or abusing others, and a greater potential to successfully reintegrate into the community (Ward and Salmon, in press). These findings speak to the importance of having therapists both demonstrate empathy and reinforce clients' demonstrations of empathy, even when such moments of empathy are relatively simplistic or rudimentary.

Relapse Prevention

Virtually all treatment programs for sexual offenders include a relapse prevention component (Freeman-Longo, Bird, Stevenson, and Fiske, 1994; Laws, Hudson, and Ward, 2000; Polaschek, 2003), despite a lack of research supporting its application to this population, as well as various problems with the theoretical model (Hanson, 1996, 2000; Laws, 2003; Laws, Hudson, and Ward, 2000; Laws and Ward, 2006; Ward, Yates, et al., 2006; Yates, 2005, 2007; Yates and Kingston, 2005). Because these problems are described in detail elsewhere in the sexual offender literature, they are not reiterated here.

The goal of relapse prevention is to help individuals identify and anticipate problems and high-risk situations that could lead to a return to sexual offending behavior as well as to teach a variety of skills to cope with these problems when they arise (Laws and Ward, 2006; Marlatt, 1982; Marques et al., 1992; Pithers, 1990, 1991). Sexual offending is viewed as a cycle of events that can be interrupted by developing an individual's ability to intervene in the offense sequence. In treatment, individuals are taught to identify and avoid high-risk situations and to develop specific skills to prevent lapse and relapse. Treatment typically involves developing a relapse prevention plan that is to be implemented in order to prevent re-offending.

The numerous problems identified in this model are beyond the scope of this book, but are described in detail in other publications (Laws et al., 2000; Ward, Yates, et al., 2006; Laws and Ward, 2006; Yates, 2005, 2007; Yates et al., 2000; Yates and Kingston, 2005; Yates and Ward, 2008) as well as in chapter 3. In order to overcome such problems, the Self-Regulation Model (SRM) of the offense process was developed (Ward and Hudson, 1998), and a few years later was integrated with the Good Lives Model (GLM) of offender treatment (Ward and Gannon, 2006; Ward and Stewart, 2003). This combined model (Yates and Ward, 2008), which is the focus of this book, more completely considers multiple pathways to offending (as compared to a single relapse prevention pathway), and individuals' goals and values and the relationship of these elements to offending. The model also situates offending within the broader context of an individual's life circumstances. The aim of treatment within the combined GLM/SRM-R approach is to manage the risk to re-offend while assisting the individual to attain important personal goals (values) and thus achieve a higher level of well-being (Ward and Gannon, 2006; Ward and Stewart, 2003; Ward, Yates, et al., 2006; Yates and Ward, 2008). This approach explicitly includes individuals' strengths, goals, and aspirations, in addition to deficits or problems, and takes a positive psychological approach to treatment (Aspinwall and Staudinger, 2003; Linley and Joseph, 2004). Thus, treatment assists clients to develop offense-specific strategies to prevent re-offending, as well as to develop their capacity to improve their lives to the degree that offending is no longer necessary to achieve important goals (Ward and Gannon, 2006; Ward and Stewart, 2003). The fundamental principles of this model are described in detail in chapter 3; the model's application to treatment and supervision is contained in parts III and IV of this book.

Release Preparation and Maintenance

Regardless of treatment orientation, it is essential to develop a realistic plan that will allow for eventual release from institutional or inpatient settings, that will maintain and reinforce gains made in treatment, and that will monitor for changes in risk and the clients' effective use of risk management skills. Within the integrated GLM/SRM-R, this plan should take the form of a good lives plan that specifies both building competencies and assisting the clients to achieve personal goals in addition to allowing them to reduce their own risk. This approach involves ensuring the implementation of offenders' good lives plans, the use of strategies to acquire important and valued goods, and the achievement of goals in the offenders' lives (see chapter 3). To achieve the objectives of monitoring and implementation of skills, many treatment programs include follow-up maintenance programming that is incorporated with supervision (Cumming and McGrath, 2000, 2005; Wilson, Stewart, Stirpe, Barrett, and Cripps, 2000; Yates et al., 2000). These release plans typically include the development of strategies for community reintegration and adjustment, expectations with respect to the community's reaction to release, reunion with family and friends, and the development of a positive support system.

ADJUNCTIVE TREATMENT

As the objective of this book is to provide therapists with information and techniques to implement the Good Lives and Self-Regulation-Revised models and to adapt them to sexual offender treatment, the focus of this chapter has been on the specific elements of cognitive-behavioral intervention, as described above. Additional elements of treatment that may be required in individual cases have not been included here, but additional information is available on those treatment elements elsewhere. Adjunctive interventions and treatment, however, in such areas as substance misuse, mental disorder, family reunification, and restorative justice, as well as general areas such as education and employment, may form an essential part of treatment for specific clients. These findings are consistent with an integrated model of sexual offending (Ward and Beech, 2006), which suggests that multiple factors—including biological factors, social, cultural, and personal circumstances, and neuropsychological factors—interact and influence all behavior, including sexual offending. Although beyond the scope of this book, adjunctive interventions for these and other areas are amenable to the application of the Good Lives and Self-Regulation-Revised models, and will be explored further throughout this volume.

Summary

Research demonstrates that programs employing cognitive-behavioral methods are the most effective in reducing recidivism among sexual offenders. Effective intervention also attends to the principles of risk, need, and responsivity. Although research is, in some areas, inconclusive, important treatment components include general self-regulation, sexual self-regulation, cognition and cognitive schemas, social and relationship functioning, emotion regulation, empathy, re-offense prevention, post-treatment maintenance, and adjunctive treatment as necessary. However, these methods and principles cannot work in the absence of genuine client motivation to change and engage in the treatment process. Client motivation is the focus of the next chapter.

CHAPTER 2

Motivation and Effective Client Engagement

The previous chapter focused on the specific orientation of sexual offender treatment and on treatment targets. As noted briefly in chapter 1, enhancing motivation and using effective methods of therapeutic intervention are essential to engaging clients in treatment and achieving maximum effectiveness of treatment. The present chapter describes the principles of motivational enhancement, as well as the characteristics of effective treatment and of effective therapists. These principles and methods can (and should) be implemented within any risk-based program, such as treatment using a cognitive-behavioral risk/need/responsivity (RNR) approach, and they are particularly important when implementing integrated Good Lives/Self-Regulation-Revised models of treatment. Also described in this chapter are specific treatment methods that combine the content (i.e., treatment targets) with these methods.

Motivation and Effective Therapeutic Methods

The importance of therapeutic processes has come to the fore in sexual offender treatment. The processes include methods by which treatment is implemented and the influence of effective therapists on motivation and treatment outcome (Blanchard, 1995; Hanson, 2006; Kear-Colwell and Pollack, 1997; Marshall, 2005; Marshall et al., 2003; Yates, 2009a; Yates et al., 2000). The early literature in sexual offender treatment emphasized that evaluators and treatment providers should be in control at all times (e.g., Salter, 1998). In some instances, this translates into a harsh, confrontational treatment style that studies have found to be unhelpful in areas such as reducing victim blame, minimization, and acceptance of responsibility. An adversarial, punitive approach can also be damaging to the therapeutic relationship with clients (Garland and Dougher, 1991; Marshall et al., 2002). It is likely to destroy trust with clients and to be ineffective in promoting well-being, as well as in avoiding unnecessary harm in treatment (Beauchamp and Childress, 2009).

Studies of general psychotherapy outcome for clients have largely neglected relational variables (Teyber and McClure, 2000), especially in the study of cognitive-behavioral sexual offender treatment. These process or relational factors, however, can have a profound influence on therapeutic change (Marshall et al., 2002, 2003; Marshall 2005; Miller, Hubble, and Duncan, 2008; Wampold, 2001). Similarly, the influence of hope on a client's readiness, willingness, and ability to change has become a topic of attention in the general psychotherapy literature (Snyder, Michael, and Cheavens, 1999) and, more recently, in the sexual offender treatment literature (Moulden and Marshall, 2009). Snyder et al. (1999) describe a theory of hope that includes thoughts related to how a client will achieve his goals as well as his ability to achieve those goals. The authors describe how even the expectation that change is possible can increase clients' ability to find ways to achieve it. Thus, instilling hope that change can be attained is becoming an important part of therapy.

Research has pointed out that basic principles taught in most counseling programs—including empathy, validation, collaboration, and flexibility—can contribute to successful outcomes for general therapy clients (Teyber and McClure, 2000). It appears that the therapeutic alliance is the bedrock upon which successful treatment stands (Miller, Hubble, and Duncan, 2007). Recent studies in the general psychotherapy literature validate this finding. For example, research shows that structured attempts to attain client feedback (e.g., how respected, heard, and understood the client felt during a treatment session, whether the session focused on goals and topics of importance to the client, and whether the therapist's approach was a good fit) helped therapists to produce better outcomes in treatment (Miller et al., 2008)

Conversely, some process variables appear to create obstacles to successful therapy and to interfere with alliance-building and positive outcome. This *negative process* occurs when clinicians fail to respond effectively to hostile, resistant, or critical sentiments expressed by their clients (Binder and Strupp, 1997; Teyber and McClure, 2000) or when those therapists simply do not listen to their clients (Miller and Rollnick, 2002; Snyder et al., 1999). Therapists of every theoretical orientation commonly respond to clients' negativity with anger, emotional withdrawal, or subtle rejection (Binder and Strupp, 1997). Therapists who treat sexual offenders may be especially vulnerable to such negative reactions, since sexual offenders may participate in treatment non-voluntarily and often enter treatment programs with resistance, denial, and a lack of motivation for change (Drapeau, Körner, Granger, Brunet, and Caspar, 2005; Jenkins-Hall, 1994; Jennings and Sawyer, 2003; Marshall, Thornton, Marshall, Fernandez, and Mann, 2001; Serran, Fernandez, Marshall, and Mann, 2003; Winn, 1996). Furthermore, subtle forms of stigmatization may negatively influence therapists' interpretation of offenders' resistant behavior, causing them to respond even more negatively (Willis, Levenson, and Ward, in press). Little research has been conducted on negative process; however, this may account for many of the treatment failures across every modality of treatment (Binder and Strupp, 1997). The findings regarding negative therapeutic processes are important, given that treatment failure (i.e., treatment non-completion) is associated with increased recidivism rates among sexual offenders (Hanson and Bussière, 1998). A question for every sexual offender therapist is whether his or her client's resistance reflects fear of change or an attempt to test the therapist's ability to handle their relationship (Drapeau et al., 2005), and could indicate that the therapist does not yet understand the client's situation (Miller and Rollnick, 2002; Prescott, 2009).

In recent years, motivational interviewing (Miller and Rollnick, 2002; Prescott, 2009) has gained currency among professionals working within a correctional milieu. Motivational interviewing uses a guiding style by the therapist to help clients explore how and why they might make changes to their lives. Motivational interviewing provides a platform for working cooperatively with others (a mindset of collaboration, support for autonomy, and evoking, rather than directing, change). Furthermore, motivational interviewing provides simple principles for therapists that serve as anchor points (i.e., supporting self-efficacy, expressing empathy, rolling with resistance, and developing discrepancy between current and desired states). The approach also provides skills for interviews (e.g., open-ended questions, affirmations, reflective statements, and summaries) that clinicians can use to replace less helpful methods of communication and to elicit additional information. Elements of motivational interviewing are used in the case examples throughout this volume. In addition, as will be seen later in this book, these techniques are also strongly consistent with, and support, a Good Lives Model approach to sexual offender treatment (McMurran and Ward, 2004; Yates, 2009a).

Ultimately, professionals can be more effective by entering each interaction with the explicit intention of collaboration and respect for the client's autonomy. From here, the therapist can create a situation in which the client makes his or her own case for change. In fact, some research shows that people who perceive themselves as having some degree of choice in an endeavor often become more compliant with it (Bem, 1972). While efforts at change frequently begin with outside pressures, long-term change is maintained through self-determination (Ryan and Deci, 2000).

As an example, let's return to the case of Bill, described in chapter 1. Bill is Native American, deeply distrusts Anglo-Saxon authority figures, and likely has attention deficit hyperactivity disorder (ADHD). Knowing that a warm, empathic, respectful, rewarding, and directive style will produce the best outcome, and that the responsivity principle requires that treatment match the characteristics of the client, the therapist will want to take extra caution at the start of treatment. As noted earlier, what may appear initially as low motivation for change may simply reflect the many concerns and/or fears the client has about the change process and the therapeutic relationship. The therapist will likely be more effective with reflective listening than with confrontation.

> *Bill:* It wasn't my idea to do this treatment. As far as I'm concerned, you've all got it in for me.
> *Therapist:* You're only here because the judge sent you here.
> *Bill:* That's right. Besides, I got a wife and kids that need me. We don't have time for these games. As far as they're concerned, they're being treated unfairly.
> *Therapist:* It's really clear that your family means a lot to you, and that you're very important to them. I also hear that you're concerned that I'm more a tool of the state than I am someone interested in your long-term well-being. Did I get that right?
> *Bill:* Yeah, I am really concerned about that.
> *Therapist:* So this situation is eating at you. You want to find a way through this and be the best you can for your family on the one hand, and on the other hand, you're concerned that I won't understand. You feel that you're involved with a system that hasn't always been fair to your people.
> *Bill:* You got it.
> *Therapist:* Given that we're from different backgrounds, what would be the best and safest way for us to work together? What else should I know about you?

Although this approach may seem time-consuming, particularly when compared to a more confrontational approach, taking time at the outset of treatment to form a deep and rich understanding of the client's world can actually save time later on in treatment:

> *Therapist:* Let me see if I can summarize where we're at with this situation. You want to be a good provider for your wife and kids, and this treatment is taking time away from that. On the other hand, you're interested in any ways to be a better husband and father. However, it's concerning to you that you're caught up in a legal system that you believe has itself been abusive to your people in the past. It can be hard to know if—and even how—you can trust me or others involved

in your treatment. You've shared that you're an action-oriented guy who would rather be on the move than sitting in therapy. Just the same, some good things about being in treatment might involve building a better life. Some not-so-good things might include how your family will react when you really do start making some changes. Where does that leave you?

Bill: *I guess that leaves me right here. I don't like any of this, but if I don't finish this program, I'm only going to have more trouble at my door.*

In this example, it is Bill himself who is making the case for being in the treatment program. The therapist has guided him in this direction by reflecting back his statements, offering summaries to ensure that Bill feels understood, and asking open-ended questions to take their conversation in new directions. Although Bill's primary motivation is mostly external early in treatment, research shows that people very often discover their own internal reasons for change once they begin treatment (Ryan and Deci, 2000).

Had the therapist argued on behalf of the treatment program or promoted the idea of personal change, it is very likely that Bill would have felt compelled to argue against both. In fact, this reaction can be quite natural for a new client. Anyone who has attempted to lose weight or give up an unhealthy habit is familiar with the phenomenon. When a friend expresses concern and recommends some sort of behavioral change ("You'll feel better about yourself when you lose weight"), it can be much easier to argue the point (It would be too hard to exercise; I'm no good at it; I don't have time") than it is to accept it ("You're absolutely right. I need to exercise regularly and I could find the time"). This subtle difference is of critical importance to therapists, who very often see themselves as directly influencing change rather than awakening the client's internal reasons for change. The therapist who argues the pro-change position creates an unacceptable risk of having a client like Bill argue the no-change position ("I'll never be able to do a white man's program").

Specific Treatment Activities

Because programs treat clients with varying levels of readiness and motivation, it is common for the first phase of treatment to focus on these areas with little or no emphasis on recounting one's history of sexual aggression. This initial phase might simply function as providing information about, and preparation for, treatment (O'Brien, Marshall, and Marshall, 2009; Yates et al., 2000). It can also include exercises to explore individuals' readiness to engage in a program (Cullen and Wilson, 2003). This early phase can also comprise a larger constellation of activities aimed at improving self-management and at ameliorating factors associated with personality disorders. Treatment targets can include cognitive skills, psycho-education, exploration of thought processes that contribute to harmful behavior, and values exploration and clarification (e.g., Wilson, 2009). Benchmarks of progress for the therapist can include signs of the client's ability to function meaningfully as a member of a group, his ability to demonstrate problem-solving skills and to identify and manage unhelpful thought patterns, his skill at managing his emotions effectively, his demonstration of acceptable interpersonal skills, and his ability to follow rules and expectations of the program.

Clients and therapists alike can wonder about the importance of this first phase. After all, this phase does not appear to address sexual abuse directly. It is crucial to remember, however, that the beginning stages of treatment are a period of intense vulnerability for both the client and the treatment process itself. Disclosing one's personal and private history too early in treatment can lead to intense anxiety for many, if not most, clients and can even cause clients to be resistant to treatment. A helpful task for therapists can include their imagining being compelled to talk about the most private area of their lives (Mann, 2009). Then the therapists need to imagine that they are compelled to talk about such vulnerable topics at length in a treatment group (which may not feel safe to the individual) while treatment providers take notes. In some cases, therapists may be asked to enact parts of their behaviors or life histories in role-play exercises. Therapists need to know, too, that it is entirely possible that the notes from their treatment might be viewed by representatives of the legal system and/or used in crucial decision-making about their future. In addition, their families and friends could also learn about behaviors of which the therapists are ashamed and perhaps about which they were untruthful in the past.

In short, from the client's perspective, there is little to be gained, and much to be lost, by disclosing personal information. It is no wonder—given the stakes involved—that many clients simply lie about their histories. This deception can become a serious obstacle to treatment progress. Not only is lying about one's history an obstacle to meaningful change, but clients can become even more ambivalent about whether they can or should tell the truth. Admitting to details about an offense is one thing; admitting to lying about it is another, even if the lying forms a self-protective function. Finally, while this first phase of treatment can help clients to develop skills that will help them to manage the demands of later treatment, it also serves a vital purpose in risk reduction by helping them to regulate their behavior and other aspects of an antisocial style known to contribute to sexual re-offense (Hanson and Morton-Bourgon, 2004).

The second phase of treatment generally consists of developing an autobiography of the relevant and formative life events that helped to shape the individual, his beliefs, attitudes, emotions, cognitive schemas, and behaviors that established offense-related dispositions. This phase typically includes developmental experiences (e.g., life in the family of origin, early sexual development), experiences of neglect or abuse, history of sexual and intimate relationships, peer influences, early criminal behavior (including both sexual and non-sexual behavior), education, and employment. Within the integrated Good Lives/Self-Regulation-Revised approach to treatment, this process also includes an exploration of the client's goals, values, and aspirations throughout his life and a specific focus on the development of self-regulation capacity and deficits (see chapter 9).

Similarly, the third phase of treatment typically consists of formulating an agreed-upon history of one's sexual offending. While treatment usually focuses on an offense "cycle"—seeking to understand clients' repetitive patterns of sexual offending—the focus is different within the integrated Good Lives/Self-Regulation-Revised Model. Specifically, this model approaches the offense progression and history from the perspective of that which the individual sought to attain through sexual offending, such that treatment can later assist the client to achieve important goals and personal states in pro-social ways and without acting in sexually abusive ways. The SRM element of the offense history focuses specifically on the progression of offending through various stages, from factors that predispose the individual to offend sexually, to specific life triggers of the offense progression, to clients' evaluation of their behavior and of themselves after they have committed a sexual offense (see chapter 10).

Traditionally, the purpose of this exercise is to identify the factors that contributed to the client's sexual offending. These factors often overlap with dynamic risk variables found in the research literature, such as sexual deviance and abuse-related sexual interests, attitudes that support and contribute to sexual offending, socio-affective/interpersonal functioning (including intimate relationships), and self-management skills including changes in substance use and dysfunctional coping styles (also see Knight and Thornton, 2007; Thornton, 2002).

This phase of treatment also typically consists of exploring some offenses in depth in order to understand each of the specific actions involved in the offense progression. Sometimes called an "active account," the fundamental aim is to explore an offense so the client moves from a more passive account to a more active account. For example, a passive account may appear as, "She hired me as a babysitter, and after a while the kids and I just got to monkeying around and having fun." With time, this dialogue can become a more active accounting of the offense. For example, "I knew she was vulnerable when we met. I was more interested in gaining access to her kids. I did not actually suggest that I babysit, but I casually mentioned that I used to babysit when I was younger. I knew she would ask me eventually, and she did. I even brought video games to her house, knowing it would be easier to gain the kids' trust."

In exploring individuals' offense progression, the aim is also to determine the chain of events beginning with the more distal life event that set the chain in motion, through to gaining access to the victim(s) and offending, and examining the individual's reactions to the offense and to their behavior after the offense occurs. With respect to the GLM/SRM-R, this process involves not only offense-related goals, cognition, and behavior, but also self-regulation styles in specific circumstances and an understanding of what the individual sought to gain by offending. For example, some individuals offend in the process of seeking sexual gratification and because they believe it will make them happy (the primary good of *happiness* in GLM terms). Others may seek intimacy or relationships (the primary goods of *relatedness* or *friendship*) (see chapter 3). Professionals also attempt at this point to assess the *self-regulation offense pathway* the individual followed during a particular offense occurrence (see chapter 5).

This disclosure work also entails determining what the individual values most in his life, both currently and historically—that is, the client's good life plan or vision of what constitutes a good life. The client and therapist also explore aspects of the client's life that they would like to improve or enhance, goals they may have sought previously but which they have been unable to achieve and may have since abandoned, and internal and external factors that have interfered with attaining what they view as a good life. Chapters 4, 5, and 8 of this book describe the strategies for obtaining this information and addressing these elements in treatment in more detail, while chapter 9 specifically examines the personal history (i.e., "autobiography") exercise, and chapter 10 examines the offense progression in the context of the Good Lives and Self-Regulation-Revised models.

The third phase of treatment focuses on managing factors in one's life that contributed to offending, and then practicing healthy alternative behaviors. This process can involve re-evaluating the justifications and attitudes that contributed to offending and practicing new strategies for coping with the circumstances and emotions they provoke. It also involves actively managing deviant sexual arousal and interests, and replacing these with healthy alternatives. Wilson (2009), drawing on the work of Haaven (2006), notes that among the components of this phase of treatment are

- developing a representation of "old me";
- developing a representation of "future me";
- doing "future me" role-plays;
- conducting a balanced, self-determined lifestyle review; and
- getting to "future me."

Case Example: José

José is determined to get the best he can out of treatment. He is very clear that he does not want to be the person he was when he was offending, although there are certain parts of himself that he does wish to maintain, such as the fact that he is a good father and a hard worker. In addition to discussing the aspects that contributed to his offending, he also created an "old me" collage, a visual representation of his view of himself at the time he was offending. It features a number of striking images that he found in magazines and newspapers. He has assembled this collage and has talked in group therapy about what each image means to him. He keeps it handy as a reminder of the changes he wants to make.

Similarly, José prepared a "future me" collage as a set of images about who he can be and wants to be. This collage process allows José to change those aspects of himself that he wants to change and to keep those aspects of himself that he does not need to change, such as his work ethic. In describing each of the images, José's therapist and group members develop ideas for role-play exercises of how he can handle the various situations he will encounter in the years to come. Alongside these discussions, he works with others to establish what a balanced and self-determined lifestyle would look like for him, with ideas for how he can get there. To this end, he also writes journal entries, and draws maps of what "the road ahead" looks like. The idea is not so much that he needs a specific roadmap, rather, it is the thought and effort that count. Incorporating this work across a range of senses (e.g., visual representations, discussions, and role-plays) helps José to understand his treatment at a deeper level.

Wilson (2009) also stresses the importance of clients obtaining a better understanding of their relationships with others. While many programs emphasize the need for clients to develop empathy for others (including victims) through specific exercises, it can also be helpful to have clients practice relating to others empathically in a more general way throughout their daily lives. This process can include

- developing a richer, better-differentiated emotional experience;
- increasing perspective-taking skills in general and specifically in situations where problems exist in seeing how others might interpret things they do and say;
- increasing the ability to share and understand emotions with others in healthy ways;
- reducing unhelpful or unhealthy responses to others' distress (e.g., self-pity, not responding at all); and
- developing and exploring empathy skills in the context of close relationships.

As indicated previously, the various components of treatment described in chapter 1 are included throughout each of these phases of treatment. For example, when a client develops a conceptualization of a "future me," the process is part of his development of a good life plan (Ward and Stewart, 2003; see chapter 12). The process creates a roadmap of goals and strategies that the client needs to have to achieve the type of life that he desires, based on what is important to him and also what is within his ability to achieve.

The final phase of treatment typically involves maintaining change and, depending on the offender's context, preparing for discharge into the community, something that may include follow-up treatment and/or supervision. The aim of such maintenance programming is to assist the client in implementing his plan to manage and to evaluate risk as he re-enters the community (Cumming and McGrath, 2000, 2005; Wilson et al., 2000; Yates et al., 2000). Specific to the GLM/SRM-R approach, the purpose of maintenance is also to practice self-regulation skills and to monitor the implementation of the individual's good life plan to ensure progress and to make any adjustments as needed.

Some clients may have considerable restrictions imposed on their behavior that might make community reintegration particularly challenging. In such situations, it is important to anticipate the re-emergence of factors that previously contributed to offending. For example, if a client was motivated to offend in part by emotional loneliness and a sense of inadequacy, community restrictions on associates or living arrangements will likely challenge the offender's newly developed ability to cope with these factors. In addition, in jurisdictions with severely restrictive community measures, therapists and supervisors will need to be creative in assisting individuals to attain important goods and goals in their newly developed good lives plans.

For example, let's return to the previous example of José. Let's assume that José's sexual offending was motivated in part by a desire to emotionally connect with others and that chief among his goals for the future are excellence at play and work. As José begins to determine who he wants to be and how he can get there, it is vital that his therapist and peers address the realities of the restrictions that José will face. They need to anticipate that the emotional loneliness that led him to offend may well be aggravated by restrictions on his residence, movement, and activities. As a result, they need to work together to explore alternatives such that José can achieve his goals in life. It is possible that others could learn about his offenses and, in some jurisdictions, that his name, picture, and residence will be available to others on the Internet. Under such conditions, it will not be enough to set a goal of emotional connection to others. Neither will it be enough to plan for setbacks and establish a list of available resources. José needs to experience himself as competent if he is to manage the frustrations he will inevitably face, and if he is to be able to create specific plans to maintain the integrity of his treatment gains. To this end, treatment will not simply be the completion of unrelated goals, but a tapestry of interwoven goals and skills. To make these points clearer, consider another case example.

Case Example: Darren

Darren presents for treatment following re-conviction for a sexual offense. Darren has sexually abused a number of pre-pubescent boys. In most cases, Darren was in a caregiver capacity, either as a babysitter or within the context of live-in relationships with their mothers.

Darren has an extensive history of his own sexual victimization. His parents pursued a semi-nomadic lifestyle, moving from one region to another while engaging in diverse drug-related activities. Initially victimized by his parents' associates, Darren was placed in foster care where he was victimized again, this time by his foster father. Ironically, however, Darren recalled his foster father as one of the few people with whom he had a positive relationship. Upon his 18th birthday, child protective services released Darren from custody with little community support. Darren was successful in securing a low-paying job at a flower shop. He interacted well with customers and met a number of women with children. In a number of cases, he was able to establish short-term relationships that provided unsupervised contact with children.

In his first treatment program, Darren presented himself as highly motivated and insisted that he simply loved the children he supervised. However, he continued to keep a secret journal of sexual fantasies about children, and he masturbated to these several times a month. He was privately convinced that his treatment providers were unable to understand him in the way that children could, and he even mentioned this occasionally, but with no follow-up by the therapists. Darren did, however, find himself enjoying the treatment process at a superficial level.

Darren completed psycho-educational assignments and appeared quite sincere as he developed a plan for how he would prevent future abuse. His treatment goals included understanding how sexual abuse affects those who experience it, challenging and replacing cognitive distortions related to sexual abuse, accepting responsibility for his actions, exploring how he gained access to the children he abused, and developing relapse prevention plans for how he could live more safely in the future.

Darren is a challenging client. While cognitive-behavioral therapy has strong empirical support with sexual offenders, it is unlikely to work under the conditions that Darren experienced. In his case, when he presented himself as motivated to complete a treatment program, it was not the same as having a genuine motivation to change. Darren simply did not meaningfully explore his offenses deeply enough to uncover the positive aspects of life, such as his goals and needs in life that he had sought to fulfill through inappropriate means. Because he had persistently evaluated his abuse of children as positive experiences within the existing—and narrow and limited—framework of his life, he was content to present himself as harmless and in need of skills to prevent re-offending. In addition, during this treatment program, Darren's therapist did not establish the kind of relationship that would have made it possible for Darren to engage more meaningfully in treatment, and the therapist overlooked Darren's references to the fact that members of his treatment team didn't understand him. This belief, left unaddressed, reinforced itself as Darren continued to masturbate to fantasies of children. Darren's cognitive schemas were related to the impermanence of most relationships in his life and the fact that he felt others could not understand him. As such, treatment was not adequately tailored to be responsive to his needs. Future treatment for Darren needs to examine whether his attitude might be further related to a self-perceived emotional congruence with children.

Darren's failed course of treatment resulted from poor adherence to the principles of risk, need, and responsivity. Although he could present himself well, Darren's treatment program was not a successful match for his level of risk and responsivity. This lack of a match is evidenced in the program's psycho-educational nature and its sole focus on preventing re-offending rather than developing positive goals for living a better and offense-free life. The poor match was also evidenced in that it did not adequately tap into Darren's internal motivations for change. In fact, Darren strategically used treatment concepts to appear less dangerous than he actually was. Furthermore, although he was able to explore his offending and make plans to avoid such abuse in the future, the program clearly did not address the need principle in that many important dynamic risk factors remained unaddressed. Specifically, Darren's capacity for long-term relationship stability and self-regulation went unaddressed, as did his problematic cognitive schemas and goals, both of which could have brought about a more balanced and self-determined life. Although neither Darren nor his treatment team raised these as areas of need, many of them are well-established criminogenic needs that require attention. Furthermore, by not adequately addressing Darren's intrinsic motivations for change, the program violated the responsivity principle and did not provide him with adequate motivation to change.

Finally, by poorly matching Darren's treatment to these principles, any attempts the therapists made to meaningfully improve Darren's social functioning, capacity for intimacy, emotional regulation, or empathic relatedness to others could only fail. Darren could learn the words but not the meaning of genuine change and a better, more self-determined life. Had Darren's therapists better understood his cognitive schemas (including the attitudes and beliefs he had learned early in his life, as well as his tendency to keep significant areas of his life secret), treatment might have turned out differently. Darren's therapists also made a crucial error by not attending to the full information-gathering that a working therapeutic relationship needs to have. Although Darren did not bring to others' attention the fact that he was continuing to masturbate to abuse-related fantasies, he did occasionally refer to the feeling that others did not understand him. A key lesson for Darren's clinical team was not to confuse his progress in mastering treatment terms with true, internal personal change.

In Darren's case, future treatment providers would be best served to consider the following questions:

- What were the primary goods in life that Darren was hoping to gain by his sexual offending?

- What goods did Darren hope to gain in other areas of his life?

- How would he like his life and relationships to be different than they currently were, with respect to those goals?

- How important was it to Darren to obtain primary goods in life?

- How confident was he that he could obtain such goods, and do so without more sexual offending?

- What strengths and positive attributes did Darren bring to treatment on which he could build?

- How could Darren use his personal strengths to embark on a journey of change and stay the course through difficult times?

- What does Darren yearn for in his life that is not there?

- What is important to Darren that could motivate him to change?

These considerations and related ones are discussed further in chapter 8.

Summary

Knowledge and practice in the field of assessing and treating sexual offenders has improved dramatically in recent years. Cognitive-behavioral methods adhering to the principles of risk, need, and responsivity have gained considerable support, even though practitioners have rightly noted that that many questions remain to be answered. Despite the emerging consensus regarding what works to build healthier lives and safer communities, it is clear that unless therapists can engage with clients at a meaningful level, their best efforts can be for naught. True public safety comes from providing opportunities for clients to realistically pursue the same primary goods as other human beings.

CHAPTER 3

Fundamentals of the Good Lives, Self-Regulation, and Integrated Models

In order to effectively deliver any type of treatment in a clinical setting, it is essential that the practitioner be familiar with the underlying theoretical model of intervention and its objectives and methods. As indicated previously, it is not the intent of the authors to provide a comprehensive overview or even instructions to guide a risk-based cognitive-behavioral treatment with sexual offenders in the pages of this book. Information provided in this chapter specifically pertains to the theoretical bases of the Good Lives and Self-Regulation models and the combined GLM/SRM-R. The GLM is a broad rehabilitation theory or framework, while the SRM-R is a specific treatment model. That is, the GLM gives practitioners a flexible framework within which to work with sex offenders. It states the aims of therapy, the core values of treatment, and the general assumptions about causes of offending, and it provides guidelines on how to work with offenders (Ward and Maruna, 2007). By contrast, the SRM-R is embedded within the GLM and translates these more general ideas into concrete treatment methods and techniques. The information provided in this chapter provides an overview that focuses on the clinical implementation of the GLM and SRM-R. Additional detail on these models is available elsewhere (Ward and Gannon, 2006; Ward and Hudson, 1998, 2000; Ward and Maruna, 2007; Ward and Stewart, 2003; Ward et al., 2004, 2006; Yates and Kingston, 2005; Yates et al., 2009; Yates and Ward, 2008).

BASIC FOUNDATIONS OF THE GOOD LIVES MODEL

The original Good Lives Model (GLM) presupposes that people commit sexual offenses because they lack the opportunity and/or the ability to acquire important things in their lives (Ward and Gannon, 2006; Ward and Maruna, 2007; Ward and Stewart, 2003). Sexual offending results when various personal, physiological, and social conditions lead an individual to achieve his goals in life through offending. Other people, without such predisposing offense inclinations, do not make the same behavioral choices (Ward and Beech, 2006). Recently, the GLM has been fully integrated with the cognitive-behavioral approach to the treatment of sexual offenders (Yates and Ward, 2008), which research indicates is effective in reducing recidivism (Hanson et al., 2002; Lösel and Schmucker, 2005). As stated earlier, the GLM is an overarching theory of rehabilitation stipulating the essential values that should underlie treatment. Those values consist of two main elements: (1) the importance of the relationship between individuals' goals and objectives and their sexual offending behavior, and (2) the focus that treatment should take so that the client can meet those needs while reducing risk. Also essential is how treatment can overcome the limitations evident in a strictly risk-based approach to treatment (Ward and Gannon, 2006; Ward et al., 2006, 2007; Ward and Stewart, 2003).

The GLM takes a positive psychological approach to the treatment of sexual offenders (Aspinwall and Staudinger, 2003; Ward, Mann, and Gannon, 2007). Thus, an important foundation of the GLM is the idea that sexual offenders, like all other human beings, are goal-directed and seek certain experiences, outcomes, and states of being in their daily lives. In the GLM, these goals are termed *primary human goods*. All individuals seek to obtain these primary goods because acquiring such goods leads to better psychological health and to a good life in general (Kekes, 1989; Ward and Stewart, 2003; Ward et al., 2006). Research in this area (Aspinwall and Staudinger, 2003; Cummins, 1996; Deci and Ryan, 2000; Emmons, 1999; Linley and Joseph, 2004; Murphy, 2001; Nussbaum, 2000) suggests that individuals seek to obtain at least 10 types of primary human goods.

- **Life:** Healthy living and functioning—the basic needs in life
- **Knowledge:** Desire for information and understanding about oneself and the world
- **Excellence in Play and Work** (including mastery experiences)
- **Excellence in Agency:** Autonomy, independence, and self-directedness
- **Inner Peace:** Freedom from emotional turmoil and stress
- **Friendship:** Connections to others through intimate, romantic, familial, and other types of relationships
- **Community:** A sense of belonging to a larger group of individuals with shared interests
- **Spirituality:** A broad sense of finding meaning and purpose in life

- **Happiness:** A state of being of overall contentedness in one's life; the experience of pleasure
- **Creativity:** The desire to have novelty or innovation in one's life

While primary human goods are somewhat abstract constructs, the GLM differentiates between these higher-level goods and *instrumental* or *secondary goods*, which are the specific and concrete ways individuals attempt to obtain primary goods. Examples of instrumental goods include specific activities to gain knowledge (e.g., attending school), creative activities (e.g., artistic pursuits), and activities to support autonomy, such as developing new life skills (or, in the case of sexual offending, dominating or controlling others).

Clients are often unaware of the primary goods that are important to them and that they seek to obtain. For example, some offenders may engage in sexual activity with children because they value and seek the primary human good of relatedness. Because sex is, to these individuals, part of an intimate relationship, the relationship with the child becomes a sexual one in order to fill the primary need. During treatment, however, clients will be more likely to describe the secondary goods rather than the broader construct of relatedness. Similarly, some individuals may have a strong need for the primary good of agency (i.e., autonomy or personal power), which they only know to achieve via sexual aggression or by dominating, controlling, or manipulating others. Thus, in assessment and treatment, determining the primary goods that a client values is an inferential process, and an assessment protocol is available for use in determining primary goods (Yates et al., 2009). Assessment of primary human goods, their value to the individual, and their role in offending, is further discussed in chapter 4.

The basis of the GLM is that all individuals often have an implicit good life plan that represents what conditions, for each individual, will lead to happiness, a good life, and well-being. Each good life plan is highly individualized—individuals place different weight on different primary goods. For example, some individuals may value family as one of their most important goals in a good life, whereas others may value excellence in work more highly. According to the GLM, when problems arise in an individual's life, it is because of specific flaws or problems that prevent the individual from attaining the goods he desires (described on page 41). With respect to sexual offending, these flaws result in socially unacceptable (and often personally frustrating) attempts to pursue primary human goods. Therefore, in treatment, the therapist's role is to: (a) determine the primary human goods that are important to the individual, (b) to reinforce the importance of those goods or goals, (c) to help the client to overcome barriers to obtaining the goods; (d) to understand the relationship of primary goods to offending and to other life problems; and, (e) to build the client's capacity to attain these goods in socially acceptable, non-offending ways. In addition, similar to the identification of "old me" and "future me" described in chapter 2, the GLM proposes that all individuals construct a narrative or personal identity. An important part of GLM treatment is to help each client create a more adaptive and satisfying personal identity on his own terms (e.g., Maruna, 2001; Ward and Marshall, 2007).

As described in previous chapters, treatment within the GLM framework begins with assessment and the development of a comprehensive case conceptualization that forms the basis of the treatment plan (see chapter 7). In addition to addressing standard elements of treatment and managing risk, this case conceptualization also contains the various primary goods that are important to clients and includes a plan to help them obtain these within the context of their lives and environmental and contextual considerations. A GLM treatment plan takes into account each client's strengths, goals, and personal circumstances, accepts the client as an autonomous individual, and respects his capacity to make certain decisions himself. This philosophy is in direct contrast to previously recommended practices in the treatment of sexual offenders, where therapists were cautioned not to allow offenders to participate in decision-making (e.g., Salter, 1988) and in which the therapist assumed the role of "expert" while the offender was the passive recipient of "treatment." It is easy to see how such an approach would not be motivating to the client. In contrast, a GLM approach aims to increase engagement with the treatment process and to stimulate motivation for the client to participate in treatment. The GLM approach stresses that treatment needs to be made relevant to the client (Ward and Maruna, 2007; Yates, 2009a).

The GLM approach also attempts to explain the origins of sexual offending beyond solely risk considerations. Simply put, individuals may lack the opportunities and/or the capacity to acquire what is important in their lives, or they do so in antisocial ways as a result of a variety of factors, such as early life experiences. Such influencing factors can, for example, include parental modeling or childhood neglect or abuse suffered by the client. The GLM does acknowledge the importance of risk factors, however, in that these factors are considered *internal or external obstacles* that often prevent the acquisition of primary human goods (Ward and Stewart, 2003). An individual's responses to these obstacles are learned throughout his life. Furthermore, an individual's ability to obtain the goods in his good life plan results from specific flaws. The GLM proposes four primary flaws—means, scope, conflict, and capacity—which are to be addressed in treatment, with the objective of developing clients' ability to obtain primary human goods in effective and non-harmful ways. (Ward and Maruna, 2007; Ward et al., 2006).

FLAWS IN THE GOOD LIVES PLAN

As indicated earlier, in treatment within the GLM approach, it is not the individuals' overarching goals (e.g., obtaining happiness, pleasure, autonomy, and so forth) that are problematic. In treatment, one of the therapist's roles is, therefore, to reinforce and strengthen these needs, rather than to change or eliminate them. What is problematic is the secondary goods—that is, the activities or strategies clients use to obtain certain primary goods. In obtaining these, four problems (flaws in the good lives plan) may be evident.

1. **Means Used to Obtain Goods:** This problem occurs when the individual uses inappropriate or harmful strategies to obtain a particular good or goods. For example, an individual may socialize with children (the strategy) in order to achieve the primary good of relatedness.

2. **Lack of Scope in Good Lives Plan:** This flaw occurs when an individual's good life plan is too narrow, with important goods left out. For example, the individual may be missing the good of autonomy and, as a result, may then feel disempowered and chronically inadequate, and may offend as a result of too great a focus on one good.

3. **Conflict among Primary Goods:** This problem occurs when a conflict exists between two primary goods and/or the ways the individual goes about obtaining them. The conflict results in psychological stress, unhappiness, and the attainment of neither good. For example, an individual who strongly desires both relatedness and autonomy may attempt to gain both by attempting to control or dominate a partner. In addition to creating conflict, this approach also has the ironic effect of making it less likely that either good will be acquired. In the GLM, this approach is also referred to as a *lack of coherence* among goods sought.

4. **Lack of Internal or External Capabilities:** This flaw occurs when the individual lacks the skills or opportunities to obtain certain primary goods. For example, an individual who lacks the skills needed to plan and to solve problems in life and who responds to life events impulsively, demonstrates a problem with *internal capacity*. Furthermore, because he is impulsive, he may have alienated other people and, as a result, will not have access to social relationships (a problem with *external capacity*). In addition to not getting his needs met, this situation may increase his level of frustration.

Treatment within the GLM Approach

Treatment using the GLM as a broad guide is described in detail in chapter 8. Briefly, treatment focuses on assisting clients to obtain primary goods, to overcome flaws in their good lives plans, and to manage and reduce their risk to re-offend. Thus, in addition to changing risk factors and building clients' abilities to manage risk, a major focus of treatment is to assist clients to develop the skills, values, attitudes, and resources necessary to lead a different kind of life—one that is personally meaningful and satisfying, and one that does not involve inflicting harm on others. Simply put, treatment focuses on helping clients to understand what they value in life, how to obtain what is important to them, how to overcome obstacles in achieving these goals, and how to effectively and appropriately obtain primary human goods. Treatment assists the clients to become better practical decision-makers who are then able to identify and formulate their core values, to arrive at the most effective ways to achieve those values in the form of a coherent plan, and to implement their plans in ways that are practical and contextually sensitive (Laws and Ward, in press).

An important construct in the GLM is the notion of *approach goals* (Austin and Vancouver, 1996). Treatment typically focuses on avoidance goals developed to reduce risk. For example, clients learn in treatment how to monitor situations that pose a risk for offending and how to avoid or escape from these situations. Thus, a client may learn to avoid being lonely and to cope with loneliness should it occur despite his efforts to avoid it. In treatment using the GLM, the focus is also on helping the client to actively approach situations and life conditions that will bring him satisfaction as well as meet his goals and needs. Thus, for example, in addition to avoiding situations that may pose a risk or create loneliness, treatment also helps a client to learn to seek out situations that will meet such needs as relationships with others and how to build a life in which loneliness rarely occurs. In using this approach, it is essential that a balance be created between risk-management avoidance goals and active approach goals to meeting needs. To do anything else can result in disastrous social and personal consequences for the therapist and offender. Promoting goods without managing risk will potentially result in clients who are happy and well-adjusted, but who remain dangerous and at risk to re-offend. Conversely, attempting to manage risk without concern for goods promotion or well-being could result in punitive therapist practices, and could bring about disengagement and lack of motivation on the part of the client.

As can be seen from the above brief discussion, the GLM adopts a constructive, positive, humanistic approach to treatment. Offenders are viewed as people who, like all human beings, are attempting to live meaningful, worthwhile lives in the best way they can, given the specific circumstances confronting them. Clients are regarded in the GLM as goal-directed individuals who are worthy of therapists' respect as well as therapists' belief in those clients' capacity to change. Offending behavior is viewed as directly or indirectly related to attempts to acquire the things that are important in their lives, and therapists are the agents of change who can assist clients to lead a better life. In other words, treatment within the GLM framework is, therefore, aimed toward having the work be collaborative, motivating, and positive.

BASIC FOUNDATIONS OF THE SELF-REGULATION MODEL (SRM) AND THE REVISED SELF-REGULATION MODEL (SRM-R)

The self-regulation model of sexual offending is based on self-regulation theory (Baumeister and Heatherington, 1996; Carver and Scheier, 1981, 1998). Self-regulation is a broad theory, while the SRM is a model that is specific to the sexual offense process. The SRM was developed to help provide an alternative approach to the traditional Relapse Prevention Model and its shortcomings (Ward and Hudson, 1998; Ward et al., 1995, 2004; Yates, 2005, 2007; Yates and Kingston, 2005).

Self-regulation is a multifaceted, comprehensive theory of the complex processes of goal-directed behavior and decision-making (Baumeister and Heatherton, 1996; Baumeister and Vohs, 2004). This theory describes numerous internal and external processes that guide or direct behavior (Karoly, 1993). The processes focus on the planning, monitoring, evaluation, and modification of behavior. Self-regulation also provides details on the complex processes that are involved when self-regulation fails and an individual acts in a manner that is not congruent with his own goals.

When applied to sexual offending in the development of the SRM (Ward and Hudson, 1998; Ward et al., 1995) consideration was given to the specific motivations and path ways followed by sexual offenders, with the aim of understanding the sexual offending process more comprehensively, and the goal of developing a more wide-ranging treatment approach than that which was previously available (i.e., the Relapse Prevention Model; Ward and Hudson, 1998; Ward et al., 1995).

The revised SRM (the SRM-R; Yates and Ward, 2008) is a 10-phase model of the offense process that includes four distinct pathways to offending based on the combination of offense-related goals and the strategies individuals use to achieve those goals. The SRM-R also explicitly incorporates elements of the GLM—to make it more consistent with this rehabilitation theory—including primary goods and their relationship to offending. This 10-phase model describes background and vulnerability factors and the development of the offense progression from the occurrence of a life event that triggers the desire to offend, through two post-offense phases. During post-offense phases individuals evaluate their behavior and formulate their attitudes and intentions with respect to future offending, a process that takes into account the factors that predispose individuals to sexual offending (see figure 1).

It is important to note that the SRM-R is a model of the *offense process*, and is not an *offender typology* model. That is, the SRM does not aim to classify individuals into specific categories or types, but it rather is intended to be used to understand the motivations and dynamics that underlie offending. Thus, the SRM-R describes the *offense progression* or the chain of events that occurs during a specific sexual offense or series of offenses, in order to identify the cognitive, behavioral, emotional, and situational factors that culminate in offending. Although the SRM and SRM-R posit four offense pathways, these pathways represent patterns of cognition and behavior in specific situations, rather than types of offenders. Thus, while it is correct to classify an individual's offense behavior as following an avoidant or approach pathway, it is not correct to regard the individual as being avoidant or approach-oriented in terms of his overall functioning, personal characteristics, or self-regulation style. The goal of using the SRM-R in treatment is to understand the various facets of behavior in offending situations, such that therapists providing treatment can plan and implement individualized treatment accordingly. The basis of the SRM-R involves offense-related goals and strategies surrounding offending behavior, and is described below as it has been embedded within the GLM (the integrated GLM/SRM-R; Yates and Ward, 2008). Using the model to prepare a personal history ("autobiography") is found in chapter 9. Offense disclosure exercises are found in chapter 10. Treatment methods for using the SRM-R are provided in part III of this book.

Within the self-regulation model, two types of problematic self-regulatory styles exist that apply to sexual offending, as well as functional or intact self-regulatory capacity (Baumeister and Heatherton, 1996; Carver and Scheier, 1990; Ward and Hudson, 1998; Ward et al., 2006; Yates and Kingston, 2005). These self-regulatory styles include the following:

- **Under-regulation:** This self-regulation style involves a failure to control behavior. It results in an individual acting in a disinhibited manner in which he does not attempt to exert control in a specific situation.

- **Mis-regulation:** This self-regulation style involves attempts to control behavior, but the attempts are misguided or counter-productive. Mis-regulation results in failure to achieve goals and in a loss of control when these attempts at control fail.

Fundamentals of the Good Lives, Self-Regulation, and Integrated Models   45

Figure 1: Revised Self-Regulation Model of the Sexual Offense Process

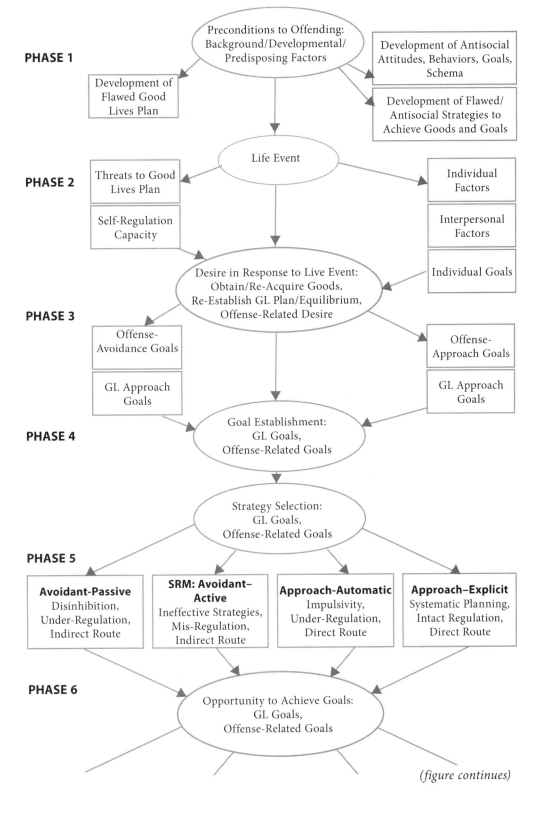

(figure continues)

46   Chapter 3

(figure 1 continued)

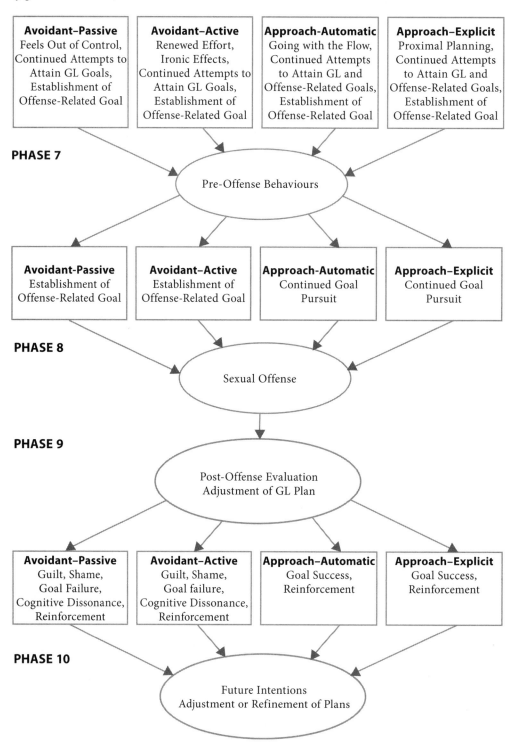

(This figure was reprinted with permission from Yates and Ward, 2008)

- **Intact self-regulation:** This self-regulation style is not considered dysfunctional with respect to self-control—that is, individuals with this style are able to use effective self-regulatory strategies or to exert control in achieving desired goals. In this case, it is the individual's goals (e.g., antisocial schemas or beliefs) that are problematic and that require intervention, rather than deficits in self-regulation per se.

OFFENSE-RELATED GOALS

As is the case with the GLM, goals are an important construct in self-regulation theory generally and in the SRM-R when it is specific to sexual offenders. While the GLM focuses on goals in the context of attaining primary and secondary human goods, the SRM-R's emphasis is on goals specifically related to sexual offending behavior during the offense progression. In the integrated GLM/SRM-R, good lives goals are also integrated in understanding offending behavior. This deeper understanding is because Ward's earlier analysis indicated that offenders were indeed preoccupied with seeking outcomes allied with, or alongside, sexual offending that were important to them (Ward and Maruna, 2007). Within the SRM-R, these goals are referred to as *offense-related goals*, and are more closely related to dynamic risk factors than are GLM goals. In the GLM, dynamic risk factors are indicators of flaws in an individual's ability to attain what is important to him (i.e., his good life plan), while in the SRM-R, dynamic risk factors provide essential information related his offense progression and motivations for offending. In a sense, dynamic risk factors or criminogenic needs are reflected in individuals' pursuit of secondary goods in the form of the four good lives plan flaws noted earlier. For example, the choice to associate with antisocial peers may result from a lack of a person's external opportunities for other types of relationships and/or certain social skill deficits.

In the SRM-R, offense-related goals can be either *avoidance-based* or *approach-based* (Cochran and Tesser, 1996).

- *Offense-related avoidance goals* guide behavior so as to enable the individual to avoid or prevent an undesired outcome, specifically with respect to sexual offending.

- *Offense-related approach goals* guide behavior so as to achieve a desired state or outcome during the offense progression.

Thus, some sexual offenders strive to avoid or prevent offending when the situation presents itself, and may attempt to control their behavior in order to do so. Others approach offending as an opportunity to secure valued outcomes, either intentionally or as a result of entrenched cognitive and behavioral patterns and scripts, when these emerge during the offense progression (Ward et al., 1998, 2004, 2006; Yates and Ward, 2008).

Examples: Offense-Related Avoidant Goals versus Offense-Related Approach Goals

Ricardo is 20 years old and lives with his girlfriend. They have been arguing about money in recent weeks, and in Ricardo's view, she has become cold and distant. For Ricardo, her coldness only makes matters worse. He tries repeatedly to calm himself down, but he keeps thinking about his financial problems and the fact that his girlfriend is much less willing to have sex with him than she used to be. One day his girlfriend returns to their apartment and finds him smoking marijuana. She demands to know where he got the money for this, and he becomes intensely angry. A fight ensues, and he forces her to have sex with him. He is soon remorseful and is confused by his own actions.

Ricardo's initial intentions were not to engage in sexual abuse. He had attempted to cope with the problems within his relationship, albeit unsuccessfully. His immediate goal in this situation was to regain a momentary sense of equilibrium and to establish himself as "the man" within the relationship.

Andrew lives by himself and works nights in a paper mill. He does not feel as though he fits in with the others who work there and views himself as defective in some way. He has spent many years trying to dissuade himself about his sexual attraction to boys. During a Saturday morning after a shift at work, Andrew is watching a young boy playing in the yard and decides that he can no longer fight the urge. Andrew has observed this boy over several months and is aware of some of the boy's interests. Andrew makes a point to go a shop specializing in sports-related trading cards so that he can approach the boy. He believes that if he can gain sufficient access, he can then show the boy some pornography and get him interested in having sex. After he pursues the boy and engages him in sex, Andrew feels very satisfied and tries to think of other ways to maintain sexual access to the boy.

Ricardo has followed an *avoidant-passive* pathway. This pathway is evident by his desire to avoid offending, which was associated with trying to re-assert control. By contrast, Andrew has followed an *approach-explicit* pathway. His explicit intent throughout the experience was to engage in sex with this boy. While Ricardo evaluated his offending behavior as negative, Andrew evaluated the experience as positive.

OFFENSE-RELATED STRATEGIES

The strategies individuals select to help them achieve their goals are related to their self-regulation capacity and whether behavior is under-regulated, mis-regulated, or intact. Individuals utilize either *passive* or *active* strategies in the offense progression in order to achieve an offense-related goal.

- *Passive strategies* involve situations in which an individual fails to implement any strategies to prevent offending. In such a case, the individual may ignore offense-related desires or urges, or may simply not use any strategies in the situation. Passive strategies may also involve poorly planned or impulsive strategies that occur relatively automatically in response to cues in a specific situation.

- *Active strategies* are used in the offense progression to prevent an offense from occurring. Active strategies may involve such choices as removing oneself from a risk situation or attempting to cope with a charged emotional state that is associated with offending, such as the presence of deviant sexual urges. Active strategies also occur when individuals explicitly plan to offend and then implement strategies to achieve this goal.

Examples: Offense-Related Passive Strategies versus Offense-Related Active Strategies

Rafael came home from a long day at work and took a shower. His brother's girlfriend arrived shortly afterward. Rafael was sexually aroused upon leaving the shower and then was surprised to see this woman in his house. Although he knew he probably shouldn't, Rafael thought it was worth seeing if she was interested in at least "playing around." She rejected his advances, so he then ignored her and went into another room to watch television. At this point, she walked into the room and tried to talk to him. He then took off his bathrobe and began groping at her breasts and vagina. When she rejected him a second time he knew he had made a mistake.

Francis collected and viewed child pornography on a regular basis, although he never intended to act out sexually with a "real" child. One day, however, his neighbor asked him to babysit her daughter for a few hours while she ran some errands. Francis had no intention to offend, but when he saw the girl, all of his fantasies that had occurred while watching child pornography suddenly emerged. He told himself that the children in the images hadn't been harmed, so neither would his neighbor's daughter be. He then began to fondle the child, at which time his neighbor returned and called the police.

Rafael had not planned to engage in a sexual crime. He knew he should not approach his brother's girlfriend sexually and so, after trying once, he simply tried to ignore her and distract himself by watching television, both of which are passive strategies. Rafael followed an *avoidant-passive* offense pathway. By contrast, Francis responded to situational cues in the environment (i.e., the presence of his neighbor's daughter, which brought forward his sexual fantasies). He acted impulsively based on this cue, which was interpreted through his cognitive schema that children were not harmed by sexual activity. Francis was following an *approach-automatic* pathway.

When an individual holding an offense-related avoidant goal utilizes no strategies or passive strategies in the offense progression, the pathway to offending is described as the *avoidant-passive pathway*. In contrast, an individual holding an offense-related avoidant goal utilizes active strategies to prevent offending in the offense progression. This pathway to offending is called the *avoidant-active pathway*. Concerning approach goals, when an individual holding an offense-related approach goal utilizes passive strategies in the offense progression (to achieve offending), the pathway to offending is the *approach-automatic pathway*. If an individual holding an offense-related approach goal utilizes active strategies in the offense progression (to achieve offending), the pathway to offending is the *approach-explicit pathway*. These four pathways are described below.

Offense Pathways

Both the original SRM and the revised SRM (SRM-R) include four pathways to offending. As indicated, each pathway is constituted by the combination of *offense-related goals* (approach versus avoidance) and the *strategies* the individual selects to achieve the goal in the offense situation (passive/automatic versus active/explicit). Each pathway is associated with a distinct regulation style and, as such, different treatment approaches and targets will be required for each pathway the client has followed (see part III of this book). As indicated previously, the SRM-R provides a model of the offense progression. Thus, individuals may follow different pathways for different types of offenses. For example, an individual who has offended against both adults and children may follow, for example, an avoidant-active pathway when offending against children but an approach-automatic pathway when offending against adults. Which pathway the offender utilized is determined during assessment (see chapter 5) and during treatment (see part III). The four SRM-R offense pathways are as follows:

Avoidant-Passive Pathway

This pathway is associated with an under-regulated self-regulation style. Individuals following this pathway wish to prevent sexual offending from occurring (and so hold an avoidant goal with respect to offending). Because their behavior is under-regulated, however, they fail to control their behavior and offending occurs because they do not take steps to stop the offense progression. At best, they will deny their urges or try to distract themselves in some minimal way from what is occurring in the offense progression. During the offense progression, they are typically unaware of the progression of events or their interpretations of, and responses to, these events. When they become disinhibited and when cognitive deconstruction occurs, they abandon their higher level goal (to refrain from offending) in favor of proceeding in the immediate situation (Ward et al., 1995). After offending, they experience negative affective states, a negative post-offense evaluation, and cognitive dissonance (i.e., because their goal to avoid offending and their actual behavior (offending) are inconsistent). They may resolve not to offend, but do not have the strategies in place to do so when the next risk situation arises.

Example: Avoidant-Passive SRM-R Offense Pathway

Doug was raised in a home in which he observed his mother and father having sex and using drugs. His sister was removed from the home due to behavioral problems and was placed in a residential program. Doug was 19 years old at the time his sister came back to their home to live. Not long after her return, he gave her drugs and alcohol and asked her about her experiences in the program. As the night progressed and they continued to take drugs and alcohol, Doug became increasingly sexually aroused but wasn't sure if she was attracted to him or not. Although he tried to ignore and deny his urges, they kept occurring. He interpreted her open discussion as an invitation and so he reached over and kissed her. When she froze in place, afraid to move, Doug understood this as tacit acceptance of his advances. Doug quickly disrobed her and began having sex with her. In Doug's mind, the fact that she wasn't saying "No" seemed to mean that she was enjoying it and okay with it. He expected to be satisfied by the experience, but he wasn't. He realized that things between them would never be the same. He regretted the incident, and said he would try never to do that again.

In this example, Doug did not set out to cause his sister sexual harm. He initially tried to deny his sexual urges, but made little effort to stop himself from carrying them out. As he became disinhibited, he quickly abandoned his goal of not offending and engaged in sexual behavior. His post-offense evaluation of the situation was negative; he did not want a similar situation to happen again. As such, Doug followed an avoidant-passive pathway to offending.

Avoidant-Active Pathway

This pathway is associated with mis-regulation. Similar to individuals who follow an avoidant-passive pathway, these individuals wish to prevent offending from occurring. In contrast to individuals following an avoidant-passive pathway, however, those following an avoidant-active pathway implement active strategies to attempt to exert control, such as suppressing urges or arousal, in order to achieve their goal to not offend. The strategies they use, however, such as substance use to control mood or the use of pornography, are ultimately ineffective. In fact, such strategies can actually increase the risk to offend. For example, substance use may disinhibit an individual, while the use of pornography may function to increase and entrench his deviant sexual interests. When his strategies to prevent offending fail, disinhibition and cognitive deconstruction occur, and he abandons his higher level goal (to avoid offending) in favor of proceeding in the immediate situation. Following the offense, an individual will then negatively evaluate himself and his behavior, given his failure to achieve his desired goal to avoid committing an offense.

Example: Avoidant-Active SRM-R Offense Pathway

Paul, 29, was in a tenuous relationship with his girlfriend, Anna. She frequently talked about other men, and indicated displeasure with the hours Paul kept at work. For her part, Anna was uncertain about the direction she wanted their relationship to go. Paul thought it might help if he took her out for a night on the town. They went to a club downtown in their city, danced, and spent some time with old friends. Throughout the course of the evening, Paul kept thinking that Anna was flirting with others. He tried to push these ideas aside and enjoy the evening, but she kept appearing more interested in other men than she was in him. Worse, she seemed to be having a better time than he had seen her have in almost a year. He grew increasingly jealous. He tried to talk to a friend to see whether he was right, but his friend said that not only had he not noticed, his attentions were elsewhere. Paul's friend told him not to worry about it.

Deciding that it would be better to talk about it, Paul confronted Anna on the drive home. By the time they arrived, she acknowledged in a frustrated tone that she was not sure what she wanted out of the relationship anymore. Experiencing this as a slight against his masculinity, he slapped Anna across the face. He quickly apologized and took a step back. Anna stood for a second, shocked. She slapped him back, and called him a name. Paul wrestled with her and told her never to do that again. Paul then sexually assaulted her, and afterward begged her not to leave him.

In this example, Paul had not planned to sexually assault Anna that evening. To the contrary, his goal was to re-establish their relationship. Through the course of the evening, his escalating jealousy became greater than his resources to regulate himself. He tried to use some rudimentary cognitive skills to manage his mood state, and attempted, albeit unsuccessfully, to check his perceptions against those of his friend. Paul's decision to sexually assault Anna happened quickly in response to her slapping him, at which point he abandoned his long-term goal of improving their relationship for the short-term goal of gaining mastery and control over her.

Approach-Automatic Pathway

This pathway is associated with under-regulation and with *acquisitional* or *appetitive* goals with respect to offending—that is, individuals following this pathway do not wish to avoid offending. Instead, they actively welcome (approach) the opportunity to sexually offend, although the offending occurs in a relatively automatic manner. These individuals become disinhibited and fail to control their behavior during the offense progression. The offenses committed by individuals following this pathway are activated by cues and triggers in the immediate situation, and may appear impulsive. If planning is evident, it is typically rudimentary, unsophisticated, and implicit. During offending, individuals following the approach-automatic pathway are guided by entrenched cognitive and behavioral scripts that support offending and of which they may not be consciously aware. Because this pathway is characterized by an appetitive goal (i.e., seeking out a desired state and reflecting a positive view of sexual offending), individuals following this pathway will exhibit predominantly positive emotional states, both in the phases leading up to the sexual offense and after the offense has occurred. When negative affect is present, this emotional state tends to be associated with grievance, hostility, retribution, anger, and so forth, for which he is seeking relief. When the offender evaluates himself and his behavior after offending, his attitude tends to be a positive one, since he has been successful in achieving his goals.

Example: Approach-Automatic SRM-R Offense Pathway

James had always found pre-pubescent girls attractive, even though he was married and attracted to his wife, her friends, and other adult females, as well. He lived in a rural area and had always offered his house for parties and various neighborhood gatherings. Very often, afternoon gatherings would continue late into the night with drinking and bonfires. James had sexually abused his daughter in the past and had convinced her it was in her best interest not to tell anyone. Likewise, he was a stern disciplinarian with his sons when they did not keep the house clean. At times he could become angry and abusive for no apparent reason. However, James could be quite endearing to others, as well.

One afternoon, James and a number of neighborhood children played a game of hide and seek. Finding himself alone behind the house with a neighborhood girl, he quickly fondled her breasts and groin area over her clothes. He laughed, explained that this was part of the game and was no big deal, and he encouraged her to return to the front yard and join him with the other guests.

In this example, James did not attempt to prevent himself from offending. Although he did not engage in extensive deliberate planning, he engaged in offending quite impulsively. James has poor general and sexual self-regulation skills, and is quick to seize opportunities for sexual gratification when they occur in his immediate surroundings. To others, he can appear quite impulsive. James' offending behavior is fueled by an appetite for sexual activity, and he appears to evaluate these experiences positively.

Approach-Explicit Pathway

This pathway is associated with intact self-regulation and an approach or appetitive/acquisitional goal with respect to offending. During the offense progression, individuals following this pathway demonstrate few or no deficits in their ability to monitor, evaluate, and modify their behavior in order to achieve their goal (to offend). Thus, offending occurs as a result of the individual's explicit, intentional, active attempts to attain antisocial goals rather than from any kind of impaired ability to control his behavior. The individual's goals arise from early learning and other experiences that have led to the development of his cognitive schemas supporting sexual aggression (Ward and Hudson, 1998; Ward and Maruna, 2007). Individuals allocated to this pathway typically demonstrate positive affect throughout the offense progression, and their strategies used in offending are well planned. In fact, offenders following the approach-explicit pathway are typically able to control and postpone offending if the conditions are not "right" (e.g., if a potential witness is present). Following the offense, these individuals will evaluate themselves and their behavior positively, as they have successfully achieved their goal. Cognitive dissonance and inhibition are absent in the offense progression and the individual appears to present as an "expert" (Ward and Hudson, 1998).

Example: Approach-Explicit SRM-R Offense Pathway

Tom has been interested in sexual contact with children as long as he can remember. He is gainfully employed as an information technology specialist and has no criminal record. In recent years, he has developed computer skills sufficient to network with others interested in having sex with children, and he has engaged in sharing computer files of child pornography with them. Tom also engages in sexualized conversations with children whom he meets on-line with the screen name "Tommie12."

Tom is actively involved in his church, and saves his vacation time to travel to impoverished areas of the world to participate in missionary activities. During these sojourns, he also seeks out and has sex with children. Often, Tom organizes these encounters in advance, through the use of international contacts. In some impoverished countries, he has simply sought out child prostitutes in the cities where his church is working.

In this example, Tom clearly and explicitly plans offending in advance and implements his plans in a skillful and reflective way. He desires and enjoys sexual activity with children and has intact self-regulation in most areas of his life, including his offending behavior. Tom is aware of the inherent risks of offending, and is able to consider these when constructing his offense plans. For example, he is able to delay many of his actions until he can travel to a region where law enforcement is scarce. Because his goal is to offend and his planning is explicit, he clearly follows the approach-explicit pathway in each of his offenses.

Offense pathways are determined using the 10-phase offense progression model per the integrated GLM/SRM-R (Yates and Ward, 2008), described below.

OFFENSE PROGRESSION MODEL

The original SRM was a nine-phase model of the offense progression that focused solely on sexual offending behavior and did not include other goals, such as primary goods (Ward and Hudson, 1998; Ward et al., 1995, 2004). The revised model is a 10-phase model that explicitly incorporates elements of the GLM and analyzes their relationship to offending behavior (SRM-R; Yates and Ward, 2008). The phases of this revised model are described next and are illustrated in figure 1.

Phase 1: Background and Predisposing Factors

This phase does not form part of the offense progression per se, but was added to the SRM-R because the original model did not include the influence of an offender's individual background and predisposing factors and those factors' influences on the offense progression. Each individual responds differently to life events that occur, with sexual offenders being predisposed to respond in a sexual manner to this event (Phase 2). Specific responses are dependent upon individuals' developmental and learning histories and psychological, social, and biological factors, each of which affects the individual's risk to commit a sexual offense. For example, clients with histories of being abused during their own early development may then be, depending on other factors, more likely to abuse others. Clients who have witnessed abuse between their parents or between other partners may be predisposed to use violence in their own intimate relationships, though again that choice is dependent upon other factors and experiences in that same individual's life. For example, the end of an intimate relationship for such an individual may trigger a desire to regain intimacy or to re-establish the relationship, which may then cause the person to attempt to re-acquire his relationship need through control and through sexual or other violence. These important predisposing factors are acknowledged in the SRM-R and are included in treatment (see chapter 9).

Phase 2: Life Event

During the initiation phase of the offense progression, a life event occurs that triggers a desire (sexual or otherwise) in response to the event. The life event may be relatively minor in nature (e.g., an argument) or may be more significant (e.g., loss of employment). The event that triggers the offense progression will be unique and personal to each client. In addition to the event itself, the individual will appraise the event and evaluate or interpret it within the context of his own experience, cognitive schemas, and the like. Thus, for example, an individual who holds the view that the world is a hostile and dangerous place is more likely to interpret an ambiguous event as a threatening experience. That assessment will, in turn, trigger his desire for self-protection or will make him inclined to harm others before he himself can be harmed. He is likely to ignore or discard evidence that runs contrary to his personal perception of the situation. Although all human beings can engage in similar processes, these elements are particularly important in understanding sexual abuse.

In addition to an offense-related desire, the life event may trigger the desire to achieve a particular primary human good (which may or may not be related to offensive behavior). For example, the potential loss of a relationship could lead to a threat to the primary good of relatedness. Because the individual is predisposed to offend sexually, this life event may threaten the individual's good life plan in addition to triggering the offense progression.

Phase 3: Desire in Response to Life Event

As indicated in Phase 2, the life event and the client's interpretation of this event triggers some type of desire. In addition, during this phase, the individual will also evaluate his capacity to tolerate the desire as he decides what his response will be to the event. His desire may be sexual or non-sexual in nature at this phase, and may be deviant, aggressive, or appropriate. For example, in response to a threatened relationship, an individual who desires to regain intimacy is demonstrating an appropriate goal at this phase in the progression. Alternatively, the desire that is triggered may be sexual (but not deviant), as when the event triggers a desire for consensual sexual activity. Similarly, the desire may be non-sexual, such as when the individual's goal is the re-establishment of intimacy. In addition, the desire may be non-sexual and non-deviant when the life event triggers anger, hostility, or a desire for retaliation instead of a sexual urge. Lastly, the desire may be appropriate, such as would be the case when the desire is for the re-establishment of elements in the individual's good life plan. It is because of the individual's predisposing factors that this desire eventually results in sexual offending later in the offense progression.

Phase 4: Goal Establishment

Once a life event triggers a desire, the individual will establish goals in response to the desire. These goals can be appropriate and/or pro-social goals (as in the case of a goal to re-attain a primary good) and/or offense-related goals, as described in Phase 3. For example, for an individual for whom the life event triggered the desire to re-acquire the primary good of relatedness, the goal established at this stage could be directly in service of acquiring this good (e.g., re-establishing a relationship—a secondary good). This choice will be the influencing factor even though the ultimate result is committing a sexual offense. Alternatively, or additionally, an offense-related goal will be established at this phase in the offense progression, with the individual either desiring to prevent an offense from occurring (an offense-related avoidant goal) or wishing to continue with behavior that actively provokes offending to occur (an offense-related approach goal). Offense-related goals and non-offending goals may co-exist during this phase. For example, an individual who has an avoidant goal with respect to offending may nonetheless simultaneously hold an approach goal with respect to goods sought. As such, the individual may want to avoid acting on offense-related desires while simultaneously seeking out a particular non-offending goal. As an example, an individual whose goal is to refrain from acting out sexually against a child may at the same time have the goal of obtaining intimacy or sexual gratification, something he lacks the capacity or opportunity to acquire appropriately. As this conflicting situation unfolds, it is likely that the individual will experience cognitive dissonance, and will rely on cognitive schemas and established behavioral and self-regulation patterns in order to continue in the offense progression. Thus, while he wishes to refrain from offending, he simultaneously wishes to obtain an appropriate goal (intimacy or sexual gratification), although he does so via offending.

As described above, the type of goal at this phase of the offense progression determines the offense pathway followed during the commission of the offense, in conjunction with the strategies selected to achieve the goal (Phase 5).

Phase 5: Strategy Selection
During Phase 5 of the offense progression, the individual selects the strategies he will use to achieve the goal established in Phase 4. These strategies are predominantly related to offense-related goals, although the individual may also have other goals, such as achieving certain primary goods. The strategies selected at this phase are in service of these goals. Thus, an individual holding offense-related avoidance goals will implement either passive or active strategies to achieve this goal. For example, he may do nothing or may simply attempt to deny or ignore urges that signal offending (passive strategies), or he may actively try to prevent offending through attempting to implement specific strategies, such as removing himself from the situation (active strategies). In either case, he is ineffective in preventing offending, and the offense progression proceeds.

Individuals holding offense-related approach goals establish strategies that will move them closer to offending. These strategies may be selected relatively automatically or in some cases, impulsively, or they may be explicitly selected. For example, some individuals may relatively impulsively select the strategy of abuse or aggression to right a perceived wrong in a particular situation, whereas others may deliberately seek out a victim against whom they will offend or against whom they will seek an opportunity to offend.

Phase 6: Opportunity to Achieve Goals
In many offense models, this phase is traditionally referred to as the occurrence of a high-risk situation. Because of the focus on achieving appropriate goals (e.g., primary human goods) in the integrated GLM/SRM-R, however, this phase of the offense progression is conceptualized as one in which the opportunity to achieve goals is presented as a result of the goals and strategies established during Phases 4 and 5. Thus, although events at this phase of the progression pose a risk for offending to occur, they may simultaneously or additionally present as an opportunity to achieve other (appropriate)

goals. So, for example, although the occurrence of the opportunity may represent the possibility of meeting the primary good of intimacy, because the individual achieves this goal through offending, this opportunity involves a child or an unwilling adult. The individual may wish to avoid offending (Phase 4), but nonetheless may also regard the situation as an opportunity to establish an intimate relationship.

With respect to offense-related goals specifically, individuals who established avoidant goals in Phase 4 of the offense progression abandon this higher level goal in favor of more immediate goals in the situation, such as the possibility of sexual gratification, which essentially overrides the avoidance goal. For individuals following this pathway, the occurrence of the opportunity signals failure and goal conflict—that is, they have failed to achieve the avoidance goal and are now approaching offending—and they experience predominantly negative affective responses, disinhibition, and cognitive deconstruction at this stage. For individuals holding offense-related approach goals, the opportunity is goal-congruent, signals success in meeting the goal, and is predominantly associated with positive affective states.

Phase 7: Pre-Offense Behaviors

During Phase 7 of the offense progression, the individual engages in specific behaviors that lead to offending. Individuals holding offense-related avoidance goals become disinhibited, and they switch temporarily to an approach goal with respect to offending. Individuals' actions at this phase may represent either or both offense-related behaviors or actions in service of achieving a primary good. Ultimately, regardless of the nature of offense-related or other goals, the behavior in which the individual engages during this phase functions to create an acute risk to offend. At this stage, the individual may be engaging in behaviors such as deliberately creating access to a potential victim, or acting aggressively in order to gain retribution, which, for the individual, is associated with sexual acting out.

Phase 8: Commission of Sexual Offense

During the commission of the sexual offense, the individual achieves his offense-related goal of offending and may also attain non-offending good lives goals, albeit in harmful and maladaptive ways. With respect to offense-related goals, individuals following avoidant pathways have either committed the offense because they did not implement strategies (passive pathway) or because the strategies they attempted were not effective (active pathway). Among individuals with offense-related approach goals, the commission of a sexual offense represents the intended end result of the offense progression as well as a success experience with respect to achieving goals. In either case, committing a sexual offense may also represent the means by which primary goods were also obtained. Furthermore, offending may be incorporated into individuals' good lives plans as a way to attain primary goods.

Phase 9: Post-Offense Evaluation and Adjustment of Good Lives Plan

As the first of two post-offense phases, Phase 9 occurs in the time period immediately following the offense. Phase 9 is the time when the individual evaluates his behavior and also the time during which reinforcement contingencies are present. Because reinforcement for behavior is a powerful process that functions to entrench and/or increase the occurrence of the behavior, it is important that treatment address what the individual gained from offending. Even individuals holding offense-related avoidance goals are likely to experience some reinforcement, such as sexual gratification (positive reinforcement) or the alleviation of negative emotional states (negative reinforcement). Even if this gain is temporary or transient, it will provide reinforcement for behavior and increase the likelihood that the behavior will recur in the future. Evaluation of behavior within individuals' good lives plans also occurs, with individuals who have successfully obtained a primary good viewing the offense as a positive experience, at least in part.

With respect to offense-related goals specifically, individuals following an avoidant pathway will experience negative affect, cognitive dissonance, and so forth, because their behavior is inconsistent with their higher order goals and their views of themselves. Offenders following an approach pathway are unlikely to experience this negative evaluation of their behavior and will, in fact, evaluate the experience quite positively.

Phase 10: Future Intentions and Adjustments to Good Lives Plan

The second post-offense evaluation in the offense progression relates to additional longer term intentions about offending (while Phase 9 evaluations occur immediately after the offense). At this phase, individuals develop, refine, and formulate future intentions and expectations with respect to offending. This process might entail further entrenching of behavior or might bring about a change in behaviors and attitudes regarding the acceptability of offending. Individuals with avoidance goals typically attempt to reassert control and may resolve not to offend in the future. However, they lack the conditions and capacities to achieve this goal. Conversely, some individuals originally following avoidant pathways may abandon this goal and take a more approach-oriented goal with respect to future offending. Individuals holding an approach goal learn from the offense experience and refine the strategies they will use in the future to achieve this goal, further incorporating offending into their personal identity. Conversely, these individuals may experience and evaluate offending in negative terms, and may develop an avoidance goal with respect to offending. Finally, regardless of offense-related goals, individuals may also formulate future plans, intentions, and expectations with respect to achieving their good lives plans.

Summary

The GLM builds on the presupposition that sexual offending results from various personal, physiological, and social conditions that lead an individual to achieve his goals in life through offending. This model includes 10 primary human goods that all people seek to achieve in various ways, and four potential flaws in peoples' pursuit of those primary goods.

The SRM-R is a model of the *offense process* that posits four offense pathways and a 10-phase process, reflecting decision-making and different dynamics of offending across offense situations. The model is anchored in research examining self-regulatory styles, including under-regulation, mis-regulation, and intact regulation, as well as approach- and avoidance-based offense-related goals and the active and passive strategies that people employ in achieving them. Having covered these models, the next chapter focuses on assessment as a fundamental basis for intervention.

PART II

Assessment and Treatment Planning

CHAPTER 4

Assessment of the Components of Good Lives

As explained in chapter 3, treatment begins with the therapist completing a comprehensive assessment of the various factors involved in an individual's offense behavior. Within the integrated GLM/SRM-R approach (in addition to risk, need, and responsivity factors) this assessment needs to include gathering an understanding of the individual's primary human goods and the secondary goods he uses to acquire the primary ones. It also needs to include an assessment of the individual's self-regulation capacity and his specific offense pathway.

Recall from chapter 3 the proposal that all individuals seek out 10 types of primary human goods in order to achieve a fulfilling life.

1. **Life:** Healthy living and functioning—the basic needs in life

2. **Knowledge:** Desire for information and understanding about oneself and the world

3. **Excellence in Play and Work** (including mastery experiences)

4. **Excellence in Agency:** Autonomy, independence, and self-directedness

5. **Inner Peace:** Freedom from emotional turmoil and stress

6. **Friendship:** Connections to others through intimate, romantic, familial, and other relationships

6. **Community:** A sense of belonging to a larger group of individuals with shared interests

7. **Spirituality:** A broad sense of finding meaning and purpose in life

8. **Happiness:** A state of being of overall contentedness in one's life; the experience of pleasure

9. **Creativity:** The desire to have novelty or innovation in one's life

As noted previously, clients are unlikely to be able to identify these goods explicitly. Understanding the goods a client values and the means he uses to obtain these goods is an *inferential* exercise on the part of the therapist. Thus, assessment of primary goods is conducted via an interview process as well as through observation during treatment (see Yates et al., 2009, for a semi-structured interview and coding protocol). This assessment includes

- the goods that are important to the client (primary goods);
- the activities (the secondary goods) in which the client engages in order to obtain his primary goods;
- the relationship between the client's attempts to attain a particular good and sexual offending; and,
- problems or flaws that exist in the client's good life plan that block his attainment of those goods.

Assessment of Primary Human Goods

In beginning the interview process, the therapist or evaluator seeks to identify the main primary human goods that form the basis of the client's good life plan. The goal is to understand what qualities of life are important to the client. These goods will be addressed in treatment in order to help the client attain a satisfying life and adequate levels of personal well-being. This assessment may take place through a series of increasingly detailed questions about the activities, situations, and experiences that are important to the client in his life and the activities into which he puts his energies on a regular basis. In addition, a second assessment strategy is to infer what goals are evident in both the client's general life functioning as well as his offense-related behavior. The assessment has both backward-looking and forward-looking aspects to it. The former is evident in the examination of the individual's offense patterns and associated developmental history, whereas the latter is reflected in the clinician's attempts to identify the offender's aspirations, future plans, and fundamental commitments he associates with his own future. As with enhancing motivation, the goal is to have practitioners relate to offenders in a collaborative way.

Some examples of the values that individuals associate with primary goods are noted below, although it is important to understand that what follows are examples only. Specific primary goods and their values are unique to each individual.

PRIMARY GOOD	SAMPLE INDICATOR OF VALUE PLACED ON GOOD
Life	• Places importance on basic needs such as housing • Places importance on diet, nutrition, or exercise
Knowledge	• Places importance on education • Places importance on specific information or personally relevant knowledge (e.g., related to work) • Desires to understand own behavior or others' experiences
Excellence in Play and Work	• Places importance on success and gratification in leisure or recreational activities • Places importance on mastery in work or career advancement • Has a desire to engage in pleasurable activities
Excellence in Agency	• Places importance on self-sufficiency and independence • Places importance on living life consistent with own values, beliefs, principles (whether pro-social or antisocial)

Inner Peace	• Places importance on gaining emotional or psychological stability and understanding; copes with or attempts to cope with emotional states
Relatedness	• Places importance on relationships with friends, family, partners, children
Community	• Places importance on being part of social groups or groups with shared interests • Places importance on contributing to one's own community
Spirituality	• Places importance on a connection to a higher being or a broader spiritual awareness • Values sense of being part of a larger whole • Participates in groups that seek or share a common broad purpose (e.g., environmental concerns)
Happiness	• Places importance on general life satisfaction, contentment • Places importance on sense of purpose in life • Places importance on experiencing pleasure
Creativity	• Places importance on artistic or creative activities, or creating a product • Places importance on novel experiences

This part of the assessment should result in an understanding of the basic elements of individuals' good lives plans—what it is they need to have in their lives in order to feel fulfilled.

Example: Assessing Primary Human Goods

Scott is a 22-year-old man who was recently convicted of sexually abusing his partner, Patrick. In this initial interview, Scott presents as anxious and in despair. He has requested to see a psychiatrist so that he can be considered for antidepressant medication.

Interviewer: Welcome, Scott. Would it be okay if we went directly to the circumstances that brought you here?

Scott: I guess we'd better.

Interviewer: I understand—and can see—that you've had a difficult time of it lately.

Scott: Yes. I can't believe what's happened in the past several weeks. I've lost just about everything.

Interviewer: How so?

Scott: Well, as you know, I got arrested for having sex with a younger man. This isn't something I would normally do. You see, I've been going with my partner, Patrick, since we were both 16 years old. We kind of grew up together. We were everything to each other. We're both from a small town about an hour north of here. Growing up gay, we were about all we each had. Then we got a place together closer to town. It was great because we felt at home there; there's a small but tight-knit gay community there. But that's when things started to go wrong. Patrick started changing, being different, and we kind of grew apart. Sometimes we got back together and sometimes things were tough. This went on for a good two years. It seemed like things were getting better, but then he went away for a couple of weeks. I mean he was just gone. He wouldn't return calls or texts, and I had no idea what had happened. I went wild. Patrick was my whole world. None of our friends would tell me what was happening, and I knew something was really wrong. There was something going on and all of a sudden our friends were treating me differently. I started hanging around downtown and probably spent too much time in the bars.

Interviewer: It sounds as though you were really missing Patrick and that he is really important to you.

Scott: He was my whole life. Anyway, after a couple of weeks, Patrick finally came home. I had stopped off for a few beers on my way home. He said he was sorry, and I wanted to know where he'd been. He wouldn't tell me what I wanted to know, and I just went crazy. I beat him up really badly. I raped him every way I could and then I beat him up some more. I've never done anything like this in my life. This isn't who I am [sobs]. I hurt Patrick, I lost the only group of friends I ever had and who I related to, and you can bet I won't hear from my family or Patrick again for a long, long time.

Interviewer: It sounds like you had trouble dealing with your feelings and with what had happened, and you lashed out at Patrick. Would that be accurate?

Scott: Yeah, maybe. Probably.

Interviewer: It also sounds like you are upset that you also lost your friends and family, and possibly Patrick. Have I got that correct?

Scott: Of course! Who wouldn't feel that way?

Interviewer: It also seems like you're worried how this has affected others—and your future.

Scott: [long pause] Yeah.

Interviewer: Let me see if I have this right. You and Patrick are both from a small town. You grew up together and eventually became partners. It was hard growing up gay in a small town and so for years you've felt lucky to have each other. Now that you're both a little older you've felt a real connection to others in the gay community. After you had lived alone for a long time, you finally had people you felt could understand you. However, all this positive growth came with a huge price tag when it seemed that Patrick was losing interest and even disappeared for a couple of weeks. Do I have that right?

Scott: That's about the size of it, yeah. And then I screwed everything up.

Interviewer: You got violent—sexually violent—toward the person you love most. You're concerned you've lost your partner, your community, and your freedom. Is that about the size of it, too?

Scott: Yeah.

Interviewer: And with everything you've got going on, you're still willing to explore this with others. That's a huge step. What other things concern you about what lies ahead?

Scott: Well, I guess I wonder how I'm going to support myself. I've only ever worked dead-end jobs. Now with a sexual offense on my record, I'm not sure what I'm going to do. To tell you the truth, I'm not sure I really care; I just need to work on getting my own place when I'm done here.

Interviewer: You're more of a cash-in-pocket kind of guy. Who you are and who you're with are more important than career choices at this point in your life.

Scott: Yeah. I suppose that sounds strange. I just want a job. Working makes me feel like I'm good at something.

Interviewer: You're not too picky about what you accomplish, but you want to accomplish <u>something</u>.

Scott: You got it.

Interviewer: So, if we were to peel back the layers of all of your life so far, I wonder if there aren't some similar themes that are very important in your life...things you've really strived for. As we've been talking, it seems clear that you want a sense of inner peace, of balance. For some people, careers are everything, but for you, inner peace comes in a different form.

Scott: Yeah. When I raped Patrick, I was definitely not feeling peaceful. I mean I wanted him back, and I wanted him back for good. Maybe I've relied too much on others for what you call "inner peace."

Interviewer: We can call it whatever makes sense to you. It's apparent that growing up gay in a small town doesn't provide a lot of inner peace, and neither does a relationship in trouble. It also seems that having a sense of community is very important to you. Part of your situation prior to your arrest was fearing the loss of the only group of people where you've felt like you fit in, and also your family.

Scott: You got that right.

Interviewer: And of course, your relationships are of the utmost importance to you. Tell me if I'm off base here.

Scott: No, you're right. I haven't had that many relationships. That's part of why this hurts so much.

Interviewer: And finally, it's clear that you want to be happy and experience pleasure. When you're not having fun and you're feeling alone, it's much more likely that you'll drink more than you feel you should. Did I get that right? Is it maybe possible that drinking gave you that sense of inner peace, but that it also led to what happened with Patrick?

Scott: Yes, I just want to be happy. I never really thought about it, but I'm sure I would never have hurt Patrick if I hadn't been drinking. I love him! But right before I attacked him, after a few drinks, I did feel a bit better, just a bit more relaxed.

Interviewer: Okay, thank you, Scott. I appreciate your being willing to talk with me today.

In the above example, the evaluator approaches the interview ready and willing to listen for what is important to Scott. She actively probes for those indicators of Scott's important goods. While Scott does not state the goods directly, obvious clues he gives allude to them and the interviewer is able to pick up what matters most to him. The interviewer uses open-ended questions in order to make sure that Scott's perspective is clear, and then she offers summaries back to him what he has said. She also verifies that she has drawn the correct conclusions, and does not make assumptions based on what she has heard. By obtaining a sense of the primary goods that are important to Scott, she can then re-cast Scott's personal narrative into a summary of areas on which he can work in treatment to reduce his risk of re-offense and to increase the chances of moving in the direction of a good life. So far, Scott has identified that some of the primary goods that are important to him are inner peace, community, relatedness, and happiness. As is often the case, these elements were involved in his offending. The interviewer also explored Scott's sense of agency by discussing his work history, which is important to him but of lower priority than the earlier mentioned primary goods. That is, it appears that Scott is driven more by the relational aspects of his life than by his desire for influence or accomplishments.

Assessing Secondary Goods

During the assessment of primary human goods, the interviewer should be alert to indications of the secondary goods that the client seeks and uses to attain his primary goods. As indicated previously, secondary goods (also known as *instrumental goods*) are the concrete activities, or means, by which an individual seeks to attain primary goods. For example, in seeking the good of excellence in play (the primary good), the client may engage in team sports and stay physically fit in order to play effectively, which is the means by which he attains excellence in play.

The aim, therefore, of this part of the assessment is to understand the specific means by which the client attempts to gain the primary goods he values. Secondary goods are more likely to be obvious to the client and, as such, he will likely be better able to provide better information on these goods than his primary goods. Numerous indicators of secondary goods in one primary good domain can suggest that the individual highly values that particular good. In discussing secondary goods, the interviewer should be alert to any primary goods that can be inferred and that should then be reflected back to the client. As with all effective interviews, the evaluator should not make assumptions about these inferences, and should always verify conclusions with the client—as well as take into account any available collateral information—to confirm that the inference is accurate.

Some common indicators of secondary goods are noted below, although, as with primary goods, these are only examples and specific secondary or instrumental goods will be unique to each client.

PRIMARY GOOD	SAMPLE INDICATORS OF SECONDARY/INSTRUMENTAL GOOD
Life	• Engages in activities such as work or criminal activity to meet basic needs • Engages in regular physical exercise • Pursues good nutrition • Manages specific health problems • Engages in activities to reduce stress
Knowledge	• Attends school or training courses • Actively attempts to understand self and/or others • Attends treatment
Excellence in Play and Work	• Participates in sports or other leisure or recreational activities or hobbies • Works or seeks to obtain employment and/or to be successful in work
Excellence in Agency	• Engages in activities to ensure self-sufficiency • Actively asserts self with others; communicates needs • Controls, dominates others; engages in aggression, manipulation of others
Inner Peace	• Actively engages in specific activities to regulate emotional states or to achieve equilibrium (e.g., exercise, stress reduction techniques, use of sexual activity) • Uses substances to regulate mood or to cope with emotions • Attempts to manage impulsivity

Relatedness	• Engages in social activities or spends time with friends • Discusses important issues with others • Attempts to acquire intimacy and/or romantic partners
Community	• Participates in community or volunteer activities (e.g., social service groups) • Becomes member of pro-pedophilia group • Provides practical assistance to others in times of need • Engages in activities in treatment that contribute to cohesion among group members
Spirituality	• Attends formal religious/spiritual events (e.g., church, sweat lodge); participates in activities such as meditation/prayer • Actively attempts to develop and/or implement a personal philosophy
Happiness	• Engages in activities that result in a sense of satisfaction, contentment, fulfillment • Engages in activities that result in a sense of pleasure (e.g., leisure activities, sex) • Engages in activities that contribute to sense of purpose in life (e.g., work, friendships, family) • Attends treatment
Creativity	• Engages in new or novel experiences • Engages in creative activities • Dislikes routine

This part of the assessment should result in additional information on primary goods and a sound understanding of the client's efforts to achieve these goods.

Example: Assessing Secondary/Instrumental Goods

In this example, the interviewer from the previous example continues the interview with Scott.

Interviewer: Scott, we talked last time about the importance of inner peace, and how it seemed to play a role in your behavior toward Patrick. Can we talk about that some more?

Scott: Sure.

Interviewer: Tell me more about the times when you've found inner peace throughout your life.

Scott: [laughs] I'm not sure I have. I mean, I don't go to church. I don't really even believe in God very much. I tried a yoga classes, but that didn't go anywhere. To be honest, I mostly just enjoy a few beers when I can. You know, with my friends, sometimes by myself. And I like having sex. Maybe I shouldn't say this, but having sex always calmed me down. Now that I'm here, I also try to do things like deep breathing and stuff, but I'm not very good at it. Maybe I should exercise more.

Interviewer: So inner peace is important, and it's also not been as much of your life as you would like. You've thought about some relaxation techniques and feel that maybe if you exercised more that would help, too.

Scott: Yeah. I've never really made the time for that. I used to play softball and that was always really good for me. I really liked that.

Interviewer: So there have been some times when you've been closer to maintaining inner peace than others. It's something you've thought about or wanted during your life.

Scott: Yeah. I guess that's true.

Interviewer: And in fact, when you've been taking good care of yourself, you've been able to experience some measure of it even though you've also felt lonely and felt like you weren't a real part of the town where you grew up. Would that be accurate?

Scott: [chuckles] You might be right. Where there's a will there's a way.

Interviewer: Where does inner peace fit into your future?

Scott: Well, I guess I can use the time that I'm here to get back into sports, Also, I saw that there are some classes in things like meditation and Tai Chi and stuff like that. Maybe I can give that a try. I need to take care of myself before I can be close to anyone, and Patrick is really gone from my life now, I suppose.

> *Interviewer:* It seems like it's time for you to take this part of your life seriously. You've had some successes in the past, and you're willing to give it another go.
>
> *Scott:* Yeah. You know, I think that if I'd been able to take care of myself better, this whole thing might never have happened.

In this part of the interview, Scott has indicated that inner peace has been important to him throughout his life. Thus, having a sense of emotional equilibrium is something he highly values (in addition to being a factor in his offense). He has tried several means to gain this sense of inner balance, through sports, sex, yoga, and meditation. Scott clearly wants to attain inner peace in his life, and he appears willing to try different means or means that worked previously (i.e., physical activity) to achieve this goal. He also appears to value the primary good of life, in that he indicates that he may want to take better care of himself.

At this point, the interviewer can also start to make links to risk factors that are related to inner peace, such as the use of sex to cope with negative emotional states and impulsivity in offending. Furthermore, the strength orientation of the GLM can be signaled clearly by letting Scott know that treatment will help him to acquire competencies to achieve things that are important to him while he is also reducing his risk.

Relationship of Primary Goods to Sexual Offending

The third element of assessment in the GLM involves evaluation of the role that each primary human good plays in offending, and particularly in sexual offending. This third step includes assessment of the primary goods that were particularly important to the client prior to and at the time of offending, or that were implicated in, or associated with, offending. The process also includes identifying the specific instrumental means used by the client to attain the good, because some of those means also represent the client's dynamic risk factors for offending.

In conducting this part of the assessment, the evaluator examines the offense progression (see chapter 10) and notes those specific activities in which the client engaged in the progression to offending, as well as the strategies used in the various circumstances and opportunities that presented themselves throughout the progression. In addition, practitioners of the GLM recommend that the evaluator attend to *themes* that are apparent in the commission of the offense. For example, the interviewer needs to inquire about whether the commission of the offense reflected a specific theme, such as intimacy, personal control, emotional control, pleasure, novelty seeking, retribution, and so on. By examining these themes, the client's specific cognitive schemas that relate to offending can also be assessed, primary goods inferred, and the means used to achieve these goods and their link to sexual offending understood.

Example: Assessing Relationship of Primary Goods to Sexual Offending

In this example, the interviewer continues to talk with Scott.

> ***Interviewer:*** *How did inner peace fit into your life when the situation with Patrick happened?*
>
> ***Scott:*** *The short answer is that it didn't. Not at all. I was desperate, climbing the walls for two weeks. I didn't know what to do. I drank even more than usual that night. I'm not using that as an excuse; I was in a really bad mood. Then I saw Patrick. What a roller coaster ride that was! I thought I'd gotten my lover back, but he wouldn't tell me where he'd been. In fact, he seemed distant. He'd clearly been fucking around with someone else. I still don't know who. All I wanted right then was to have him back, and I was hurt and angry when he was there in front of me, but it was like he belonged to someone else. I just wanted him back, and I also wanted to know how could he do this to me? It was the rug pulled out from under me for the second time. So we started yelling and arguing, and I hit him. He started talking about how he had been with someone else and wasn't going to tell me about it. I hit him some more and right then as that was going on I actually kept thinking about him with that other guy and—I know this sounds crazy—but it got me horny. I wanted him back so I beat him really bad and had sex with him. The funny thing is that the sex wasn't any good at that point. So when you talk about inner peace? That whole idea was there—and it wasn't there.*
>
> ***Interviewer:*** *I remember last time you spoke about how it's really important to you. How about your sense of relatedness? You've shared a lot of how important that is to you. How did that fit into the situation with Patrick?*
>
> ***Scott:*** *Well, it's funny, because just thinking about him having sex with a stranger made me want him more. I was imagining it and I didn't like it, but that image made me want sex right then and there. Maybe I'm crazy getting horny thinking about my lover with someone else, but that was a big part of it. And also I was half-drunk and feeling mean.*
>
> ***Interviewer:*** *You'd had a lot of time to think about this. Just imagining Patrick with someone else was arousing, but at the same time, it was infuriating and heart-breaking.*
>
> ***Scott:*** *Exactly.*

In this example, the primary goods and their relationship to offending are becoming clearer. Scott has confirmed that inner peace, relatedness, and happiness were factors in his offending; he was trying to re-acquire these goods. Scott was also indicating that he felt a threat to his good life plan (in which relatedness is important). He also sensed that the offense could have been related to re-establishing autonomy—in this case, via sexual assault—and related to the dynamic risk factor of sexual self-regulation.

Example: Relationship of Primary Goods to Sexual Offending

Phil is a 46-year-old man with an extensive history of undetected sexual offenses against children. He has just received his first conviction for a sexual crime.

Interviewer: What can you share with me about your life?

Phil: I thought long and hard about being here, doing this assessment, and being in treatment, and I'm not going to try to make anything less than it really is. I put myself here and I don't know if I'll ever really be free again. I grew up in a small town in the southeast. My childhood was a disaster: foster care, got into trouble for setting a barn on fire, went to a residential school as a last chance. Basically, I learned to shut up and keep my head down. I dated a woman closely for a little while when I was younger, but that was never going to work out. Heck, I lived with my mother until I was 43 years old! I just don't like adults that much—no offense. I like kids, and I like dogs. Kids are better friends than adults can ever be. The thing is, though, when I want to get something, I can make up just about any story I want, and I can mean something totally different. For example, I made a lot of friends with single women so that I could gain access to their kids. I really wasn't that interested in the women, you know, but I got really good at making friends with them, helping them with mowing their lawns, getting the groceries, and looking after their kids. Honestly, I never even cared all that much about anyone, even my mother.

Interviewer: So what kinds of things are important to you?

Phil: Well, if you'd asked me before I got caught and I was honest, I would have told you that I'm one of the best sex offenders who ever lived. I was a real master. Persuading people is something I'm really good at. It was like a hobby, a skill set. I read the newspapers and books, and I learned how other people like me operate. I was much more creative than the guys I would read about. I was really proud of how I could make things happen and leave people wanting more. I always figured I'd get caught someday, but that was okay for me. This is who I am. It's my place in the world. It's the one place where I can say I am truly accomplished.

Interviewer: *So, feeling like you're good at something is really important to you. Does that sound right? On the one hand, you were aware that you would eventually get in trouble, and on the other hand, this activity was the one thing that gave you a sense of mastery, pleasure, and competence.*

Phil: *Yes. Like I said, I'm not going to make it less than it was.*

Interviewer: *So, using the words we talked about before, having a sense of excellence, of mastery, and of creativity, happiness, pleasure, and knowledge are all important to you, and they played a role in your actions. Would that be accurate?*

Phil: *Yes. I know that sounds terrible, but I felt very powerful being all of those things while I was out there and while I was doing what I was doing.*

Interviewer: *Offending was just about the only way you had to feel like you had those things.*

Phil: *That's right.*

Interviewer: *And there are some other things that are less important to you—for example, your relationships with adults.*

Phil: *I'm not sure I agree. I know I said I'm closer to dogs and kids than I am to adults, but that's only because I've never really trusted adults. I wouldn't rule out having friends someday. However, I'm aware that my options now aren't what they used to be.*

Phil has gained a sense of mastery, creativity, and knowledge through offending sexually, and views himself as highly competent at it. He appears to have pursued the primary good of autonomy by offending as a part of his good life plan. Further assessment, however, will uncover the extent to which he values relatedness with others.

For purposes of a more in-depth exploration, one method that clinicians can use under these circumstances is an options menu (see figure 2, page 80). Essentially, this figure is two pages of circles. Some of the circles contain the primary goods described throughout this volume. Other circles are blank, in case the client has additional goods of importance to him. The purpose of this format is to provide a menu that is free of any hierarchical appearance. For example, a simple list of primary goods may give the impression that the first good listed is the most important, or that there is an order to each good. Having the sort of handout provided above also offers therapists and clients a tangible, visual aid.

Figure 2: Primary Goods Options Menu

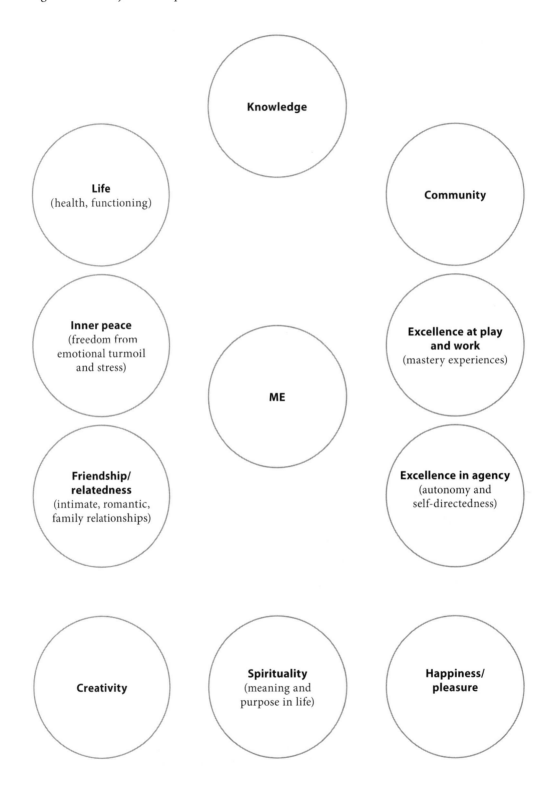

Essentially, the clinician using these circles can pursue a method such as the following:

Interviewer: Phil, here is a menu of areas that serve as goals at one time or another for just about all human beings. I wonder if there is an area here that you would like to talk with me about.
Phil: We could talk about spirituality.
Interviewer: Okay, thank you. What made you choose spirituality?
Phil: Well, because I've never really gone to church, even though when I was a kid I sometimes went with my mother when I visited her. It's mostly like it says here on the sheet. My meaning and purpose in life has been to persuade people to let me into their lives in ways that are not good for them. It's pretty much what I've done. I've been proud of that, like I told you. It's no use lying about it now.
Interviewer: Let's consider a scale of zero to ten, with zero being not at all important and ten being very important. What number represents the importance of spirituality in your life?
Phil: If we mean religion, it's not very high. If we mean finding purpose and meaning in life, then it's really high right now, because I just don't know what the future is going to bring. I'll say an eight.
Interviewer: Given that you've said you don't care that much about others, and since persuading people to let you into their lives has given you such meaning and purpose, why you didn't rate yourself lower?
Phil: I guess because I want to be able to have at least some contact with adults, especially since I'll be spending a lot of time in the company of adults now that I'm here. Also, I guess I need to figure out what I'm going to do with my life now that everything's changed.

In this example, Phil is making his current state clearer with respect to spirituality. He is ambivalent about giving up sexual offending as a primary source of his life's meaning and purpose. At the same time, he is wondering about the directions his life is taking him and second-guessing his place in the world around him. Many of Phil's concerns also overlap with the primary goods of community and relatedness. Evaluators and treatment providers can explore these goods in subsequent assessment and treatment interviews.

Example: Relationship of Primary Goods to Sexual Offending

Chris is 19 years old. He molested his sister at the age of 14 and was sent to a residential facility. The therapists in the program felt that Chris had achieved as much as he could when the facility discharged him to a group home a few months prior to becoming a legal adult. The hope was that Chris would prepare himself for independent living in the community. Instead, Chris absconded to his parents' home, and his supervising agency closed his case. Chris was recently convicted of a sexual offense following an incident in which he rubbed the breasts of his sister's friend without her consent during a party at his house.

Interviewer: Please tell me what happened.
Chris: We were having a party and she was really high, so I gave her a feel. I know I shouldn't have done that. I thought she might enjoy it. I guess not.
Interviewer: Sounds like a wild time.
Chris: Well, yeah, I like to party. It's the best time I have with my friends and my sister now that I'm home.
Interviewer: So, you were spending a lot of time partying with your friends and your sister.
Chris: Yeah. I mean, I couldn't find a job. No one will hire me. What I want more than anything is to stand up for myself and make my own money, but everyone around here knows who I am and where I've been.
Interviewer: It's important to you to stand on your own two feet. Would that be true?
Chris: It's been really depressing. I'm a young guy, and I want a chance to make my mark and have some fun along the way. What I really want to do is be a professional stock car racer, but I can't find a job that will help me get there. In fact, I don't even have a driver's license. And now I'm in trouble for trying to hit it off with my sister's friend. I just can't get a break. I was actually really hoping she'd go out with me, but that's not going to happen now. I wanted to have some fun; being in trouble isn't fun. Everyone thinks I'm a worse loser than I was before.
Interviewer: It's like there were lots of things you wanted to do and they all crashed into each other.
Chris: Yeah. I was going too fast again.
Interviewer: Would it also be true to say that you don't like being thought of as a loser?
Chris: Of course! Who does?

Chris' good life plan to the present has focused on the primary good of happiness (mainly via pleasure), relatedness (his attempts to gain a girlfriend), mastery in work, and agency. These primary goods are hallmarks of late adolescence. However, Chris attempted to attain the goods through maladaptive and poorly conceived means, in ways that led to offending.

ASSESSMENT OF FLAWS IN THE GOOD LIVES PLAN

The last component of the GLM portion of assessment examines clients' good lives plans for the four flaws—means, scope, conflict, and capacity—that can lead to problems when it comes to implementing the plans.

Assessing the *means* the client has used to attain primary goods includes determining both strategies that are successful and those that are inappropriate and/or counterproductive. The evaluator also needs to determine the means that the client uses in his life in general, as well as when offending. For example, an individual who seeks to attain intimacy via sexual relationships with children is demonstrating the flaw of means, as he is using an inappropriate strategy (a relationship with children) to attain a primary human good (relatedness).

The evaluator also seeks to determine whether the client's good life plan is restricted in *scope*—that is, does he focus more on obtaining one or a few primary goods, while neglecting others? For example, an individual who overemphasizes autonomy and mastery but underemphasizes relatedness may be chronically unsatisfied with a lack of friends or a partner.

Assessing *conflict* among goods involves detecting those situations in which the client indicates priorities or goals that cannot co-exist easily, such as the desire for emotional intimacy with a romantic partner (the primary good of relatedness), while simultaneously seeking sexual freedom with a variety of partners (the primary good of happiness, manifested as pleasure).

Assessing a client's capacity or capability to enact his good life plan involves assessing both *internal capacity* or skills as well as *external opportunities* that are available to the client. For example, he may state that he would like to marry and have children (the primary good of relatedness), but also that he is timid and unassertive and unable to approach an adult partner. In this case, he lacks the internal skills he needs to form such a relationship. Additionally, the client may have restrictions on where he can go and, as such, an external capability issue may be denying him access to activities that would allow him to meet appropriate partners.

Example: Assessing Good Lives Plan Flaws

Previously, in Phil's case, it appeared that his goals of mastery, creativity, happiness, and knowledge are in conflict with his goal of autonomy. Specifically, his pursuit of happiness is in conflict with his goal of having a life that he spends largely by himself. Furthermore, his goal of mastery is in direct conflict with autonomy and self-directedness—that is, his attempts to attain happiness mean that he must depend on the cooperation and confidence of others when he generally prefers to be alone. Finally, his attainment of knowledge is in conflict with his need for agency because he cannot attain knowledge freely or in any open way. Ultimately, his attempts to attain these goals—by his own admission—were destined to bring him into contact with the law and resulted in serious long-term harm to others as well as to himself. In other words, he used sexual offending as a means to attain these goals, and this decision ultimately affected his good life plan in a negative way. Further assessment will uncover to what extent the scope of his good life plan takes into account areas of his life such as relatedness.

Example: Assessing Good Lives Plan Flaws

In Chris' case, it is clear that his good life plan contained all four of the flaws. Attempting to attain relatedness by grabbing the breasts of an intoxicated woman represented a problematic means to attaining this good. Likewise, Chris' goal of becoming a professional car racer, particularly when he has no license to drive, displays a lack of external capacity for attaining excellence in work—that is, he would be unable to attain this goal without a drivers' license and training. He may also lack the internal capacity to attain this goal (i.e., the skills to be a race car driver), although the presence of Chris' skill or abilities in this area is unknown.

Chris also has a limited scope of primary goods in his life plan. For example, he appears to place emphasis on the primary goods of happiness (pleasure) and excellence in work, but many goods are missing from his life plan. His focus appears to be on pursuing immediate gratification. Finally, his attempts to pursue those goods that are immediately important (happiness through pleasure-seeking and relatedness) were clearly in conflict when he attempted to gain the company of his sister's friend by taking advantage of her intoxication.

INTEGRATION

Once the GLM assessment is complete, the evaluator should have a comprehensive picture of the client, what he values in life, how his valued goods were associated with offending, and what problems he is currently encountering while implementing his good life plan. Treatment priority given to attaining primary goods is established based on the importance of those goods to the individual and the extent to which those goods are implicated in his offending. The GLM assessment is also incorporated into an integrated assessment that includes the evaluation of self-regulation and risk, need, and responsivity concerns in order to formulate a comprehensive case conceptualization and treatment plan (see chapters 6 and 7, respectively).

Summary

Assessment identifies the primary goods that clients have sought to achieve and identifies what clients need to have in their lives in order to feel fulfilled. As a part of the assessment process, the evaluator should also be alert to indications of the secondary goods that the client seeks and uses to attain his primary goods. The third element of assessment relates to the role that each primary human good plays in offending. The evaluator also examines the specific instrumental means used by the client to attain each good. This evaluation is important because some of those means also represent the client's dynamic risk factors for offending. Lastly, the flaws or problems encountered in implementing the good lives plans are identified and evaluated. Understanding these elements helps the therapist to develop a comprehensive understanding of the client and, in conjunction with self-regulation and risk assessment, it forms the basis of treatment planning and implementation. The next chapter focuses on the assessment of self-regulation styles in offending and offense pathways.

CHAPTER 5

Assessment of Self-Regulation: Determination of Offense Pathway

While chapter 4 described the assessment of primary goods and their relationship to offending and to treatment priority, this chapter focuses on assessment of the self-regulation pathway in the commission of offending. The reader should also be familiar with the theoretical underpinnings of the self-regulation model, as described in chapter 3.

Additionally, chapter 10 will offer a detailed description of how to conduct a relevant personal history ("autobiography") exercise that is focused on Phase 1 of the offense progression (predisposing factors to offending). Chapter 10 similarly will provide a detailed description of how to conduct an offense disclosure exercise using the integrated GLM/SRM-R approach. Specifically, chapter 10 focuses on Phases 2 through 10 of the offense progression, in which participants complete an offense chain exercise commencing with the life event that triggers the sequence and proceeding through to post-offense evaluations. In conducting this exercise, participants examine offense-related goals and the strategies developed to achieve these goals, which in combination form an individual's offense pathway.

Recall from chapter 3, that each pathway is offense-based (rather than offender-based), and that a given individual may follow different offense pathways, either historically or when he commits different types of sexual offenses. (Detailed information and an assessment protocol can be found in Yates et al., 2009). The four offense pathways are described in chapter 3 and elsewhere and so are not reiterated in detail here. Briefly, however, the four pathways are as follows:

Avoidant-Passive Pathway

When an individual follows an avoidant-passive pathway to offending, he enters or encounters the specific situation that triggers offending with the goal of avoiding or preventing sexual offending from occurring. Prior to acting out, the individual legitimately commits to restraint, although because of lack of insight, he is unable to identify this state easily or explicitly. Because of certain vulnerabilities, however, such as unfulfilled needs or deficits in skills required to meet needs and achieve goals, self-regulation abilities in the specific situation are under-regulated or disinhibited. Thus, an individual focuses on meeting his needs in the immediate situation, and not on his overall goal of not offending. Because he lacks insight into, and the ability to cope with, the situation, the individual following this pathway tends not to use strategies to ensure that he does not offend. At best, his "strategies" may be simply ignoring or denying that he has a problem, or distracting himself from the situation at hand. After offending, the individual tends to experience cognitive dissonance (the discrepancy between his intended goal of avoiding offending and his actual behavior) and to perceive the offense, his behavior, and indeed possibly himself, in a negative light.

Example: Avoidant-Passive Pathway

Dominic is a young man of 21. He is being assessed for admission to a new treatment program, having re-offended following completion of his previous treatment program. At the age of 15, he used bribes to persuade his sister to agree to engage in sexual intercourse, and overcame her resistance by holding her down and telling himself that she would enjoy the experience as it progressed. He was sent to a residential program and only partially engaged in treatment there. Dominic's therapists were concerned that he had difficulty acknowledging his role in abusive actions. Dominic made sporadic progress in following rules, however, and tried to manage his anger by telling himself, "It's not worth it to get angry." Dominic turned 18 years old before completing this program and so was discharged, and he has lived with his mother ever since. In the intervening years, he has had difficulty finding employment. Dominic now spends much of his time at home. He has few friends and drinks six to eight bottles of beer per day. When he feels stressed, he tends not to do anything about it except to wait until it passes.

Prior to the current offense, Dominic's sister visited, concerned about her brother's welfare. Dominic was aware that her good intentions were nonsexual, but began to experience sexual arousal toward her again. At first, he tried to ignore the feelings, but the more he tried not to think about them, the more his state of arousal was at the front of his mind. He began to hope that if he initiated sex, his sister might consent as she had seemed to in the past. He told himself that if she actively said "No," he would stop. As his impulsive attempts to initiate sex progressed, however, he became increasingly aroused and could not cope with the fact that his sister did not want to comply. She became clearly distressed, but by this point, Dominic was focused only on having sex. In recounting this offense, Dominic expresses confusion and self-hatred. He had known better at the time, and yet it had not seemed like such a bad idea at the moment.

Pre-Treatment Assessment Interview with Dominic

Interviewer: Let's go back to the hours before your sister visited. What was going on and what happened?

Dominic: I don't know. Things haven't been going so well, and I've been bored. My mother thinks I've been grumpy and to tell you the truth, I'm not sure what I'm going to do with my life. That night, I was watching TV when my sister came over. She said she was worried about me. I tried hard not to think about it, but I got horny. I don't know what came over me, but the next thing I knew, I tried to have sex with her. She didn't take that so well.

Interviewer: You say you tried not to think about it. What else might you have tried?

Dominic: I don't know. I wasn't really thinking. It just got the better of me.

Dominic's initial intent was to avoid sexual offending, but he made little effort to prevent it beyond simply trying not to think about it. In this instance, he had little ability to reconcile the conflicting goals of gratifying his urges and avoiding re-offending. He states that he was not thinking, and in some ways his assessment is accurate. He was aroused and focused on sexual behavior, and anxiously unable to distract himself. Dominic's general strategy for managing problem situations is to avoid them or to try not to think about them. Further assessment by the therapist can focus on Dominic's self-regulation style and skills in general, as well as on his cognitive problem-solving skills. Dominic was assessed as following the avoidant-passive pathway in the current offense for which he is undergoing assessment. Although other pertinent factors play a role, this assessment is based on Dominic's obvious avoidant goal (his desire to not offend) and his passive efforts to achieve this goal, as indicated by his initial attempts to ignore his sexual arousal to his sister.

Avoidant-Active Pathway

When an individual follows an avoidant-active pathway, like the avoidant-passive pathway, his goal is to avoid or to prevent offending from happening. In order to achieve this, when the individual recognizes that a specific situation involves risk, he uses active strategies explicitly to control or suppress desires, arousal, fantasy, or behavior in order to avoid acting out (even though these are ultimately unsuccessful). Therefore, individuals following this pathway have some awareness of the offense progression or chain, since they are able to identify problematic situations and to take action to deal with them. The problem, however, is that the strategies they select are ultimately misregulated—that is, they are not likely to be effective in preventing an offense and may, in fact, actually increase the risk that sexual offending will occur. For example, an individual who uses alcohol to regulate his mood may offend as a result of the loss of inhibition and behavioral control associated with intoxication. After offending, the individual following this pathway tends to experience cognitive dissonance (the discrepancy between an individual's intended goal of avoiding offending and his actual behavior) and to perceive the offense and his behavior in a negative light.

Example: Avoidant-Active Pathway

Ken had long been conflicted about his sexual orientation. Deeply religious, he spent much of his life attempting to convince himself that he had no sexual interest in males. He married a woman at the age of 21 and became active in his church. In this context, he developed an interest in a number of young men involved in the choir, and he also volunteered at the church's Sunday school. Ken knew he was in a position of authority and so, when he felt attracted to the boys, he immediately reminded himself of the importance of his role and immersed himself further in church activities. Nonetheless, he offended against a 14-year-old boy in the church choir. The boy's parents quickly found out, and Ken received a four-year prison sentence.

Ken entered a treatment program, where he quickly decided that he had not been observant or fervent enough in his faith, and that this failing was a primary factor in his offending. In fact, Ken became an informal religious leader within his prison, offering counseling to others. Ken became increasingly convinced that strict religious observance would prevent future offending. He expressed disgust about his past attraction to young males.

Upon release from prison, Ken became involved with a small fundamentalist church in his neighborhood. Within weeks of his reintegration into the community, his family made it clear that they wanted only minimal contact with him. His peers at church seemed distant, and he grew increasingly lonely. He found himself attracted to young men in the area around the church and felt he had no one with whom he could talk openly. Desperate, he made contact with several young men, telling himself that he would remain brave in his "struggle with evil" and that they could benefit from the wisdom he had accrued through years of his devout faith. His stated resistance quickly became futile, however, when a discussion he conducted with a 15-year-old male turned to the topic of homosexuality. It was clear to Ken that the young man with whom he was talking seemed to be unsure of his own sexual orientation. Despite Ken's better judgment, he quickly made sexual overtures and progressed to a sexual activity. Afterward, Ken sank into despair and self-loathing as he realized that his attempts to reconcile his sexuality had failed.

Ken is undergoing assessment for re-admission to his previous treatment program.

Ken's Assessment Interview

Interviewer: Please tell me what happened.

Ken: I was involved in a church activity with some young men. One of them was talking about sex and sexuality. I knew this was a bad situation to be in, but I really wanted to ease his pain and make a connection with him. I had struggled with a lot of the same things he had. I knew I was thinking more and more about having sex with him—I thought it could be kind of like an initiation for him—but then it got to be too much. I tried the prevention skills I had learned in treatment, like stopping my thoughts and remembering that immediate gratification is not good for anyone. This situation was different. I don't know. I guess I kind of snapped. It's not like I really even planned any of this, but the more I thought about how to avoid being turned on, the more I wanted sex. I thought maybe if I could make the kid be willing, it wouldn't be bad—it wouldn't be a sin. I expected better of myself.

Where Dominic (in the previous case) had few, if any, skills to avoid re-offending, Ken actively tried to use a number of cognitive skills that were, unfortunately, ultimately unsuccessful. Among the techniques he tried were his self-talk related to immediate gratification, his use of religion to prevent re-offending, and his over-reliance on thought-stopping. His attempts to subdue and master his interest in teenage boys by being in close proximity to them not only failed, but made it more likely he would re-offend. Although spirituality can play a vital role in building a good life, Ken's reliance on it as a tactic of avoidance was ill-conceived. As a result, his attempts to avoid re-offending failed quickly. Typical of an approach-avoidant pathway, each of Ken's attempts could work under other circumstances, and he truly believed these strategies would be effective. Ken's attempts to deploy one skill after another happened after many other areas of his life (e.g., his social isolation) were left unattended. This topic will receive more attention in chapter 11.

Approach-Automatic Pathway

When an individual follows an approach-automatic pathway, he more actively works toward offending and does not attempt to prevent himself from offending. In the case of the approach-automatic pathway, individuals offend in a relatively automatic manner, and do not tend to reflect on their behavior. Behavior with respect to self-regulation is under-regulated and disinhibited because these individuals do not successfully or effectively control their behavior in situations that pose a risk. They respond automatically to cues in the situation or the environment and, in some cases, the behavior in the offense progression appears to be quite impulsive. What triggers offending are the individual's perceptions and interpretations in the specific situation that then lead him to act in accordance with well-entrenched cognitive schemas or implicit theories that guide behavior, and that do so in a relatively automatic manner. For example, an individual who believes that women are sexually responsive all the time is more likely to interpret a woman's friendly behavior as indicating sexual interest or willingness than someone who does not hold this belief. Individuals following the approach-automatic pathway tend not to plan their offenses, or they may plan the initial contact with victims but thereafter respond rapidly to cues in the environment and in the situation. They may not be consciously aware of these cues, nor of their perceptions, interpretations, and reactions to events. They may be guided by sexual scripts or by negative views about the world, victims, or others, and respond with hostility, retribution, or anger.

Example: Approach-Automatic Pathway

Jay grew up in a home where his father dealt drugs and abused his mother. Jay periodically lived with relatives and in foster care when his parents were in trouble with the law. Jay developed few emotional ties to others, and came to view the world as a place where one has to have fun when opportunities arise, and as a place in which authorities can be hostile, controlling, and unpredictable.

Jay was eventually placed in a juvenile detention center where he forced sex onto younger teens during staff shift changes and while the overnight staff slept. These happened to be periods of time during which the residents were left alone without supervision, and their conversations would turn to talking about the things they would do when they got out of detention. Jay did not overtly plan his assaults during these times. He indicated that something "just came over" him, and he saw the opportunities when they presented themselves. Jay was regarded as a "tough guy" and the others looked up to him, which made him feel superior and worthwhile. His attitude toward these assaults was that the behavior itself was pleasurable and worth the risk.

After his discharge from this program, Jay subsequently sexually assaulted a woman in a bar after she went into a bathroom a few minutes before closing time. He held a general belief that women could not be trusted to tell the truth, particularly in sexual matters, and felt that because this woman had flirted with him, it made little difference that he assaulted her, because, in his view, "she owed him." He had actually not had any particular plans to assault anyone that evening, Jay viewed his actions of the evening favorably, because his behavior involved sex and alcohol. To others, this assault seemed to come from "out of the blue."

Jay's behavior in prison was frustrating to others, as he seemed unperturbed by his actions. He attempted to flirt indelicately with staff members and became involved in illicit sexual activities and other rule violations.

Pre-Treatment Assessment Interview with Jay

Interviewer: Tell me what happened on that night at the bar?

Jay: It was simple. I was at the bar and she was high, so we went into the bathroom and had sex.

Interviewer: She was high? How do you know?

Jay: That's what I said. I don't know where people get off saying it was abusive. It must be because of my record. She just lied afterwards to make it seem like it was something bad I did to her. I can't help it if she wanted to have a good time.

Interviewer: You were out for a good time, too.

Jay: Why else would I be out? She wants a good time, I want a good time. There's nothing wrong with that.

Interviewer: So for you it's kind of like you're out on the town looking for opportunities for a good time.

Jay: Yeah. Look, with my record, someone's going to be looking to throw me into jail, so I'm gonna get what's coming to me when I can.

The schemas resulting from Jay's early life experiences have contributed to his template of offending. He has focused his efforts on the opportunistic pursuit of pleasurable experiences. In a world in which he believes that all authority is hostile and women are untrustworthy, Jay is relatively automatically aware of opportunities to get what he wants. As a result, his behavior can seem impulsive and surprising to others. Individuals following this pathway may not always be impulsive in the classical sense of blurting out the answers in class or being unable to refrain from telling dirty jokes in inappropriate situations, but their behavior does seem unprovoked at times. Because Jay is able to adhere to social norms when it suits him, his sexual aggression, therefore, seems swift and impulsive to those around him. A key aspect is his positive appraisal of his sexually aggression actions.

Approach-Explicit Pathway

Individuals following the approach-explicit pathway carefully plan their behavior in order to achieve their goals, which are supportive of offending. They achieve their goals by approaching them in a very explicit, planned manner. In following this pathway, these individuals typically have offense-supportive attitudes and beliefs, but they also have the ability to monitor situations and their behavior. They have intact self-regulation ability in the situation as they are able to carefully plan and restrain their behavior, depending upon what would be the best strategy in a specific situation. For example, they would be able to suppress urges to offend if too great a risk were present in the situation, such as the presence of police.

Example: Approach-Explicit Pathway

William's upbringing was uneventful. He had obtained a Master of Arts degree in Asian studies, and had made frequent trips to the Orient, where he sexually assaulted children. He gained access to these children by becoming a teacher through the Peace Corps and other charitable organizations. He gained the trust of the children's families and persuaded the children that his actions were in the service of their education and that this behavior was acceptable, particularly in some parts of the world.

William was aware that the laws of Asian countries were often not enforced with the same rigor as they were in North America and Europe, and that sexuality was perceived differently. He attributed this variation, in part, to a naïve stance by the Western world toward sex with children. William believed strongly that sex with children, under the right conditions, was a matter of love and mentorship, and outside the bounds of what government should decide on behalf of its citizens.

William was successful in avoiding detection in Asia. He was eventually apprehended after molesting a number of children in his capacity as a substitute teacher back home in North America. Upon his arrest, a search of his records found that he had been a member of two organizations that regarded sex with children as acceptable and that promoted the idea that society's laws regarding sex with children are unacceptable. His correspondence with children made it clear that he viewed those he molested as works of art. He expressed disdain at the more "cavalier" attitudes he often encountered in others who abused children.

Pre-Treatment Assessment Interview with William

Interviewer: Please walk me through one of your sexual encounters with a child.

William: These weren't "encounters," as you say. These events took place within a context of caring mentorship. I have been a teacher for many years, and I am devoted to all of my students. I didn't have sex with all of them. Rather, some of my students have either sought out a deeper level of connection and understanding, and some of them have actively asked for initiation into a part of their development that I could help them understand.

Interviewer: Okay. What might that look like?

William: Well, for starters, I had many students who would attach themselves to me. We would talk about their lives and their futures, and I would ask them what kind of person they hoped to be when they grew up. Many of them were interested in sex, and I helped them to understand sex in the context of a gentle and patient relationship. Please understand that these were helpful relationships. None of the children ever fought back.

William has followed an explicit and conscious path of sexual offending on each occasion he offended. He has made regular trips to areas where sexual abuse of children goes largely undetected, and has worked in positions of trust and close contact with children. He has also established networks with others interested in sex with children, including becoming a member of two such organizations. His appraisal of such behavior—before, during, and after offending—is positive, and he deliberately seeks out opportunities to engage in this behavior. His overall self-regulation is intact and purposeful, but his goals are inappropriate and harmful. William actively believes that society is wrong in its condemnation of child abuse.

Assessing Offense Pathways

When assessing an offense pathway, the evaluator begins with the individual's most recent sexual offense, and works through the assessment protocol for similar offenses, particularly recent crimes. Similar offenses generally are expected to follow the same pathways. It is not necessary to determine the self-regulation pathway for *every offense* the individual has committed. To do so would be excessively time-consuming and of little added benefit. However, it is useful to assess the offense pathway for different offenses in three types of cases. First, if an individual has committed different types of offenses, he may have followed different pathways for each offense. For example, a mixed offender, who has offended against both adults and children, may follow an approach-explicit pathway when offending against children, but then may follow an approach-automatic pathway when offending against adults. In addition, an individual with an extensive history of offending may show different offense pathways over time. For example, he may have followed avoidant pathways when committing earlier offenses, but may have switched to approach pathways with the passage of time, after having more experience with offending. The third possibility involves individuals who may have received treatment that was effective in changing their goal regarding offending, for example, from an approach to an avoidant goal. However, such individuals encountered a high-risk situation in which they did not implement strategies and then re-offended. In such cases, it is possible that a change in an individual's pathways had previously occurred as a result of treatment or intervention, and that the re-offense was associated with a different self-regulation pathway than were prior offenses. In general, however, assessment seeks patterns in offending and evaluates recent pathways, as these are important for treatment in the present.

Understanding the offense pathway followed should be reached via assessment (e.g., per the formal assessment protocol; see Yates et al., 2009) and/or via assessment in conjunction with offense disclosure (see chapters 9 and 10). Regardless of the method chosen, the information that follows describes the factors on which offense pathways are determined.

Offense-Related Goals

As described above, the offense pathway followed is a combination of the individual's goal in a specific offense progression and the strategy he chooses to achieve this goal. In assessing a self-regulation pathway, the evaluator first determines the individual's overarching goal when the offense occurred. Unlike goals in the Good Lives Model, the goals examined here specifically refer to those in the SRM-R offense progression (see chapter 3 and figure 1). Final determination of the goal (and ultimately, the pathway) is based on what has occurred overall or predominantly in the individual's behavior throughout the chain of events in the offense progression. That is, offenders may demonstrate both avoidant and approach goals, but it is what is *most evident or predominant* in the offense progression that determines the goal.

In assessing an offense goal, four factors are considered and described below:

1. The individual's desire to prevent or avoid offending

2. The individual's overall attitude toward offending

3. Cognitive distortions in the offense progression

4. Post-offense evaluation of self, the offending, and the behavior enacted during the offense

Desire to Prevent Offending

In the SRM-R, desire is evident formally in Phase 3 of the offense progression; however, for assessment, information is obtained from other phases as well. Generally, the interviewer seeks information that indicates that the individual, both overall and early in a specific offense situation, wanted to prevent offending from occurring and/or was anxious about the possibility of offending. This attitude is independent of the individual's actually committing an offense later in the offense progression. When sufficient evidence suggests that the individual did not want to offend, particularly in early phases and post-offense, an avoidant goal is indicated. When sufficient evidence suggests that the individual's goal was supportive of offending, an approach goal is indicated. Following are examples of statements indicating either avoidant or approach goals with respect to desire to avoid offending:

- "I was afraid I would so something to her, but I wasn't sure how to handle the situation. I didn't want to do what I did, but it also felt good." (avoidant desire/goal)

- "I just got really mad at her. I had tried to treat her right, but she just kept getting on my case. I mean, how could she do that? I tried all the anger management stuff I learned before, but got to the point where I needed to stand up for myself." (avoidance desire/goal)

- "When she said 'No' to me, I just thought to myself, 'I'll teach her a lesson not to do that.'" (approach desire/goal)

- "I knew I was onto a good thing when we met. I knew she had kids and needed a lot of help. I knew she would need someone to help out around her house and maybe do some babysitting." (approach desire/goal)

Attitude Toward Offending

In the SRM-R, the attitude the offender has toward offending reflects his relatively stable core beliefs or schemas about himself, others, victims, and the world. All of these beliefs influence the individual's attitudes about offending. In assessing those attitudes with respect to offense-related goals, the evaluator goes beyond specific cognitive distortions in a particular instance (e.g., "She should not have been out drinking in the bar alone") to uncover patterns of thinking that reflect more global belief systems (e.g., "Women who drink alone are looking for sex"). In assessing the influence of attitudes toward offending in the offense progression, avoidant goals are associated with the relative absence of attitudes that support the occurrence of offending. This assessment involves both evaluation of attitudes in general and also in the context of committing the offense, such as the offender's assessment of the desire to offend. Examples follow:

- "I didn't seem able to control myself, despite knowing it was wrong. Children are innocent and are too young for sex." (avoidant goal attitude)

- "I knew I was close to the edge spending all that time alone with him, but I thought I was strong enough to stop. I tried to get myself out of there, but he seemed to be enjoying himself so much, I just thought it would be okay." (avoidant goal attitude)

- "Children are able to consent to sex and intimacy; it is modern society that is prudish." (approach goal attitude)

- "Believe me, if you'd been there, you would know that she is no 'victim,' as you call it." (approach goal attitude)

Cognitive Distortions

Cognitive distortions are more specific to a situation or state of being than are attitudes. In fact, such distortions have been referred to as cognitive "products" (Gannon, 2009). In other words,, the distortions result from broader cognitive schemas, attitudes, or core beliefs and are indicators of a particular belief. For example, deferring responsibility to a child for provoking sexual behavior may be suggestive of a more general belief that children are sexual beings. By contrast, the cognitive distortions arising from such beliefs allow an individual to give himself permission in a specific situation to proceed with his behavior (i.e., offending), reduce cognitive dissonance in some cases, and assign responsibility for the offense. With respect to assessing offense-related goals, cognitive distortions that reflect internal responsibility for offending, or that the offender uses to reduce guilt or dissonance, are reflective of an avoidant offense-related goal. Conversely, cognitive distortions that externalize or deny blame or responsibility and that reflect that the behavior is common or acceptable indicate an approach goal. Examples follow:

- "Doing something like this is just not me. But I was just so depressed and so lonely that I felt like I couldn't stop myself." (avoidant goal distortion)

- "I tried all the things my last treatment program taught me, but they didn't work." (avoidant goal distortion)

- "What I did was not really that bad. After all, she is a prostitute so she is used to it. It was just rough sex, the way most of them like it, anyway." (approach goal distortion)

- "I'm actually not that different from you. I like to help others work through their problems. I'm sorry if she thought it was harmful." (approach goal distortion)

Post-Offense Evaluation

The SRM-R has two post-offense phases during which individuals evaluate their behavior and the offense and during which they form intentions with respect to acting similarly in the future. Individuals who have offense-related avoidance goals tend to respond negatively to committing the offense. They tend to experience negative emotions, a negative evaluation of themselves, and cognitive dissonance, and they typically express a desire to better restrain themselves in the future. In short, to them, the offense is a failure, since they did not achieve their initial goal (i.e., to avoid offending). Individuals holding offense-related approach goals tend to respond positively and to evaluate their behavior and the offense as an experience of success in meeting their goal. Examples of indicators of goals during the post-offense phases follow:

- *"I was disgusted with myself afterward. I felt so much guilt. I am never going to offend again."* (avoidant goal evaluation)

- *I was never so scared in my life. It was actually a relief when the police came. Even though I wanted the sex, it really wasn't even worth it."* (avoidant goal evaluation)

- *"Okay, so I probably shouldn't have been so aggressive, but I was really angry and even though I felt bad after, I felt like she knew not to diss me."* (approach goal evaluation)

- "Well, I certainly learned my lesson. I learned that I shouldn't go to that particular park as it is full of police and nosy people. Next time, I won't make that same mistake." (approach goal evaluation)

Offense Strategies

As indicated above, the offense pathway is a combination of an individual's goal in a specific offense progression and the strategy he chooses to achieve this goal. After determining the goal, the next step for the assessor is to determine the actions the individual undertook in order to achieve the goal. Strategies are generally either active or passive. As with determining the offense-related goal, assessing offense strategies is based on what is *most evident or predominant* in the offense progression. Strategies to achieve goals are selected in Phase 5 of the offense progression, but information on strategies selected and employed will be evident throughout the various phases of the SRM-R.

In assessing strategies used to achieve offense-related goals, three factors are considered and described below:

1. The individual's self-regulation skills

2. The degree of planning of the offense

3. The individual's control, or perceived control, over his offending behavior

Self-Regulation Skills

Self-regulation skills include the ability to engage in goal-directed behavior in order to achieve a desired outcome or to avoid an undesired outcome. The skills may also include abilities to cope with emotional states, such as anger, loneliness, sexual arousal/desire to offend, and so forth. In determining the offense pathway followed, the evaluator assesses the offender's general self-regulation skills and strategies demonstrated during the offense progression. If an individual has few or minimal skills to cope with life events, regulate emotional states, or solve problems, he may use passive strategies to achieve goals. In the offense progression, indicators of passive or automatic strategies include failing to attempt to prevent offending from occurring, offending impulsively, and having little or no ability to cope with offense-related desires and events. Indicators of the use of active or explicit strategies include some general abilities to cope with life events, solve problems, formulate plans, and make attempts to intervene, even if ineffectively, in the offense progression.

- "I don't really know what happened. We were dancing, and I wanted to be with her and just didn't want to stop. It was like my urges were controlling me." (passive/automatic self-regulation strategy)

- "I went to a party and got really stoned. I had my old friends there, and I thought that with everyone there knowing me and all, there should be no problem." (passive/automatic self-regulation strategy)

- "When I felt the urge to be with my neighbor's son, I knew it was wrong, so I went on the Internet and found some kid porn and masturbated. It wasn't a really good idea, because I thought of the pornography the next day when I saw him, which was when I offended." (active/explicit self-regulation strategy)

- "I don't have any problems. If I need something, I steal it; if I want something, like sex, I take it." (active/explicit self-regulation skill)

Offense Planning

The degree of offense planning throughout the offense progression provides indications of the types of strategies used to achieve the offense-related goal. Individuals plan their offenses to varying degrees. Some demonstrate no or minimal planning while others employ active or explicit planning. In some cases, evidence of planning offending will be absent, with the commission of the offense occurring relatively impulsively. In other cases, planning will be covert (e.g., accompanied by some mental rehearsal) and in still others, overt (e.g., done with explicit selection, in advance, of victim and/or location). Indicators of offense planning are found throughout the offense progression and include evidence of intent to commit an offense, forethought in selecting strategies, awareness of planning, and grooming potential victims. With specific respect to avoidance goals, active strategies also include those intended to help the individual refrain from acting out and to help him manage the desire to offend.

- "I have had fantasies of young girls, but have never acted on them. The night I offended, I was really upset that my girlfriend had left me, and it just happened when I saw that girl." (passive/automatic offense planning)

- "I couldn't believe it when we were alone all of a sudden. I was kind of surprised when she wanted another drink. When her sister went off to bed, it just seemed like the thing to do." (passive/automatic offense planning)

- "I usually take that particular subway line—mostly in the morning. It is always crowded and easy to get in a rub and disappear practically before they know what happened." (active/explicit offense planning)

- "I had looked after those kids before. This time, I made sure we watched some wrestling shows so that they would want to monkey around." (active/explicit offense planning)

Control over Offending Behavior

Control and perceived control over one's behavior varies across offense pathways. Generally, individuals who perceive their actions as beyond their control are likely to utilize passive strategies, while individuals who perceive their actions as within their control are likely to use active or explicit strategies. To assess control of offending behavior, the evaluator considers factors such as the offender's degree of disinhibition, his passive or active efforts to meet offense-related goals, his selection of strategies, and his ability to delay gratification during the offense progression. In addition to considering the offender's evident control over his behavior during the offending, the interviewer also assesses the individual's perceptions or beliefs about whether or not he was in control of his behavior. Despite an offender's ability to control behavior, an individual who *perceives* that his actions are influenced by factors beyond his control or external to him may be more likely to have used passive strategies to achieve the goal.

- "I have trouble controlling myself. It's like I have too much testosterone or that I was born deviant." (passive/automatic control)

- "I got to a point where I wondered if this isn't just who I am." (passive/automatic control)

- "I knew she would be alone that night and that, if I could just get to her, she would realize she had made a mistake and would take me back." (active/explicit control)

Determining the Offense Pathway

As indicated previously, allocation to an offense pathway is determined by combining the offense-related goal and the strategies the individual uses to achieve this goal. Each is evaluated separately. When the goal is avoidant and strategies are passive, the individual has followed the *avoidant-passive* pathway in the offense progression. When strategies are active, the individual has followed the *avoidant-active* pathway. Approach pathways are assessed as being *approach-automatic* when strategies are passive and as *approach-explicit* when strategies are active. These choices are illustrated below:

		STRATEGY	
		PASSIVE/AUTOMATIC	ACTIVE/EXPLICIT
GOAL	AVOIDANT	Avoidant-Passive	Avoidant-Active
	APPROACH	Approach-Automatic	Approach-Explicit

Once an offense pathway is determined, treatment methods and targets are determined in conjunction with other factors such as static and dynamic risk, primary goods, and individual responsivity concerns. Treatment tailored to individual pathways is described in chapter 11.

Summary

This chapter has focused on the four pathways in the SRM-R, with attention to thought processes, attitudes, planning, and post-offense evaluation. The evaluator begins with the individual's most recent sexual offense, and then works through earlier similar offenses. Similar sexual crimes generally are expected to have followed the same pathways. It is not necessary to determine the self-regulation pathway for every offense the individual has committed. However, it is useful to assess the offense pathway for different offenses in three types of cases, including when an individual has committed different types of offenses, has engaged in an extensive offending over time, or when prior treatment may have been effective in changing his goal regarding offending (for example, from an approach to an avoidant goal).

CHAPTER 6

Integrating Assessment

Chapters 4 and 5 described how to conduct the assessment of the self-regulation pathway and primary goods, how these are attained, and how they are linked to offending. As noted previously, the GLM/SRM-R is designed to be utilized within the context of comprehensive cognitive-behavioral treatment that takes into account risk, need, and responsivity. This chapter provides an integration of these elements in order to formulate an overall evaluation that includes other pertinent factors and clinical phenomena in individual cases. This evaluation allows the therapist to have a relatively complete picture of their clients, what they value in life, what areas are problematic and why, how they regulate their offense behavior, and what the dynamics and motivations are of their offending behaviors. The evaluation forms the basis of the case conceptualization of clients and treatment planning (see chapter 7) as well as treatment implementation (See part II).

Assessment of Risk

As noted previously, within the risk/need/responsivity approach to intervention (Andrews and Bonta, 2007), clients present with different levels of risk to re-offend and with different risk factors that are associated with offending. According to the risk principle, treatment should be tailored to these factors (in addition to responsivity characteristics; see chapters 1 and 2). Specifically, to be effective, treatment intensity (i.e., duration, number, and frequency of contact hours), should be higher for those clients who are at higher risk to re-offend, while minimal or no intervention should be applied to clients at lower risk to re-offend. This graduated approach also makes the best use of limited treatment resources and allows treatment to be focused on those individuals at moderate to higher risk, where treatment is most needed and is most likely to be effective. Thus, one aim of assessment is to determine the relative risk posed for purposes of placement in a specific program. Ideally, separate treatment programs of varying intensity are available for clients with varying risk levels. While variable treatment approaches are essential to treatment effectiveness, it is also important to allow for the variation because offenders who receive higher levels of intervention than is required can actually be harmed by treatment, potentially causing increased recidivism (Andrews and Bonta, 2007; Gordon and Nicholaichuk, 1996).

When evaluating risk, both static and dynamic risk factors are assessed. *Static risk factors* are those factors demonstrated to be empirically related to recidivism that cannot be changed through intervention (Andrews and Bonta, 2007). Among sexual offenders, such factors include being a younger age, offending against males, having committed previous sexual offenses, committing non-contact sexual offenses, and performing acts of non-sexual violence during sexual offending (Hanson and Thornton, 1999). *Dynamic risk factors* are also assessed. These are factors that are associated empirically with re-offending, are ones that can be changed through intervention, and are ones that represent criminogenic needs to be targeted for change in treatment. Dynamic risk factors include such factors as problems with general and sexual self-regulation, deviant sexual interests, intimacy deficits, and lack of positive social support (Hanson et al., 2007). The combination of static and dynamic risk factors can be used to establish a baseline level of risk for an individual client and for treatment placement decisions, while dynamic risk factors form the basis of the risk-based component of cognitive-behavioral treatment.

Consider the following example:

Example: Risk Factors and Treatment

Jeremy is a 24-year-old man on supervision in the community following his incarceration for a sexual offense against his girlfriend's infant son. He was convicted for this crime at the age of 19. Prior to that, he had spent much of his adolescence in inpatient programs following revelations at the age of 13 that he had molested a number of boys and girls in his neighborhood. The juvenile court system placed Jeremy in increasingly restrictive settings due to his disruptive and violent behavior toward others. In one program, he was found to have secreted a number of weapons, including a straight razor that he kept hidden in the drain of his shower. Jeremy possesses schemas relating to the world as being a dangerous place in which only those who are powerful can survive.

Upon his recent release from prison, Jeremy befriended a woman with two children. Within several weeks, the woman learned that he had molested her children. Jeremy blamed her for these offenses, saying that he only did it as revenge for her not having sex with him. He also stated that, because he was motivated by revenge, these offenses could not be considered sexual crimes.

Jeremy scores in the moderate range on actuarial measures of static risk. His age at the onset of offending and age at release, as well as the persistence of his offending, place him in a moderate risk population. Furthermore, Jeremy has abused males and has engaged in a high volume of sexual crimes. Jeremy has an extensive and diverse criminal history.

Jeremy's level of dynamic risk is high. He has a strong sexual interest in children and a very high level of sexual preoccupation. He has no history of stable, intimate relationships, and he possesses a high level of psychopathic traits. Jeremy professes little interest in what the future will bring to him, preferring to engage in pleasure-seeking in the present moment. He holds many attitudes and beliefs that are supportive of sexual abuse, and possesses few skills for overall self-management, including both general and sexual self-regulation. He is prone to angry outbursts and ruminates angrily. He possesses few skills for establishing and maintaining long-term relationships, and it is unclear what these skills would entail if he were interested in such relationships.

Protective factors for Jeremy include his absence of mental illness and his level of education (he was able to earn a high school diploma while in prison). Jeremy possesses good verbal skills and is very intelligent, although he has clearly used these skills in the service of criminal behavior.

Jeremy's good life plan to date has focused on happiness (via achieving pleasure), creativity (through developing a diverse and persistent means of doing as he pleases), and agency (by maintaining his sense of autonomy without conforming to others). His plan has been flawed by his inattention to the primary goods of life, spirituality, relatedness, excellence at play and work, and the other goods mentioned throughout this volume (illustrating his lack of scope). Although he possesses the ability to develop and maintain a healthy good life plan, Jeremy has not spent any meaningful time focused on realistic, long-term goals (revealing his lack of internal capacity). He therefore has few means to attain primary goods. Jeremy's pursuit of the primary goods of agency (or autonomy) and happiness (through sexual pleasure) have long been in conflict, since his behavior results in severe restrictions on his autonomy and his ability to attain happiness.

Jeremy follows an approach-explicit pathway in his sexual and other offending behavior. He holds cognitive schemas that are supportive of offending and actively plans his offenses. He does not desire to refrain from offending, nor does he attempt to prevent offending from occurring.

Jeremy's treatment programming and motivation to change will doubtless be challenging. Proper assessment and development of a good life plan for Jeremy will take time as he explores the difference between where he is and where he wants to be with respect to each of the ten primary human goods. One difficulty in assessment and treatment will be that Jeremy has a long history of mostly thinking in the short-term. In addition, his distrust of authority and his schemas related to a dangerous world will mean that his therapists must be willing and able to proceed slowly as they work with him. His explicit approach to offending and abusing others will also require changing his cognitive schemas, a process that will also require considerable time and that will proceed slowly and, most likely, with many setbacks. Jeremy will need to become motivated to examine his cognitive schemas and the ways in which these both interfere in his life and result in offending. He will also need to begin to question their validity and to reformulate these schemas.

A key component will also be to ensure that Jeremy uses the time he is not in treatment to demonstrate his progress and make changes relating to his treatment goals. Patience on the part of the therapists will be required, as progress is likely to be slow. The collection of collateral information from those involved in supervising Jeremy will be vital in order to provide feedback and to corroborate his self-report. All of this work needs to be done in addition to targeting Jeremy's multiple dynamic risk factors, which are significant.

Case Example: Larry

Larry is a 37-year-old man who works at an automotive parts store, although his goal is to one day become a hunting and fishing guide. Larry has been married for three years and was recently arrested for arranging a sexual encounter with a 15-year-old girl on the Internet. He had visited a number of sexually-oriented networking Web sites while his wife was working and had become acquainted with a young woman in his area. Her parents found out about Larry and notified the police. Larry has no prior criminal record, although he reported viewing appropriate (i.e., adult consensual) pornography on a semi-regular basis, as well as going to strip clubs. He indicated during the interview that he felt he might be "obsessed with sex more than a normal person." Although his wife is understandably distraught, she has stayed with Larry, and she intends to support his efforts in treatment.

In his initial interview, it became clear that Larry frequently views himself as less competent than others around him. He tends to cope with challenging situations either by attempting to avoid them or by ruminating on how he cannot seem to accomplish his goals. His sense of inadequacy has strained his marriage, and, with his wife appearing more distant to him and also because she is working in the evenings, he has engaged in a sexual self-regulation pattern of frequent pornography use and masturbation (approximately 10 times per week). Larry has a number of "buddies" with whom he shares an occasional drink after work, but he is generally unhappy with his situation and hopes one day to have a closer relationship with his wife and to guide hunters and anglers in the wilderness. However, the costs of setting this business up are very high, and he feels stuck in a dead-end job selling automotive parts.

Larry has followed an avoidant-active pathway in his offense. His intent was to avoid sexual offending. Larry has made attempts to cope with challenging situations through avoidance, rumination, and excessive masturbation. However, these attempts have been ineffective and misdirected, and have also likely increased his risk of re-offense. Larry's attempts to plan, monitor, and evaluate his behavior were effortful (in contrast to the avoidant-passive pathway), but were ultimately unsuccessful. Larry evaluates his offense as a negative experience.

Larry scores in the low-risk range on actuarial measures of risk. He has no prior sexual offenses and no history of other criminal behavior. He was acquainted with the victim, and has lived in an intimate relationship for more than two years. The victim of his offense was a female. He is currently in an age category associated with reduced sexual re-offending when compared to younger men. He scores low on measures of psychopathic traits, but his interview and phallometric assessment results indicate some sexual interest in pre-pubescent girls. These issues, in conjunction with his dynamic risk factors, indicate that his overall risk is in the low to moderate range. These dynamic risk factors include some difficulty with general self-regulation, his level of sexual preoccupation, and a lack of emotionally intimate relationship skills.

Larry requires minimal intervention and will benefit from being guided in addressing a number of dynamic risk factors while in treatment. These factors include his sense of inadequacy, his lack of competence in relationships (i.e., intimacy deficits), and his ability to cope effectively. Treatment should focus on these areas and on sexual self-regulation. Larry would also benefit from working on his employment plan and determining how realistic setting up a guiding business would be and, if not possible, what other employment he might seek that would be equally gratifying.

Protective factors for Larry include his low static risk and his capacity to maintain his employment and his marriage. He has a generally pro-social orientation, and his sexual preferences do not involve prepubescent children or other non-consenting partners. Larry is committed to doing what it takes to remain offense-free in the future, and is amenable to whatever treatment programs are available to him.

Larry's good life plan to the present has emphasized agency, relatedness, inner peace, and excellence in work. He has given less thought to areas such as spirituality and community, but does not appear to have a lack of scope in his plan. He could expand his good life plan and his career, however, by doing such things as pursuing creativity or knowledge. This direction would not require a significant area of focus in treatment. Larry's attempts to gain inner peace by pursuing an illegal relationship on the Internet were bound to bring him into conflict with the legal system (a problem with means). Furthermore, his goal of happiness (which resulted in his Internet use and illegal sexual pursuits) is in clear conflict with his goal of relatedness in his marriage. His goal of excellence at work also appears to be compromised by a lack of external capacity, although this capacity may change depending on how well he can meet other goods related to his employment prospects and pursue his goals in those areas. Such topics need to be a key focus in Larry's treatment.

Because of his low overall risk, Larry does not require a high level of treatment intensity. A low-intensity, cognitive-behavioral therapy program with a psycho-educational component will suffice and will comply with the risk principle of treatment. Periodic meetings between Larry, his therapist, and his wife will help his wife to better support her husband.

Larry's assessment results indicated that he would benefit from developing a good life plan that builds on his goals related to agency, relatedness, inner peace, and excellence at work, particularly focusing on his means and his internal and external capacity. These elements can assist him in managing the dynamic risk factors of interpersonal functioning, general coping skills, and sexual self-regulation. Because he lacks sufficient scope in meeting the primary goods of knowledge, creativity, and spirituality, he will most likely benefit from exploratory work in those areas, as well.

Considerations in Risk Assessment

When assessing risk, it is important to consider the question of "risk to do what?" That is, some clients will be more at risk to re-offend—to commit a new sexual offense—whereas others will be most at risk to commit a non-sexual violent offense. Still others will be at risk to commit both types of offenses in the future, or to re-offend in other, non-sexual and non-violent ways. For example, in the above cases, Jeremy is likely to re-offend both sexually and non-sexually. Should Larry re-offend, however, it would most likely be sexually.

In fact, research indicates that sexual offenders as a group overall are most likely to re-offend non-sexually, although of course each case is unique to each individual. As such, it is important that the evaluation process includes assessment of each type of risk, and that treatment be tailored according to each individual's needs. Various research-based measures are available to evaluators for this purpose,* a discussion of which is beyond the scope of this book.

Case Example: Maarten

Maarten is a 27-year-old man who consented to an evaluation following his conviction for sexually assaulting his girlfriend. Although he has an extensive criminal history, this incident is his first known sexual offense. In fact, his previous convictions have been for possession and distribution of street drugs. In his most recent prior offense, he seriously injured a man in the commission of a drug deal. Maarten reports very little concern about any of his past wrongdoing, and appears to have only consented to assessment in the hopes of influencing the evaluator to give him a positive report. Subsequent assessment shows that Maarten scores very low on actuarial measures of sexual re-offense risk such as the RRASOR and Static 99 (Hanson and Thornton, 1999). However, he scores very high on measures of general and violent risk, including the Sex Offender Risk Assessment Guide (Quinsey, Harris, Rice, and Cormier, 2005), which examines violence risk among sexual offenders. At this point, the evaluator experiences a dilemma. The purpose of the evaluation is for a sexual offender treatment program. However, it seems that Maarten is at far greater risk for non-sexual violence and general criminality, and, therefore, the evaluator will more prudently recommend a program for violent offenders instead of a sexual offender program, as the former is most likely to reduce his risk to re-offend.

In addition to variations in types of risk, different risk factors carry different weight in the assessment, with certain risk factors being stronger predictors of future offending than others and with various factors being associated differentially with sexual versus non-sexual recidivism (Hanson and Morton-Bourgon, 2005, 2007). Among sexual offenders, the two strongest predictors of sexual recidivism include *deviant sexual interests* and *anti-social orientation*. Anti-social orientation refers to such factors as anti-social personality, psychopathy, and anti-social traits such as impulsivity and problems with general self-regulation, substance abuse, reckless behavior, and a history of rule violations (Andrews and Bonta, 2007; Hanson and Morton-Bourgon, 2005). Dynamic risk factors most strongly associated with sexual recidivism include sexual attitudes, sexual deviancy, sexual preoccupation, intimacy deficits, and emotional identification with children.†

---

* For a review of measures commonly used with sexual offenders, see Yates & Kingston (2007).
† Although most strongly related to sexual recidivism, some of these factors have a smaller effect on recidivism than others.

Lastly, some factors that are commonly considered as risk factors have actually been found to be unrelated to recidivism. These include such factors as an adverse childhood environment, a negative family background, general psychological problems, and clinical presentation factors such as denial and low motivation for treatment (Hanson and Bussière, 1998; Hanson and Morton-Bourgon, 2005, 2007; Yates, 2009b). This complexity of factors can present a dilemma for evaluators and treatment providers. According to the RNR approach, these factors should not be addressed in treatment as they represent non-criminogenic needs that, even if they are changed, will not result in any positive impact on re-offending. In the GLM/SRM-R approach, however, addressing such factors in treatment can be important in that they may help to create a strong therapeutic alliance and assist clients to improve their lives. Thus, some of these factors, such as motivation or denial, may represent significant responsivity characteristics that will influence engagement in treatment and capacity to change (Yates, 2009b).

Given the above, treatment should concentrate on the risk factors most strongly associated with re-offending and should differentiate between the type of offending behavior in which the individual is most likely to engage according to risk assessment. Additional factors not necessarily related to recidivism are assigned more minor importance, however, and are assessed and included in evaluation with respect to their impact on self-regulation, their influence on treatment engagement and participation (i.e., as responsivity factors), and the attainment of a good life.

Risk Assessment and Treatment Planning

Many tools are available for assessing static and dynamic risk and for treatment planning, many of which are based on, and validated by, empirical research (Yates and Kingston, 2007). Regardless of the specific measure used, most instruments result in estimates of risk that involve a comparison of individual offenders with the overall population of sexual offenders, resulting in ratings such as low, moderate, and high. Generally, the more factors that are present, the higher the level of risk. Some assessment measures allow for determining risk using a combination of static and dynamic risk factors and that provide guidelines for establishing treatment and supervision priority (e.g., Hanson et al., 2007), The weight of these factors (as described above), however, also plays a role in treatment planning.

In using risk assessment for treatment planning, a combination of static and dynamic risk factors will serve as a baseline for determining treatment intensity, in accordance with the risk principle. For example, clients demonstrating lower risk should receive no intervention or only minimal intervention, such as a short psycho-educational intervention and/or routine community supervision. Clients assessed as being in the higher risk range will require treatment that is longer and comprised of more treatment hours.

Once a baseline level of risk is established, treatment intensity may be adjusted depending upon other factors, such as level of cognitive functioning, mental disorder, or other elements. For example, a client assessed as falling within the moderate risk range, but who has additional treatment needs in the area of mental health or substance abuse, may require additional treatment outside sexual offender treatment, or may require a higher intensity program, if these factors are addressed in the context of sexual offender treatment instead of externally by different treatment programs or providers. Similarly, clients who demonstrate considerable responsivity concerns may require separate programming or more intensive intervention. For example, clients with learning disabilities or low cognitive function should be placed, when possible, into a separate group that proceeds in a manner that is responsive to their level of functioning. This placement will require additional assessment, which is described below.

ADDITIONAL ASSESSMENT FOR TREATMENT

There is no question that an adequate assessment of risk is crucial for determining treatment intensity and supervision and for providing information for resource allocation. Likewise, evaluations must take into account criminogenic treatment needs (dynamic risk factors) in accordance with the risk principle. Just as vital for guiding treatment, however, are measures that provide information for adhering to the responsivity principle. For example, intelligence testing is critical for decision-making about programming. Measures of cognitive flexibility (such as the Wisconsin Card Sort; Grant and Bergs, 2003) can provide useful information about a client's ability to think about his life and circumstances. Recent research has also highlighted the prevalence of such problems as Attention Deficit Hyperactivity Disorder, Autism Spectrum Disorders, and Fetal Alcohol Syndrome/Effects among sexual offenders. Assessing the presence of such conditions can be vital to treatment success. Likewise, assessment of learning disabilities also provides important information about a client's ability to access the services that are available and their needs with respect to treatment participation. Measures of personality can also be very helpful, although it is well established that these measures cannot provide information about risk. Some personality scales, however, such as the Millon Clinical Multiaxial Inventory (Millon, Millon, Davis, and Grossman, 2009), can yield important information about the depth of a client's involvement in true therapeutic change (e.g., changes in suppressed or socially desirable responding) and can indicate whether in-depth interventions such as schema therapy (Young, 1999) are needed in treatment. An assessment of psychopathic traits can also provide important information about how best to match services to the individual needs of clients. For example, while the *Psychopathy Checklist –Revised* (Hare, 2003) is not a risk assessment instrument, it can still provide useful information in terms of risk and responsivity considerations in treatment. For example, clients scoring high on items related to grandiosity and shallow affect will likely be more difficult to engage meaningfully in treatment. Likewise, high scores on items related to both impulsivity and irritability ("poor behavioral controls") can yield information about how clients behave when angry or when provoked. Factor Two on this instrument is a measure of social deviance, and so can, therefore, provide information about a client's overall ability to manage himself (i.e., self-regulation). Likewise, high scores on Factor One, relating to internal affective states and interpersonal style, can provide important information about amenability to treatment and can serve to guide therapists as to the best ways to be responsive to a client demonstrating these characteristics.

Integration and Treatment Planning

As can be seen from the foregoing discussion, multiple factors are included in pretreatment assessment. In addition, within the GLM/SRM-R approach, additional assessment includes evaluation of elements such as primary goods and offense pathway (see chapters 4 and 5). Once all assessment has been completed, the full evaluation provides the basis for planning treatment for each individual client. This treatment planning is comprehensive and, within the GLM/SRM-R approach, takes the form of a good lives plan. This approach allows the treatment plan to be positive and approach-oriented and conceptualizes treatment as an exercise for clients to lead fulfilling lives and achieve their goals. Risk management is also addressed in this context, because both goods promotion and targeting risk are essential to treatment. Near the end of treatment, clients will construct their own personal good lives plans, which, in the GLM/SRM-R, will replace the traditional relapse prevention plan. This work is described in chapter 12.

As indicated previously, sound, effective treatment is based on comprehensive assessment. As stressed throughout this book, a thorough assessment needs to include the client's static and dynamic risk, his good lives constructs, his self-regulation with respect to the offense process, and any additional need areas based on the client's unique levels of functioning and needs. While risk-based approaches focus predominantly on changing dynamic risk factors, the comprehensive approach described here is designed to be inclusive so that treatment planning can be comprehensive and can also meet the goals of risk management and the attainment of a good life.

As indicated in chapter 1, common areas of dynamic risk that treatment programs address include sexual deviance (including both the type/nature and intensity of sexual interests), antisocial orientation (including self-regulation and dysfunctional coping), intimacy deficits, and interpersonal functioning, including the offender's ability to feel competent within relationships (Hanson et al., 2007; Knight and Thornton, 2007; Marshall et al.; 2006; Yates et al., 2000). Treatment programs often seek to help clients develop competencies in problem-solving and other cognitive skills, management of cognitive distortions, development of interpersonal skills, and the regulation of emotions. Programs also focus on compliance with the rules and requirements of treatment and supervision, healthy sexual functioning, the productive use of one's time, and positive and cohesive behavior in group settings (e.g., offering supportive feedback, listening to others) (Prescott, 2009; Wilson, 2009). From the GLM/SRM-R perspective, these competencies are wrapped around a good lives plan and, more specifically, take account of offenders' overarching goods. These goods are those associated with a person's core commitments and are rooted in his practical identity (Laws and Ward, in press).

A comprehensive treatment plan needs to address all relevant factors evident in an individual client's case. Within the GLM/SRM-R, this approach also includes the development of a treatment plan that explicitly and actively helps the client to attain what he values most in life. Thus, for example, while also targeting such areas as deviant sexual interests, intimacy deficits, and/or impulsivity, treatment also concentrates on actively meeting sexual needs, having intimate relationships in one's life, and using problem-solving skills to achieve important goals.

In developing the treatment plan, the therapist amalgamates all available information and designs a plan that is tailored to each individual client. Treatment typically follows a predetermined plan—for example, it often starts by establishing group norms, relevant personal history disclosures (i.e., "autobiography," see chapter 9), specific modules that address the risk factors described above, offense progression disclosure (see chapter 10), and the development of a risk management plan and release preparation (see chapter 12). These procedures are, at present, standard, well-supported elements of treatment. Within the GLM/SRM-R, however, treatment planning goes beyond these standard elements. Although the structure of treatment may be similar each time, it is essential to include all the elements that a client views as essential to achieving a good life, and to then determine how to attain these goals. Furthermore, within this structure, treatment is tailored to each client's responsivity characteristics and self-regulation pathways and styles. Such treatment pertaining to these characteristics and pathways are explored in more detail in later chapters. It is necessary, however, that treatment be structured to adhere to all of the principles described thus far, and that it is prescriptive insofar as it addresses relevant areas of concern and risk. Within this framework, therapists must have flexibility to implement treatment in a way that is responsive and relevant to clients' concerns. This degree of tailoring is an integral part of the GLM/SRM-R approach, since the aim of the approach is to wrap the specific components of treatment around each individual's primary goods and associated practical identities (Laws and Ward, in press). In short, it is recommended that therapists are trained and that they follow an established treatment process and content (i.e., a book), but that they have sufficient flexibility to utilize the most effective methods within this framework. To do otherwise runs the risk of implementing treatment that fails to engage offenders and that fails to offer them the possibility of a worthwhile life that does not target criminogenic needs, or that is oriented toward process rather than outcome, all of which is ineffective in changing behavior (see Hanson and Yates, 2004). It is this unique combination of goods promotion and risk reduction that is at the heart of the GLM approach to offender rehabilitation (Ward and Gannon, 2006; Ward and Maruna, 2007; Ward and Stewart, 2003).

Treatment plans function most effectively when clinicians prepare them using goals that are specific, measurable, attainable, realistic, and time-limited. Thus, establishing a goal of "reducing risk for sexual offending" would violate most of these principles (i.e., it is vague, difficult to measure, and has no time limit). These principles are particularly important when working within the GLM/SRM-R framework. As such, these factors must be operationalized in order to assess progress. For example, therapists need to define toward what goods a client is working to successfully obtain, how well he is working in specific treatment areas—such as cognitive schemas or plans to attain primary goods—and the best ways to address criminogenic needs. To do otherwise results in establishing goals that cannot be measured and puts the client at risk for making progress that cannot be demonstrated, either to treatment providers or to officials within the criminal justice system requiring such information, such as for decision-making purposes.

Although many options certainly exist for setting up a treatment plan, it can be most helpful to keep the format as simple as possible: a description of a specific concern or treatment area, a carefully stated goal, a handful of strategies for achieving the goal, a description of who is responsible for each of the strategies, and operational definitions of progress in these areas that includes specific, measurable indicators. It needs to be stressed, however, that these plans should also be comprehensive, coherent, and able to ultimately address offenders' basic needs, core commitments, and risk factors in ways that engage them and that reduce risk. These plans are specific and must updated regularly as treatment unfolds.

Treatment planning will be most meaningful and relevant to clients when they take an active role in developing their treatment plans. In fact, failure to include clients as active collaborators is against the spirit of the GLM/SRM-R, which is an inclusive rather than coercive approach and, as such, respects the dignity and agency of offenders. For that reason, clinicians seek to maintain a highly collaborative stance that supports the client's autonomy and self-efficacy to the greatest extent possible. It is the therapist's job to possess expertise about sexual offending; however, the clients possess the greatest expertise about themselves. Treatment planning should, therefore, involve a skillful choreography that takes into account both assessment-driven criminogenic needs and the need for clients to be actively and directly involved in developing good lives plans. This process takes the form of the clinician listening carefully to clients' desired personal identities and future states and exploring how these relate to both primary goods and to identified dynamic risk factors. For example:

> *Therapist:* Jon, what I've done is put together a list of the factors that the evaluator said were important to address during your time in treatment. As you can see, I also have this menu of areas that almost all human beings seek to attain at some time or other in their lives. You would have talked about these during your assessment. This might seem like a lot of information, but the idea is that we come up with a plan for what we can work on in the next several months. Remember, the focus of treatment is to help you live a better life. Before we go any further, I wonder what thoughts you might have about these concepts.
>
> *Jon:* We can go over these items, if you'd like. The main thing I'm concerned about is trust. I don't know that I can trust this system, or the people I work with.
>
> *Therapist:* Treatment feels dangerous to you.
>
> *Jon:* Yeah. I tried being in treatment before and it didn't go well. I didn't fit into the group, and I think someone in group talked to others about my private business.
>
> *Therapist:* It's really important to you to feel like you belong, and that your connections to others are solid.
>
> *Jon:* Exactly.
>
> *Therapist:* In fact, the whole notion about being part of a community and feeling like you can relate to others are some of the areas I was talking about before, the areas that make up a good life.

> **Jon:** Okay.
>
> **Therapist:** For now, would it make sense to establish a goal of being better able to judge when you can trust others? That part of the discussion will involve how trust fits into your future. It may also be the case that as you explore this issue in treatment, that perhaps trust played a role in some of the things that got you into trouble.
>
> **Jon:** That works. We can talk about all the big issues in treatment. I just want to make sure this one is in my treatment plan because it is a big deal to me.

Note that, in this example, the therapist is actively listening to Jon's statements and gently drawing out his concerns and associated values. The therapist has inferred, based on Jon's statements, that the primary good of agency is very important to Jon, and so the therapist has built achieving this goal into Jon's treatment plan.

In addition, note that the process should honor the client's voice at the same time that the clinician guides the client in the direction of change. The therapist's role is to create a therapeutic matrix in which the possibility of change can occur. This atmosphere cannot truly be created when the therapist is forceful or overbearing, or when the therapist is unable to listen or infers or assumes what is important to the client without seeking verification. Likewise, if the clinician simply defers to the client to set the treatment agenda, it is likely that treatment will proceed inefficiently at best, will lack authenticity (as clients' real interests and commitments may be missed), and will fail to address important treatment goals.

Clinicians involved in treatment planning will also need to keep clients' self-regulation pathway in mind when developing plans for meeting treatment goals. For example, it may be perfectly appropriate to offer behavioral methods for managing sexual arousal such as covert sensitization or thought-stopping to highly motivated clients who have followed an avoidant-active or avoidant-passive pathway. These skills can be a first step to self-regulation, but this technique should occur within a broader, approach-goal context. For avoidant-passive clients, the task will likely involve raising their awareness of abuse-related sexual interests, while clients following the avoidant-active pathway may require special attention in order to develop repertoire of skills needed to manage their sexual arousal. It often happens that avoidant-active clients have difficulty being able to recognize deviant arousal patterns, while avoidant-active clients recognize them but lack adequate self-regulation abilities.

In addition, therapists will want to exercise caution in the timing of addressing abuse-related sexual interests. For avoidant-passive clients, it may be necessary to improve their overall coping and self-regulation skills first, while for avoidant-active clients, it may be necessary to first raise their awareness of how they can cope with the stresses of daily life. For example, the client who masturbates to deviant fantasies in order to manage negative emotional states will benefit from a focus on developing healthier emotion regulation skills prior to directly addressing his sexual interests. To do otherwise might leave the client with no coping skills whatsoever, which in itself is a risk factor, and can also result in failing to detect the function of the masturbation and its relationship to the client's primary goods.

For clients who have followed an approach-automatic pathway, it is often necessary first to raise awareness and to help clients reflect on the interests, beliefs, desires, and needs that they have in their lives, also known as meta-cognitive control (Wells, 2000; Wells and Matthews, 1994, 1996). Clients who have followed an approach-explicit pathway will first need to explore the primary goods they have attained through offending. For example, the pursuit of relatedness through sexual activity with children will likely interfere with attempts to maintain freedom and agency and possibly intimacy, as well. Likewise, clients may also wish to explore how meeting the need of relatedness with children is likely to backfire as the child grows up and away from the offender, as well as to leave the client unsatisfied with the level of intimacy in his life. This direct a focus requires a strongly therapeutic environment and working alliance through which the client can openly disclose his behaviors, thoughts, beliefs, attitudes, and fantasies with a receptive therapist. These areas of treatment focus are often not seen as problematic by the client. Therefore, it is frequently necessary to raise a client's awareness of how these factors have contributed to his offending, how his experiences differ from those of others, and how these factors interfere with his attaining a good life.

The problem of intimacy deficits can result in different treatment for avoidance-based and approach-based offenders because of their varying goals and associated resources. For motivated, lower-risk clients who have followed an avoidance pathway, psycho-educational programs focusing on healthy sexuality can often be very helpful and frequently are all that is required. Likewise, programming designed to enhance interpersonal relationships can also be very helpful. For avoidant-passive clients, the treatment of intimacy deficits may involve exploring past relationships and raising the client's awareness of how relationships can operate. The process will assist him with skills acquisition and allow him to rehearse the development and maintenance of intimate relationships. The treatment of clients following avoidant-active pathways, however, may require examining past attempts at developing and maintaining relationships in order to understand the best way to use the skills he may already have, as well as to acquire and rehearse new skills.

By contrast, for clients who have followed approach pathways, it will be necessary to raise awareness and to analyze issues related to intimacy and cognitive schemas surrounding relationships in much greater detail so that those clients can develop a sense of discrepancy between their current state and a desirable future state. Often, this approach can be accomplished by exploring the past.

> **Therapist:** Jay, as you look back at your entire life, putting aside the present and the future, I wonder about times in the past when you felt really close to someone. It could be your mom, your dad, big brother, anyone. What do you think was the closest you ever were to someone?
>
> **Jay:** I don't know. Why are you asking?
>
> **Therapist:** You've spoken a lot about not wanting to get too close to others. I wonder about that. Some guys who have come through this program have talked about the times in their lives when they <u>did</u> connect really well to others. For one client, it was the time he showed his mom a picture he'd drawn, and she was so proud of him. For another client, it was about his dad teaching him to ride a bike. These were men who had been through all kinds of hardships, as you have been, but they remembered some good times of being close to someone, as well.
>
> **Jay:** Okay, why not? There was this one time my dad took me to the movies. I don't even remember what movie it was. But it was just him and me. I don't even know why I always remember that. You'd think it should be Christmas or something like that. The movies and my dad. Of course, that was before he went to prison.
>
> **Therapist:** What was going to that movie like?
>
> **Jay:** It was okay. He was a big person in my life back then.
>
> **Therapist:** Someone really important. And that was a time the two of you were really close.
>
> **Jay:** Yeah [sighs; rate, pitch, and volume of voice decrease].
>
> **Therapist:** There are a lot of ways to be close to someone. You and I both know you're all grown up now. I still wonder, if you look into a crystal ball 25 years into your future, what are one or two very small, and I mean just barely noticeable ways, where you might be close to someone else? It could be an old friend, a partner, a family member. I'm not talking about in a perfect world, only what's possible as you see it.
>
> **Jay:** I'm going to have to think about that, because I know I don't have that many chances left.
>
> **Therapist:** It sounds like you've got good reasons to look at your relationships. I wonder what part of this you would be willing to include in your treatment plan?

As in the previous example, Jay's therapist is actively listening to his client and inferring and verifying, based on the information provided, that the primary good of relatedness is important to Jay. The key idea is to explore a time—any time—when the client attained an important primary good, even momentarily, and then to explore what it would be like to attain that good again in the future. If a client suddenly attained this good overnight, what would be the first thing he would notice? If he could rewind his life from the future to the present, what would he see that made the difference in attaining this good?

Finally, sexual preoccupation can be a challenge for those who maintain offense-related goals. Many clients who have followed an avoidance-based pathway will be amenable to intervention in this area, including the use of medications such as antiandrogens; however, many will not. In some cases, clients have unfortunately taken such medications only to maintain the appearance of an investment in change, or as a last effort when all other interventions failed. Other clients who have taken these medications have found themselves confused as to how to cope with their lives in the absence of their past sexual outlets and their reduced sexual drives. If sexual activity or pleasure is an important goal to clients, it is likely be difficult (as well as threatening and distressing) for them to consider radically altering this facet of their lives in treatment, particularly when it has been an integral part of their personal identity. For example, clients following approach pathways are likely to have particularly well-entrenched attitudes and behaviors in this area when it is a risk factor. As such, change in this area may be slow, and therapists will need to be patient and encouraging, and will need to reinforce progress in a step-by-step fashion (e.g., through successive approximations). Furthermore, some clients view their sexual preoccupation as fixed within their character. One possible way to begin to address this might appear as follows:

Therapist: Jay, would it be okay if we talked about your sexual drive for a few moments?

Jay: You're not going to take that away too, are you? [laughs]

Therapist: You wonder whether that's going to be allowed here [smiles], and it's been a big part of your life—for better or worse—up till now.

Jay: Uh-huh. And if you can get a handle on it, I'll personally give you a medal.

Therapist: Well, we both know it doesn't work like that. Here's my question. What can you tell me about your sex drive? What's it all about?

Jay: Well, it's not just about offending. It's also about who I am as a man. It's how I get along. It's how I relate to others. Yeah, I admit, sometimes I think about sex a whole lot more than I probably should, but life is short, and I've got a right to be sexual.

Therapist: So this is really a big part of you. It's not like any program is just going to take it away.

Jay: That's right!

Therapist: I wonder, if we could make your sex drive just a little bit more of a problem for you, what would that be like? What would you have to do to make that happen?

Jay: [long pause] I'd have to be hanging out with the wrong crowd. I'd be telling myself it's okay, I won't get caught, and it's worth all the risks to get what I want.

Therapist: So if you wanted things to get worse with your sex drive, it would come down to your friends, your decision-making, and your values. Did I get that right?

Jay: Yes.

Therapist: Okay, maybe I can ask something just a little different. What if you wanted to make your sex drive just a tiny little bit less of a problem than it may have been for you? What would that take? Keep in mind, I'm not talking about losing your sexuality, I'm just asking what it would take to make it just one little bit less of a concern for you.

Jay: Now I see where you're going. It would be the same thing. I'd need to watch who I hang around with, be careful with the decisions I make, and be thinking about what's important to me in the long run. And I'm not sure I'm ready to do that.

Therapist: You're feeling two ways about this. There are some things you could do for yourself in this area, and you're not sure you want to do them.

Jay: No, I know I have to explore this, and I'm willing to look at all the options. You can put that on my treatment plan.

Therapist: It takes courage to say all this when it seems like the whole rest of the world has only seen the downsides of your sexuality. It seems to me that when you become ready and willing to make healthy changes in this area, nothing will be able to stop you.

In this example, the therapist is pursuing the principle that if a person can make a problem worse, he can likely make it better, too, one small step at a time. The therapist is also acknowledging the importance of sexual pleasure in Jay's life and is clearly giving him the message that the purpose of treatment is to improve his life in this area, not to take away its importance.

Summary

Integrating assessment and treatment planning is where the art and science of sexual offender services come together, and it is not an easy feat for the assessor or the therapist. An integrated approach with treatment founded on comprehensive assessment capitalizes on the strengths of each discipline. Furthermore, the principles and practices of enhancing motivation and including clients' needs in the process can be challenging. This integration of assessment and treatment planning may be particularly difficult when adding the GLM/SRM-R approach to assessment and treatment, not only because this integration adds additional elements to evaluation, but also because it challenges traditional models of sex offender treatment. The evaluator and the therapist need to ensure that they do not focus solely on risks and problems. They must also be able to actively and non-judgmentally listen to clients and to detect clients' strengths and needs. Although challenging, this approach will go further in building healthier lives and safer communities.

CHAPTER 7

Developing a Case Formulation and Treatment Plan

The preceding chapters in this section have focused on assessment, both using the integrated GLM/SRM-R approach and incorporating these elements in an overall evaluation that includes other pertinent factors such as risk. As indicated previously, pre-treatment assessment is essential to treatment implementation, as it provides the foundation upon which treatment is built. The aim of a comprehensive assessment is to allow the therapist to have a complete picture of the client and his strengths and areas of need. The assessment is also needed in order to adhere to the RNR principles—that is, to tailor treatment to clients' individual levels of risk, criminogenic needs, and responsivity factors.

Within the integrated GLM/SRM-R approach, the aim is also to include in this evaluation an assessment of those things that are important to the client in his life, the ways he has gone about acquiring those things, and the relationship of these factors to his self-regulation, his sexual offending, and his various life problems. The goal is also to understand the client's self-regulation style in committing sexual offenses, such that treatment can be tailored to be responsive to this style and the skills needed to respond to both the style and to the offense pathway he has followed. This chapter provides a model for incorporating assessment information into a relatively formal case conceptualization, and developing a treatment plan based on this formulation, which forms the basis of treatment as described in part III of this book.

Developing a Comprehensive Case Formulation

The case formulation should describe, for each individual client, the factors that made him vulnerable to committing a sexual offense. If the assessments described in the previous chapters have been completed, the therapist should, by this stage in treatment or pre-treatment, have a comprehensive understanding of the client that can form the basis of an individualized treatment plan. That said, the therapist must not assume that other aspects of the client and his behavior will not be discovered during treatment, and so the therapist must be flexible in augmenting or changing the case formulation when new information is presented.

What is different from other treatment methodologies using the integrated GLM/SRM-R approach is that the case formulation explicitly takes a good lives orientation. Typical case formulations (and their accompanying treatment plans) take a risk-based focus and predominantly include clients' deficits, problems, shortcomings, and risk factors. Within such a framework, those kinds of treatment plans focus predominantly on ameliorating problems, avoiding certain situations, building "coping" skills, and managing risk. Thus, those approaches are relatively negative in orientation, and it is easy to see how they do not motivate clients to participate in their treatment programs or to change their lives and their behavior (Yates, 2009a).

Such approaches also too easily become avoidance-focused, in that the aim of treatment becomes the delineation of all of the thoughts, activities, etc. in which the client *cannot* engage. Conversely, an integrated GLM/SRM-R case formulation and treatment plan is oriented toward understanding what is important to the client in his life and what his strengths are. Using this approach, the client and therapist collaboratively develop a plan for attaining a satisfying and fulfilling life for the client. Treatment is based on positive approach goals—those activities, circumstances, states of being, and so forth—toward which the client actively works, ones that the therapist actively assists him to obtain. For example, in addition to managing deviant sexual interests, treatment also actively helps the client to work toward seeking out and acquiring sexual relationships that do not pose a risk. It is easy to see how this approach is more positive than a solely risk-based approach, and more likely to motivate the client to change. Consider the following example:

Case Example: Scott

Let's return to Scott, whose case first appeared in chapter 4. Scott is a 22-year-old man who was convicted for sexually abusing his partner, Patrick. In his initial interview, Scott presented as anxious and in despair. He was concerned that he had lost everything that was important to him, including his partner, the community, and social groups that he had recently joined. As his relationship with Patrick became strained, Scott had begun to consume increasing amounts of alcohol. Following his admission to the program, Scott requested to see a psychiatrist for consideration for antidepressant medication.

In a more traditional treatment approach, treatment planning would primarily address the risk factors involved in Scott's offense. These factors would include alcohol use and abuse, and treatment discussions would center on the "cycle" of Scott's offense. Anger management would be a primary focus, and could include assessing Scott's feelings that he was entitled to greater sexual access to his partner as well as addressing his desire for immediate gratification. Treatment also might focus on developing an apology letter and on acceptance of responsibility without necessarily fully examining Scott's relationship with Patrick in detail. Scott would further be required to describe in detail what the effects of his actions were on Patrick. Scott would write a comprehensive plan that would describe all the ways he might reoffend, with a detailed list of situations and behaviors that he should avoid, thoughts and feelings that would put him at risk for acting out sexually, and a list of "warning signs" for service providers to alert them to potentially increasing risk. Scott's goals for treatment might include improved cognitive problem-solving skills, but the purpose would likely be focused primarily on managing high-risk situations and anger. He would also be asked to challenge and replace cognitive distortions related to aggressive behavior. A major focus of treatment would also be on raising Scott's awareness of the harmfulness of sexual abuse.

By contrast, in a GLM/SRM-R program, Scott would be asked about what primary goods he values the most, how the pursuit of these goods has occurred during his life and during his offending, and what instrumental goods he has sought and employed. A primary focus would be on the nature of Scott's relationship with Patrick and how this relationship fits in with his pursuit of primary goods. Does this relationship create conflicts among the primary goods that Scott is trying to attain? Are there aspects of the relationship that limit his capacity or means to attain these goods? Does the relationship limit or enhance the scope of his attempts to attain these primary goods?

Scott's therapist would also elicit from him what aspects of treatment would be most relevant to him. In order to attain primary goods, the focus would move from anger management to the regulation of emotions as a means to facilitate the attainment of goods and meeting his goals. Rather than learning to employ cognitive problem-solving skills solely for the purpose of managing risk, the focus would be on what skills Scott can use to attain primary and secondary goods that are personally meaningful and relevant to him, such as his relationship with Patrick or a future relationship. Beyond challenging and replacing cognitive distortions, a focus of treatment would be on identifying and exploring Scott's full range of cognitive schemas. This process includes examining how these schemas have influenced his behavior in the past and currently, and coming to an understanding of how he can understand these schemas in the future and change aspects of them in order to attain his goals. A major focus of treatment would also include understanding how Scott's offense-related goals and strategies (i.e., self-regulation pathway) were related to the attainment of primary goods, both during offending and in his life in general, and whether this self-regulation style is typical for him in his life.

As is evident from the example above, treatment within the GLM/SRM-R approach takes a much broader view of the client and the role of treatment than traditional risk-based approaches. Case formulation is based on a holistic and comprehensive picture of the client and his goals and needs in life, and treatment planning explicitly includes these as well as differences in offense pathway and self-regulation.

In addition to the above, although many treatment programs are diverse in their delivery methods, many have placed community safety above the needs of their clients. In fact, many programs state this explicitly. While there is no question that community safety is vital, it seems more important that programs operate from a structure that promotes both community safety *and* clients' well-being. Many programs have adopted an explicit stance that participation in treatment is a privilege and not a right. Therefore, the client is expected to participate to the very best of his abilities or be subject to dismissal. An advantage of the GLM/SRM-R approach is its explicit emphasis on serving community safety by building offender well-being and enhancing self-regulation and risk management. Beginning this process starts with developing a comprehensive understanding of the client and preparing a case formulation based on this understanding.

Constructing a Case Formulation

Phase 1

The first phase in constructing a case formulation involves the inclusion of primary human goods that are important to the client and that he actively seeks out or that he would like to have in his life. This phase is related to the first part of the assessment of primary human goods as described in chapter 4. This phase also includes those goods the client may have previously valued in his life but that he no longer seeks out, for example, because he was no longer able to attain them or lacked opportunities. If the client would like to re-acquire these goods, they are included in the case formulation and treatment plan.

Consider the following case example:

Example: Developing Case Formulation (Phase 1)

Therapist: *Welcome back, Scott. The last time we were together, we talked about your current distress and some of the primary goods that are valuable to you. Can we continue that conversation?*

Scott: *Sure. I'm doing a little better, and this would be a good time.*

Therapist: *Thank you. My understanding from our conversation was that, by moving to the city, you were able to feel a real sense of belonging to the community that you hadn't experienced in your small town up north. This change was very important to you, and you seemed to feel more a part of the city than you felt where you had grown up. Is that about right?*

Scott: *Absolutely. Being a part of the gay community is a big part of who I am. When I think of the primary good of community, urban areas with gay communities come immediately to mind.*

Therapist: *Feeling a sense of peace with people you're confident you can relate to is one of the most important values in your life.*

Scott: *Yes, and actually, that points to a couple of other things. Spirituality—the way you seem to define it as having meaning and purpose in life—is also really important. Unfortunately, part of being gay means that if you're too far from the community of your town, you're not going to find many organized religions that will accept you. And that brings me to another primary good that's really important to me: inner peace. I had very little when I was a kid, and I definitely think that absence was a major contributor to my assaulting Patrick. I need to find ways to have inner peace if I'm ever going to have a good life. The problem is, I'm not even sure how to do that. I know the inner peace of long walks and playing with puppy dogs, but I don't know enough about how to bring it with me wherever I go.*

Therapist: *I hear you loud and clear that you're looking to balance and pursue your goals so that you have inner peace, community, and spirituality. Given that Patrick has been such a key part of your life, where do relatedness and happiness/pleasure fit in?*

Scott: *Those are also really important. Mostly, I want to make sure I take care of the other ones first because that's what's going to make relationships and happiness possible. You know, I haven't valued life and agency as much as I should. I probably drink more than I should, and I don't have the knowledge or education to get anything but dead-end kinds of jobs. Somewhere in the rest of my life, I need to gain some knowledge and creativity so I can get better jobs, but I still want to work on those other goals first.*

In Scott's example, the therapist has effectively led the client in the direction of the primary goods that are important to him. The therapist has also effectively framed treatment as explicitly beneficial to the client. Once completed, the therapist moves to understanding how these goods can be attained.

Phase 2

Phase 2 involves evaluating the secondary (instrumental) goods associated with obtaining primary goods—that is, the means by which the individual goes about obtaining those things that are important in his life. For example, as indicated in chapters 3 and 4, in order to attain the primary good of life, an individual may engage in activities such as working to acquire income or eating well in order to remain healthy. These secondary goods represent the activities in which clients engage in their day-to-day lives in order to obtain the things they want in life. Some of these activities will also be related to sexual offending.

In addition, clients' strengths are also assessed at this stage, with a focus on such things as: (a) the goods that they are able to successfully acquire without offending; (b) how they effectively manage various problems in their lives; and, (c) the times during which they could have offended but refrained from doing so.

Consider the case illustrated below:

Example: Developing a Case Formulation (Phase 2)

Therapist: Scott, We've spoken about the importance of some primary goods to you, specifically community, spirituality, and inner peace. You mentioned that you would like to develop more ways to find inner peace, and that spirituality can be dependent upon one's community. What are some of the means or ways by which you've sought to attain these goods? And what are the secondary goods you've had and would like to have?

Scott: Well, for community, I need an urban area where there is an identifiable gay community. I mention that because there are smaller places that serve as popular places for gays to go for vacations, but that's not what I'm talking about. Urban areas have more options for things to do and places to go, and that's important to me. There was a lot I loved about growing up in a rural area, but I can always drive there. Spirituality is the same thing. I belong to the Unitarian church and that denomination can be hard to find outside of the larger cities. If I have access to a Unitarian church, I should be okay.

>   *The main thing is inner peace. Like I said, I just don't seem to have that element except when I stumble upon it here and there. I think that absence explains my drinking too much. Drinking has always been less about pleasure than about dealing with inner turmoil. I've seen other people find inner peace, but I just have felt left behind. That's why I said what I said. I'm not a violent guy, but I was really violent toward Patrick. I hurt him really bad, and he probably won't ever speak to me again. Maybe I counted on him too much for inner peace. I think I probably did. I need ways to find inner peace for myself if I'm going to have a life that's healthy and one where I can become good at something. I need inner peace so I can stop myself when I do get frustrated* [Scott cries]. *Sorry, but this really touches a nerve.*
>
> **Therapist:** *Tears are always okay in this program* [long pause]. *I wonder about some of the other secondary goods you've used or would like to use?*
>
> **Scott:** *Sooner or later, if I'm going to work toward agency, knowledge, or even excellence at work and play, I'm going to need an education. I put a lot of that on hold so I could move here with Patrick. I'm looking at that differently now. I need to gain these other secondary goods so that I never, ever rely on violence again.*

In the above example, the therapist has drawn from the client both his prior means to achieve his primary goods as well as problems Scott has with some of those means. Scott has also revealed his secondary goods, which may represent better means for him in the future so that he can achieve his goals.

Phase 3

Phase 3 involves identifying problems that are evident in a client's good life plan. Such an analysis is not limited to the client's sexual offending behavior but instead, includes all life problems the client reports. For example, a client may experience difficulty obtaining or keeping a job as a result of a lack of education or skills. His deficits in those areas may not be related to offending, but may nonetheless be important to him. Thus, the goal is identified and included in the case formulation, as it represents a treatment target on which the client may wish to work. Conversely, other problems in a client's good life plan may be more directly related to sexual offending, such as when the individual seeks sexual pleasure (the primary good of happiness) through sexual aggression. Such problems implementing the good lives plan are also included in the case formulation. In addition, flaws in the individual's good life plan are also identified, helping all parties to better understand the specific problems—i.e., scope, means, conflict, or capacity—that the client experiences in implementing the plan, since these flaws may lead to offending.

Consider the case illustrated below:

Therapist: *Scott, you've already discussed some of this, but what do you think are going to be some problems with the good life plan you're starting to develop? As we have discussed, the problems could be that you lack the means to make the plan happen, because you don't have the capacity or the scope, or because you have some other conflict between your different goals.*

Scott: *I guess one thing I already mentioned is that I need to develop inner peace, and right now, I'm just lacking the ability. In fact, I always have. I'm open to all ideas. Also, although I want to focus on community, inner peace, and spirituality right now, I can see that, unless I start also planning and working on the other goals, I might set up a conflict. Also, I'm pretty sure I can be a happy person in the future generally, but I'm going to need to do some things that are just plain fun. I guess that's just hard to look at right now because I feel like I owe it to Patrick to take all this really seriously. I used to do lots of different things to have fun, but that stopped some time ago.*

Also, to say it like I learned in treatment, my trying to be in control and trying to be good at my work are going to crash with my life, knowledge, and creativity unless I go back to school. I've never cared that much about work. I'm a cash-in-pocket kind of guy, but I can see that someday I'm going to want more out of life. I'm going to want ways and means to be a better person.

The last thing is that I'm going to need to watch out for is my relationships and my needing pleasure and happiness, if these don't happen together. This struggle has happened before. What I'm trying to say is that when I get into another relationship, or back with Patrick, I'm going to need to make sure that we're building a balanced good life type of plan together.

In this example, the therapist has effectively identified flaws in Scott's good life plan and has assisted him to prioritize his goals and goods.

Phase 4

Phase 4 of developing the case formulation involves understanding all clinical phenomena implicated in sexual offending. This process includes an analysis of all the factors (primary and secondary goods, risk factors, offense pathway, and so forth) that are specifically related to offending behavior and that will build upon information identified in the first three phases of building the case formulation. In this section of the case formulation, the aim is to identify links among these various factors that influence offending, as well as their relationship to offending behavior, for each individual client. Also, in this phase, the function that offending serves for the individual is identified—that is, what does the individual gain from offending, either directly or indirectly? Lastly, any additional information gained from all areas of assessment (see chapter 6) is included here.

Phase 5

The fifth phase involves identifying the context and environment in which the client is living or will be living upon completion of treatment. This look at the future allows for the development of a treatment plan and a release plan that will take into account the specific opportunities and limitations for each individual client. For example, some jurisdictions will have restrictions on movement within the community, which will need to be taken into account when developing an individual treatment plan.

Consider the case illustrated below:

Example: Developing a Case Formulation (Phase 5)

Therapist: *Scott, up to this point we've covered the main points on primary and secondary goods, and any flaws that might exist in your past and present good life plans. What we haven't discussed is the context in which much of this plan will take place. How do you envision your reintegration into your community?*

Scott: *I am scared half to death. I don't know what Patrick has done recently, but I know that a lot of our mutual friends know what happened, and they probably think I'm a monster. So I don't know if the gay community will shun me or not. I'm sure I will fit in somewhere eventually, but I'm expecting that I will have a lot of explaining to do, to say the least. I'm also going to have to work really hard to find a job. I have some leads through my family, but it's still going to be tough. The other thing is—for all the value I've placed on being in the city, I may need to live outside of it if the news reports are true that they are going to put restrictions on where I can live. I know for a fact that Unitarian churches have a process for what to do when there is a sex offender in their church, and I am willing to go through that process. I expect that my conditions of release will include no alcohol, and that will be fine with me.*

The most important things will be my getting along with others and having ways to cope with the community members who think "once a sex offender, always a sex offender." I will just have to double up on my efforts at finding inner peace. You might think I'm rattling these answers off really easily, but I've been thinking about it a lot. The big thing about the context is going to be staying focused and dealing with the disappointments of where I live and work. I'll make it, though. It's just part of building the life I'm going to build.

In this last example, Scott has identified a number of constraints in the environment in which he will be living, including, but not limited to, formal restrictions. Scott appears realistic about the barriers he will face in his reintegration into the community and has begun to make some plans to address them.

At this phase of the assessment process, therapists will have a sound understanding of a client's valued goods, how he goes about attaining these goods, the flaws in his good life plan, and the relationships between goods and offending.

In the *sixth phase,* the therapist constructs a treatment plan for the client based on the above considerations and assessment information such as risk factors and the self-regulation offense pathway. This process requires taking into account the kind of life that would be fulfilling and meaningful to the individual (i.e., primary goods, secondary goods, self-regulation and its relationship to ways of living. This also includes the likely or possible environments in which the client will be living, as well as the capabilities or competencies he will require in order to have a reasonable chance of putting the plan into action in these environments. The therapist and client can then develop a treatment plan.

Developing a Treatment Plan

As indicated above, the case conceptualization forms the basis of clients' individualized treatment plans. Because the treatment plan is based on the case formulation and lays out the direction and methods of treatment, it is important that both parts of the treatment plan are comprehensively compiled and that these are as complete as possible. Although, as has already been noted, new information may come to light during treatment, by this stage, the therapist should have relatively complete information on a client in all the assessment areas described thus far, allowing for a detailed treatment plan to be developed. The plan, developed in collaboration with the client, should include the following elements:

- Intensity (duration and frequency of contact) of treatment based on risk assessment
- Dynamic risk factors
- Responsivity factors and comprehensive plans to address these
- Specific treatment components required, based on assessed criminogenic needs (e.g., the regulation of emotions, sexual arousal reconditioning, etc.)

- Treatment targets based on dynamic risk factors
- Treatment targets based on the offense pathway(s) and self-regulation styles and issues
- Treatment targets based on primary and secondary goods and flaws in good lives plans
- Existing strengths on which treatment will build
- Specific skills and strategies to be developed during treatment
- Treatment goals developed in collaboration with the client, timeframes to re-visit, and/or revised treatment goals
- Objective, operationalized indicators of treatment progress

Treatment planning should be an explicit exercise involving the client and the therapist. The clinician must arrive at the treatment-planning meeting with the client's assessment results and case formulation in mind. This way, the clinician can guide discussion in the direction of primary and secondary goods, relevant dynamic risk factors, and offense pathways and self-regulation. The client should arrive simply with an open mind as to what he can expect in the meeting. He will have been prepared by the therapist to respond to the types of questions that will be posed and the rationale behind such questions, all based on a treatment planning process that will assist him in meeting his needs and managing risk.

Recall that, within the GLM/SRM-R approach, treatment is explicitly framed as an activity designed to assist offenders to attain important things in their lives. As such, the therapist can begin by asking each client on which areas of his life he would like to focus throughout treatment. What is meaningful to the client? What is missing in his life that he would like to have or experience? This inquiry lays the foundation for a choreography that can occur between client and therapist. The client can talk about what is important to him, and the clinician can skillfully offer reflective, summarizing statements and pose open-ended questions to guide the client in the direction of primary goods. Often, this back-and-forth discussion will involve moving through discussions of the client's desire for secondary goods and then into the primary goods themselves, which, as described previously, are most likely to be inferred from the secondary goods the client describes.

The clinician can next bring the client's strengths, talents, skills, and other positive attributes into the discussion. Although this stage may seem like common practice, it is all too easy for a therapist to begin a discussion with an overview of the client's skills and strengths and then quickly move into a discussion of his needs and deficits. Many clinicians have had prior training in deficit-based treatment planning and, as a result, bring unhelpful habits with them to treatment planning.

The therapist might, for example, tacitly pay a disproportionate amount of attention to what is wrong with the client, and in the process, ignore or minimize the client's strengths, thereby adopting a negative or judgmental stance in which the therapist portrays as the expert. For example:

> **Therapist:** Now that we've covered your strengths, it's time to explore what you need to work on. What do you think you need to address in treatment? I think anger management is a big issue for you.

In this instance, the clinician appears to pay minimal attention to a client's strengths and instead emphasizes his liabilities and makes assumptions about what the client needs to address in treatment. Although initially appearing to elicit the client's thoughts, the clinician quickly reverts to expressing opinion and giving advice. It is as though exploring strengths is a way to ease the client into weightier matters rather than using the client's attributes as a foundation for addressing his concerns and building a treatment plan. Furthermore, by moving too quickly into the clinician's agenda, the client provides too little input into his treatment plan, and the process is neither collaborative nor consistent with the GLM/SRM-R approach. This restrictive approach can risk making the treatment plan less desirable for the client and can reduce the likelihood that he will actually follow through on his goals. Instead, it can be helpful to focus first on a client's assets and strengths and ask the client how he might rely on these during the course of his treatment.

> **Therapist:** You've given a lot of thought to the strengths and positive attributes that you bring into treatment. These same strengths will no doubt help you make and sustain the changes you want to make. Some of the key strengths that I see in you include your motivation to attain knowledge, your desire to improve your relationships with others, and your focus on expanding how you take care of yourself. Let's next turn to the areas you would like to work on.
> **Client:** One thing I know I need to work on is finding out how I can re-build my relationships with my family, and to see if that's even possible.
> **Therapist:** You really miss your family, and this fits with one of the positive attributes we just discussed: your desire to improve your relationships with others. I wonder how you can include some of the other strengths we discussed.
> **Client:** [After some thought] I guess the best way to move forward is with some additional knowledge. I guess I should use treatment to learn the best ways to get back in touch with them.

Therapist: You could gain knowledge from others who have been in your situation.
Client: Yes.
Therapist: One thing you may not know is that part of the treatment program focuses on problem-solving skills. Maybe that would help, too?
Client: Yes, I think it would.
Therapist: One of the main goals of the treatment program is to help clients develop their abilities to have healthy and fulfilling relationships with others. We discuss areas like problem-solving and being able to understand other peoples' perspectives and then to act accordingly. How does that sound?
Client: That sounds great!
Therapist: How about if we set a goal for improved relationships with others, including your family. The action plan could include the steps you'll take as you prepare to re-build your family connections. That process could include identifying some problem-solving steps, collecting feedback and ideas from the others in your treatment group, and exploring how relationships have fit into your past. How does that sound?
Client: Sounds like a plan.

In this example, the therapist has avoided negative language (e.g., phrases like "social skills deficits") and has focused on the positive aspects of what the client wants. The therapist has also guided the client's goal into the broader direction of relatedness (a primary good) and the reduction of social isolation (a dynamic risk factor and criminogenic need).

In setting treatment goals, each clinician will have to establish how many goals a client can address and over what length of time. In some cases, it will be most helpful to start with smaller, more manageable goals rather than focusing on the expected end product of treatment. For example, a client may express the goal of "getting better" or re-establishing his relationship with his family, while the therapist's focus will be to reduce the risk to re-offend. In such cases, the therapist should work with a client's initial goal even though the goal may not directly reflect that the ultimate objective of treatment is to prevent recidivism. Then, gradually, the therapist can revisit progress toward these larger goals and then establish new goals later in treatment as a client comes to accept the changes he will need to make to avoid re-offending. In addition, some goals may require clarification to become more concrete. For example, if the client indicates that a goal of treatment is "to get better," what precisely does this goal mean and what does it entail? Lastly, when setting goals, it is essential that objective, measurable indices of progress and achieving goals are established. All too often, treatment programs set goals for or with clients but do not develop concurrent methods to assess whether the client is meeting these goals. For example, it may be a goal for clients to develop "empathy." But when empathy is not well-defined and indicators of progress are not set, the therapist has no way to know or demonstrate that such a goal has been attained. This situation can create considerable difficulty when decisions pertaining to release, reduced security, or treatment completion require evidence that the client has benefited from treatment and has achieved treatment targets.

In some jurisdictions, treatment plans are structured according to licensing and statutory requirements. However, it is recommended that treatment plans be kept as simple and manageable as possible. A desired end state is for the client to have a meaningful plan and to express satisfied commitment to working on it. If the client does not experience his treatment plan as relevant, important, and meaningful, he will have fewer reasons to be motivated to participate in treatment and to work toward the goals established in his plan.

Treatment plans often take the form of specific concerns, goals, and action plans. In many cases explicit statements detail which person is responsible for which part of an action plan (e.g., "The psychologist will provide individual counseling relating to previous sexual victimization" or "The religious resource coordinator will provide a comprehensive schedule of available religious activities"). The layout is best when it is deceptively simple. The focus should be on what the client can accomplish rather than having the clinician attempt to cover every base.

Example: Treatment Planning

Jim is a 38-year-old offender who was convicted for one count of sexual touching. The victim was a 10-year-old boy who was Jim's neighbor. Jim knew the boy's family very well. At the time of the offense, Jim had completed treatment and was participating in post-treatment maintenance programming. Up to that time, he had been doing very well, both managing his risk and implementing his good life plan to the best of his abilities and within the imposed constraints in the community. Jim had learned to accept his sexual attraction to males and to manage his risk and avoid contact with boys. Immediately prior to the offense, however, Jim was rejected by a potential lover, was feeling lonely and depressed, and had not yet found a job following his conviction (he is trained, and had worked, as a personal homecare aide for 15 years). At the time of the offense, Jim was feeling worthless and disconnected from his family and friends. He had been very involved in his community and church, but because of residency restrictions, Jim could no longer participate in many of these activities. When he realized he was in a high-risk situation with his neighbor, he initially ignored his sexual feelings and shut himself off in his house. Jim is shocked and depressed that he committed another sexual offense. He has been returned to treatment.

In the previous case example, Jim re-offended following treatment after a period of successful management in the community. The primary goods that are important to him include community, relatedness, spirituality, and happiness. Furthermore, the primary goods that were implicated in his most recent sexual offense include relatedness—specifically intimacy—inner peace, spirituality, excellence in work, and community. With respect to his good life plan, he demonstrated flawed means to attain primary goods as well as a lack of both internal capacity and external opportunities. His dynamic risk factors include sexual self-regulation (deviant sexual preference), regulation of emotions, general self-regulation (problem-solving), intimacy deficits, and a lack of social supports.

Jim's treatment planning meeting will begin with a review of his positive assets. As worthless as he may feel in the wake of re-offending, he was not offending the entire time he was in the community. How did he manage that? What skills and strategies did he use that contributed to his success during these times? How can he use these strategies toward an offense-free future? These existing skills represent Jim's strengths upon which Jim's treatment plan can be built. He will also benefit from understanding when things started to go wrong, and how he responded in those situations.

Next it will be time to consider Jim's good life plan. What does Jim think he needs to work on first, and what primary goods are involved? The clinician should keep in mind that Jim may choose to work toward more easily attainable goals toward the beginning of treatment. An approach such as this is certainly acceptable as long as it is clear that other, more challenging goals will become the focus of treatment in subsequent treatment planning meetings.

The following is a brief version of what an initial treatment plan might look like for Jim. Note that this provides a brief example only, and that a full treatment plan would contain additional detail. This plan will be reviewed and revised with Jim on a regular basis throughout treatment. Although the following example includes all goals that would ultimately be included in Jim's treatment plan, a plan like this will most likely not be developed in full at the outset, and will instead be expanded upon later in treatment.

Jim's Treatment Plan

Intensity of Treatment Required: Moderate (6–8 months, three times per week, followed by maintenance programming)

Risk Factors: Jim demonstrates several risk factors of importance, including deviant sexual preference, offenses against boys, difficulty with the regulation of his emotions, general self-regulation problems (specifically in the area of problem-solving), intimacy deficits, and lack of social supports. He also re-offended following treatment and while under supervision in the community, which also functions to increase his risk to re-offend. The absence of social support in his life was, in part, a result of supervision restrictions.

Responsivity Factors: Jim easily experiences a sense of worthlessness and becomes depressed. In treatment, attention will be paid to the emergence of these states, and Jim's skills will be actively reinforced and his self-efficacy will be supported. Supplementary evaluation will be conducted to determine whether antidepressant medication is warranted. In addition, because Jim's sexual orientation is toward males, treatment activities such as written work will be revised where these refer only to heterosexual relationships.

Specific Treatment Components Required: Based on his risk factors, Jim will participate in the following treatment modules:
1. Re-assessment of need for sexual arousal reconditioning
2. Offense progression (for review and update regarding the current offense only, as his offense progression was previously prepared in his treatment program)
3. Regulation of emotions
4. Self-regulation for avoidant-passive pathways (to increase problem-solving, self-monitoring, cognitive skills to prevent loss of control in risk situations, and behavioral rehearsal)
5. Developing and maintaining interpersonal relationships
6. Implementing a good life plan (see below)

Good Lives Planning: Jim highly values the primary goods of community, relatedness, spirituality, and happiness. These goods, as well as inner peace and excellence in work, were associated with his re-offense, during which he experienced flawed means to attain relatedness and happiness, a lack of internal capacity to gain inner *peace, and a lack of external opportunities to meet all needs. The regulation of his emotions and his sexual arousal control will assist in addressing the flawed means he chose to meet goals, in conjunction with inculcating strategies to achieve positive emotional states as Jim's baseline and providing opportunities for sexual and intimate relationships. He will be assisted to find new employment based on his interests and expertise, since supervision restrictions indicate he cannot return to his previous employment. He will be connected to a church, with a safety plan in place, in order to pursue his need for spirituality in his life. He will furthermore be connected with the gay community to allow for external opportunities to meet the needs of having a shared community, developing relationships, and attaining happiness and opportunities for sexual relationships.*

Treatment Goals: *In collaboration with Jim, the above treatment goals have been established, although it should be noted that he is somewhat fearful of connecting with the gay community. He has not told his parents of his sexual orientation and is not certain they will be supportive and accepting of this. Therefore, strategies in this area will be devised later in treatment to allow him to become comfortable with this treatment goal and to determine whether, and how, he will inform his family. This goal will be re-visited with Jim every 30 days.*

Indicators of Treatment Progress:
1. *Awareness of re-offense progression and pathway, as evidenced by Jim's understanding of all factors influencing his re-offense and offense patterns overall*
2. *Behavioral demonstrations of control of sexual interests (e.g., as evidenced by fantasies and masturbation recording logs) and disclosure of any problematic sexual fantasies or situations*
3. *Ability to manage negative emotional states as evidenced by fewer instances of re-emergence of these states and indicators of inner peace (e.g., participating in activities, absence of brooding, evidence of fewer negative states, all as reported by Jim, treatment providers, supervision personnel, and collateral contacts; observation of implementation and practice of skills and strategies to cope with negative affective states, use of antidepressant medications, etc.)*
4. *Increase in knowledge of primary goods and their role in his re-offense and offense patterns*
5. *Demonstration of use of self-monitoring (e.g., use of self-monitoring log, implementation of problem-solving skills in situations that arise, auto-correction of under-regulated behavior, observation)*

6. Demonstration of establishing relationships with others (e.g., developing friendships, contact with family members) and absence of contacts with potential victims (i.e., boys within Jim's preferred age range)
7. Demonstration of implementation of Jim's good life plan as evidenced by establishing contact with church, participating in church activities, establishing new friendships, developing contacts within gay community (see above) and with other communities of interest or social groups, and positive support persons (to be determined)

Timeframe for Goal Review: 30 days

Other: Jim's community management team will be enlisted to implement the above-indicated treatment goals and to monitor progress.

Case Example: George

George is a 51-year-old offender with a long history of sexual abuse of teenaged girls. George has worked as a health board inspector since obtaining his diploma in quality control and being assigned to inspect school cafeterias due to his high level of knowledge in this topic area. Although he takes significant pride in his work, George admits that his work provided him with the opportunity to meet "lots of hot young girls" who, he said, were easy to befriend because they were often in the throes of adolescent crises. The ones who had broken up with their boyfriends were easy to identify, according to George, particularly those who wanted to "get back" at their boyfriends by being seen with an "attractive, older man." George made friends with these girls, gave them money to go shopping, and bought them presents. He reports that, in each instance, they were more than happy to "thank him properly." George has never been married and states that he is completely fulfilled by his current "activity"—he gets a lot of sex from attractive young girls, he is able to "teach them about the harsh realities of life," and they are not assertive and "demanding as older women can be."

Dynamic risk factors related to George's offending appear to include intimacy deficits (including a lack of concern for others and possibly hostility toward women), a lack of sexual self-regulation (including sexual preoccupation), attitudes tolerant of sexual abuse, related cognitive distortions and schemas, and a lack of significant positive social influences. The therapist will want to explore these factors further throughout treatment. George's most valued primary goods appear to be happiness (though sexual pleasure), agency, and excellence at work (although the latter should be explored further in treatment to determine whether George truly values his work or whether it solely or predominantly provides the opportunity for him to find opportunities to offend). The primary goods implicated in his offending include happiness, relatedness, and agency. The main flaws apparent in his good life plan include a lack of scope (in that he appears to focus much of his energy in the direction of his job and access to teenage girls, to the detriment of other primary goods) and flawed means (in that his attempts to gain pleasure and relatedness are inappropriate and also limit his ability to gain them in a different yet meaningful way).

The following is a brief version of what an initial treatment plan might look like for George. Note that this is a brief example only; a full treatment plan would contain additional detail. This plan will be reviewed and revised with George on a regular basis throughout treatment. Although the example below includes all goals that would ultimately be included in George's treatment plan, a plan like this will most likely not be developed in full at the outset, and will instead be expanded upon later in treatment.

George's Treatment Plan

Intensity of Treatment Required: Moderate to high (9–12 months, four times per week, followed by maintenance programming)

Risk Factors: Although his actuarial risk is assessed as low, George demonstrates several risk factors of importance. He experiences considerable intimacy deficits, and has never been in a long-term relationship. He holds a number of adversarial attitudes toward women. He experiences same-aged women as being too assertive and demanding, and he enjoys his pursuit of women who are significantly younger than he is and who are easy to influence. George possesses a number cognitive distortions and schemas that support sexually abusive behavior. George reports engaging in sex with "a lot of attractive young girls," suggesting a possible sexual preoccupation.

Responsivity Factors: George has a low motivation for treatment participation or genuine change. He describes himself as being "completely fulfilled" by his sexual behavior with underage females and does not see a need to change. Therefore, George's primary responsivity factor is his low level of motivation to change his behavior. Motivational enhancement techniques will be essential to treatment implementation. In addition, George will require additional assessment in the area of psychopathy which, if found to be present, will result in reconsidering the *recommended treatment intensity and length due to the relationship of psychopathy to re-offense risk, particularly should deviant sexual interest or preference also be present in George's case.*

Specific Treatment Components Required: Based on risk factors, George will participate in the treatment modules focusing on:
1. Assessing for possible pharmacological interventions to help George manage his sexual impulses
2. Relevant personal history disclosure (autobiography)
3. Assembling George's offense progression
4. Helping George to learn self-regulation for approach-explicit pathways
5. Identifying cognitive schemas and their attendant cognitive distortions and the impact of both on offending
6. Developing George's perspective-taking skills (i.e., "empathy")
7. Helping George to learn how to develop and maintain interpersonal relationships
8. Assisting George with developing and implementing a good life plans (see below)

Good Lives Planning: George highly values the primary goods of happiness/pleasure, agency, and excellence at work. These goods, as well as relatedness, were implicated in his offenses. George's approach toward attaining these goods was flawed by a lack of scope in that he has been more focused on his pursuit of sexual pleasure than on other ways to achieve happiness and pleasure, or on other primary goods that he might value. His good life plan also displays a lack of means—that is, his attempts to gain happiness and pleasure are harmful to himself and others, and they limit his ability to sustain happiness in a more meaningful or longer term manner. George will benefit from using his personal history exercise to explore what has been important to him in the past, as well as what is important to him in the present. This process will set the stage for exploring what primary goods he seeks to attain, and how he might develop a more balanced good life plan. The offense progression module will enable him to better understand what factors were involved in offending, and provide ideas for how he can manage these factors in the future. It will also provide an opportunity to further explore the primary goods implicated in his offending. George can then use the knowledge he attains from participation in the approach-explicit pathway treatment component to develop a balanced and self-determined good life plan that is not flawed by a lack of scope *and inappropriate means. He can next use interpersonal skills development to practice maintaining healthier, more satisfying relationships with others. He can use his remaining time in treatment to review how he is implementing his good life plan. According to supervision restrictions, George will not be permitted to work in close proximity to adolescents in the future, and so he will work with vocational staff to explore options for health inspection outside of school situations.*

Treatment Goals: *The above goals have been developed in collaboration with George. However, it is noted that George maintains a low level of motivation to change and has taken a "wait and see" attitude toward treatment. Motivational enhancement will, therefore, be a primary aspect of treatment provision. In addition, when he is ready, he will need to undertake considerable schema work in order to become able to view himself and others differently. This goal has not yet been set with George, as he requires motivational work and needs to learn to consider change based on early treatment stages.*

Indicators of Treatment Progress:
1. *Completion of personal history exercise*
2. *Completion of offense progression module*
3. *Ability to describe the primary goods and the secondary goods he has used to attain these in the past and the ways that he can attain them in the future;*
4. *Initial shift from pre-contemplative to contemplative stage of change, followed later by movement to action stage of change (e.g., evidence of considering change, discussion pertaining to achieving goals differently in the future, etc.)*
5. *Demonstration of new and appropriate interpersonal relationships (e.g., development of adult platonic relationships)*
6. *Demonstration of self-monitoring changes made in treatment*
7. *Changes in cognitive distortions and cognitive schema (e.g., as evidenced by considering the world differently and being able to identify effects of abuse on victims and learning how to take the perspective of those victims)*
8. *Demonstration of good life plan development and implementation, including alternative means of gaining happiness and pleasure, relatedness, and agency. As George has not yet indicated motivation to achieve these goods in other ways, specific goals and indicators with respect to the implementation of his good life plan will be re-visited and more specific goals will be established in these areas.*

Timeframe for Goal Review: *30 days*

Other: *George's caseworker will initiate a referral for psychopathy assessment and sexual arousal testing. Vocational services will work with George to determine employment possibilities.*

Summary

Case formulations should describe, for each client, the factors that made him vulnerable to committing a sexual offense. Traditional case formulations have often been unnecessarily based on clients' risks and deficits rather than what they are trying to achieve in their lives. GLM/SRM-R case formulation and treatment planning is oriented toward understanding what is important to clients in their lives and what their strengths and areas of need are. In this way, the formulation can more readily inform individualized treatment planning. Collaboration, in turn, is at the core of treatment planning, which addresses dynamic risk, responsivity factors, treatment components, primary and secondary goods, and potential flaws in clients' attempts to achieve them.

PART III

Treatment

CHAPTER 8

Treatment Using the Integrated Good Lives/Self-Regulation-Revised Model

In addition to its application to treatment, the Good Lives Model was designed to provide a broad theory of offender rehabilitation that addresses not only the causes of offending and identifies the targets of treatment but also the manner in which treatment should proceed and the values of clinicians and treatment overall (Ward and Gannon, 2006; Ward and Marshall, 2004; Ward and Stewart, 2003). As indicated previously, the GLM proposes that sexual offending results from the pursuit of legitimate goals via inappropriate and harmful means and a lack of opportunities or capabilities to meet needs in ways that are both socially acceptable and personally fulfilling. This approach speaks to the causes of offending and what should be addressed in treatment. In addition, the GLM as a broader rehabilitation framework involves treatment that takes a holistic, positive, ethical approach. Treatment includes the use of the most suitable mode of treatment, positive therapist attitudes toward clients, addressing motivation and engagement with treatment, the recognition of the importance of the therapeutic alliance in treatment, and help for the client to allow him to live a satisfying life. Achieving psychological well-being among clients is an essential component of treatment using the GLM. All of these elements are included with the additional goal of reducing the likelihood of reoffending and providing protection for the community. A number of these features of treatment have traditionally been excluded from standard approaches or are regarded as beyond the scope of treatment. For example, the risk-based approach adopted by many treatment programs ignores factors such as assisting clients to live a fulfilling life. In fact, in some instances, those programs take the stance that, as a result of offenders' behavior, they are not entitled to live a fulfilling life.

When using the GLM/SRM-R approach in treatment, it is essential that treatment focus on *approach goals*, those goals concerned with realizing a desired situation, rather than solely or predominantly on *avoidance goals*, those concerned with avoiding an undesirable outcome. Thus, for example, the focus of treatment should be on reaching such goals as attaining sexual satisfaction, having intimate relationships, and being autonomous and independent. This therapeutic approach is followed because avoidance goals are negative in orientation, are difficult to achieve, and require considerable cognitive resources to attain and maintain. Such goals are also associated with failure, impaired self-regulation in times of stress, and higher levels of psychological distress (Austin and Vancouver, 1996; Emmons, 1999; Wegner, 1994). By contrast, approach goals are easier to acquire, are sustainable, require fewer cognitive resources to maintain, and are associated with positive affect (Carver and Scheier, 1990). In addition, using approach rather than avoidance goals in treatment has been found to be more motivational, clinically effective, and more conducive to a positive therapeutic environment than an avoidance-based approach (Mann, 1998; Mann, Webster, Schofield, and Marshall, 2004). As noted previously, the integrated GLM/SRM-R takes a positive, strengths-based approach that is more conducive to a focus on approach goals and on increasing motivation (Yates, 2009a). Thus, it is important in considering the material contained this chapter, and those that follow, that the therapist adopt an explicitly positive, reinforcing, motivational approach that frames treatment targets in terms of what clients can gain by both participating in treatment and by addressing factors that pose a risk.

This chapter specifically addresses steps to assist clients in meeting goals and obtaining goods in life. It also targets traditional risk factors (see chapter 1) in treatment, using the GLM/SRM-R framework. Chapters 9 and 10 describe the specific treatment activities of formulating a relevant personal history (i.e., an "autobiography") and developing an offense progression, respectively, using the integrated approach. Tailoring treatment to self-regulation pathway and clients' goals in life is described in chapter 11, while chapter 12 describes the development of comprehensive good lives/self-regulation plans. The reader is reminded that the aim of this book is neither to provide a comprehensive treatment program outline nor specific treatment activities. Rather, the purpose is to situate the elements and targets of what is known to be effective currently in treatment within the GLM/SRM-R approach.

Steps in Treatment

Previous chapters have addressed the process by which treatment unfolds, including:

- creating a strong foundation based on assessment of risk, need, responsivity, self-regulation pathway, primary and secondary goods, the relationship of goods to sexual offending, and other factors relevant to an individual client;
- tailoring treatment to risk by matching treatment intensity to clients' levels of static and dynamic risk; for example, by treating offenders whose risk to re-offend is moderate or higher, and offering separate treatment groups for individuals at different levels of risk;
- establishing a treatment process that will allow clients to have maximum benefit from treatment (i.e., tailoring treatment to individual responsivity factors);
- establishing an approach to treatment that is motivational and that takes into account clients' concerns about treatment and the change process;
- developing a treatment plan that takes the form of a good lives plan and that explicitly includes approach goals, the attainment of well-being, self-regulation, and the management of risk;
- targeting known risk factors in treatment, such as deviant sexual interests, intimacy deficits, and general and sexual self-regulation;
- differentially addressing self-regulation pathway to offending; and,
- assisting clients to meet important needs and attain important goods and goals in their lives.

In addition, as described in chapter 13, maintenance and follow-up treatment and supervision are essential parts of the treatment process (Cumming and McGrath, 2005; Yates et al., 2000).

Beginning Treatment

By the beginning of treatment, as indicated previously, the therapist will have conducted a comprehensive assessment of each client and will have gained a sound understanding of his personal identity (who he sees himself as being), things that are important to him, and factors that represent risks for an unsatisfying life and for re-offending. The therapist will have developed an individualized, tailored treatment plan for the client.

Although clients may have been provided with an overview of treatment at the assessment stage, it is helpful to all parties to provide an introduction to treatment and the process by which it will unfold. For example, the therapist may explain the treatment approach—i.e., cognitive-behavioral therapy that addresses self-regulation in offending, managing risk factors, and achieving a good life.

"The type of treatment we use here is called cognitive-behavioral treatment. This means that we will learn about the types of thinking, emotions, and behavior that

cause problems, and how these are linked to each other and to offending. We will learn about and discover self-regulation, which has to do with how we respond and react in certain situations. But, importantly, this treatment program is designed to help everyone to get what they want out of life—but of course in a way that is realistic and that does not hurt others—and to become who you want to be and have a satisfying, good life."

At the beginning of treatment, it may also help the client if the therapist discusses specific risk factors and their relationships to sexual offending, such that client understands his own risk factors and begins to consider how to address them in treatment (Yates et al., 2000). Additionally, at the beginning of treatment, group "rules" that apply (e.g., maintaining confidentiality, appropriate communication, etc.) should be developed by clients *themselves*, rather than presented as *a fait accompli* to treatment participants by the therapist, such as by providing a written list of rules and expectations. This inclusiveness will allow treatment providers to set the stage for a collaborative environment, the development of group cohesion, and ownership of the treatment process by clients (Yates et al., 2000).

Introducing the Good Lives Model: Primary Goods

Treatment may then next introduce and explain the Good Lives Model, define and illustrate primary and secondary human goods and the means used to attain them. This stage may require considerable treatment time. In order to progress effectively, it is *not* recommended that the therapist provide either a list or a description of goods to clients. Such constructs can be quite abstract and presenting such a list will not likely be conducive to creating a therapeutic environment or understanding the good lives notions. The provision of such a list could result in a less effective didactic (or teaching) approach. Instead, the therapist should introduce the concept that certain factors are especially important to people in their lives, and that people actively seek out those elements in their lives. The therapist needs to then follow up by asking clients what some of these elements might be. The therapist can use the responses generated by clients to introduce the topic and definitions of primary goods. An example follows:

> **Therapist:** *We discussed earlier how this treatment program is set up to help you get what is important to you in your lives. To accomplish this goal, we need to know what makes up a good life. We all have in our minds what a good life means for us, individually, even though people are not all the same, so their goals in life are different. We will be discussing the specific things we want out of life, which we*

actively try to go about getting. Can someone start by telling the other group members what is important to you?

Client 1: *I really miss my kids. After my offense, child protection took them away. Then my wife filed for a divorce. I don't know what I am going to do.*

Client 2: *The same thing happened to me. It's really hard and it's not fair. I didn't hurt my kid; I would never do that.*

Therapist: *So your kids are very important to both of you?*

Clients 1 and 2: *Yeah.*

Therapist: *What else is important in your lives?*

Client 3: *I didn't lose my kids, but I lost my job. My partner doesn't work because she takes care of the kids. We might lose our house. Plus, it is really embarrassing, because she has to take the kids to her parents' house to be looked after and sometimes to eat. It's humiliating. I'm supposed to provide for them.*

In this illustration, the first two clients are indicating that they highly value the primary good of relatedness, which in this case relates to their children. The third client is concerned about the primary good of life—meeting basic needs—as well as, potentially, excellence in agency, as indicated by his sense of not being a good provider for his family. Importantly, the therapist is able to uncover what is important to these clients without reacting negatively to specific statements, such as, "It's not fair." In fact, by actively ignoring such statements and reinforcing positive statements, the therapist will be able extinguish negative statements and increase positive verbalizations during treatment. After identifying goods, the therapist can then reflect the important goals back to clients and continue as follows:

Therapist: *Your awareness of yourselves is good. What I have heard from you is that family is very important to some of you, while being self-sufficient and being able to provide for your families is essential to others. In terms of a good life, these things—which are called* primary goods*—are the higher level things we want to have in life. In your cases, it means that you value a sense of relatedness, which includes family, the basic needs in life, and something called* agency, *which means being in control of how your lives play out. Does that sound right to you?*

Elaboration of primary goods also includes understanding what elements may have previously been important to clients, but which they have abandoned. And it also means coming to an understanding of why they gave up on these goods.

> *Therapist:* So far, we've heard about the primary goods involving relatedness—the connection to one's family, for example—and the fundamental primary good of life, which means being able to take care of the basics needed to survive. I wonder what other goods are important to you? And I would like to hear if something was important to you in the past, but lately has felt less important.
> *Client:* I don't know about how this fits in, but the biggest thing on my mind is that I've committed a real sin. My faith is really important to me. Well, it used to be, but over the last 10 years, I've let it slide.
> *Therapist:* For you, I am hearing that it's very important to have a sense of meaning and purpose in life, and that your faith used to be a big part of that purpose. You're concerned that you've compromised that part of your life and abandoned it, even though it is a primary good that you pursued in the past. Worse, you're concerned about where your actions are leaving you. Is that right?
> *Client:* Yeah. That's really been on my mind. My actions have left me with a hole in my life, and I'm not sure how I can fix it.

In this example, the therapist is exploring what primary goods are important to the client as well as how abandoning a previously valued primary good (spirituality) has affected him. Beyond understanding the client in his current state, this approach can provide the therapist with useful information about the factors that have contributed to offending as well as the elements that might provide a more balanced life for the client in the future.

Understanding how a client abandons his attempts to attain primary goods can also yield important information about what a re-offense process might look like, if it were to occur.

Introducing the Good Lives Model: Secondary Goods

Once the construct of primary goods is clearly understood, the notion of secondary goods is introduced to clients. This tiered approach will allow clients to understand and reflect on the means they use to achieve their goals, and will also set the stage for understanding the flaws in their good lives plans and the relationships between primary goods, secondary goods, and flaws to sexual offending, self-regulation, and life problems. The topic of secondary goods can be introduced in a manner such as:

> *Therapist:* As you think about these primary goods that are important to all people in one way or another, I also want us to talk about things called secondary goods, which are also known as instrumental goods. Secondary goods are the resources

or specific activities that human beings use to attain primary goods. For example, going to your job can be instrumental to the primary goods of meeting basic needs in life, agency, and excellence at work—working is what you need to do to meet these basic needs. Our jobs can also be instrumental to our sense of being part of a community, and to the primary good of knowledge.

Client: *That's kind of like how money doesn't buy happiness, but it sure can help along the way.*

Therapist: *That's a good observation. What other secondary goods might there be?*

Client: *I never liked going to school. I just couldn't see the value in a diploma, but I've realized that it sure is a good way to get a job, to get further knowledge, and to be independent.*

Therapist: *That's a great example; that's exactly what we mean by secondary goods.*

Introducing the Good Lives Model: Good Lives Plans and Flaws

Once the constructs of secondary goods and their relationship to primary goods are clearly understood by the client, the therapist introduces the notion of a good lives plan as well as the potential flaws in such plans. The objective is both for the client to develop an understanding of his own life plan as well as to comprehend the difficulties that can occur in his plan and the reasons such difficulties can occur. This process involves first conveying the concept of a good lives plan or, in other words, helping the client to see his own unique "roadmap" or "plan for living" that contains all of the elements that he finds important to have in his life. It is important at this stage not to restrict the development of the client's plan to those things that he is presently able to attain, but to also include how he would like his life to be in the future. This process acknowledges that the individual may hold important values in life that may not yet be realized. For example, an individual may wish at some point in his life to have children or to return to school, even though he has no current plans to do so. If such a good is important to this individual, it should be included in this discussion and in the good lives/self-regulation plan developed later in treatment. In introducing the notion of a good lives plan, the therapist may proceed as follows:

Therapist: *As you think about the primary goods we've been discussing, what are some areas that are really important to you? What's missing from your life in that list of goods that you would really like to have?*

Client: *More than anything, I want to feel like I belong in my own town again. I guess you'd call that community. I also want to get back to feeling like I had some* *kind of meaning and purpose in my life. And I want to be able to get a job again to show people that I can pay my own way and take care of myself. That way, when I do move about town or go to church, I can hold my head up high. I guess that's agency, community, and spirituality. I want friendship again, too, but I'm willing to wait for that until I can take care of these other things. Those are the things I want most in my life right now.*

Once the notion of a good lives plan is clearly understood, the therapist can proceed to a discussion of potential flaws in the plan, the manner in which these flaws prevent goods from being attained, and the way such flaws can lead to problems. For example:

Therapist: *Usually there are four ways that a person's good lives plan doesn't work out as he'd hoped, due to flaws in the planning process itself. The first way is that sometimes a person simply doesn't have the means to attain a primary good that he wants. For example, if he hopes to attain spirituality by being blessed by the Pope or having an audience with the Dalai Lama, it's important to recognize that these secondary or instrumental goods are flawed, since they are not realistic and are unlikely to happen. The question then becomes what other means might the person have at his disposal.*

A second flaw in a good lives plan is when the plan is restricted in scope. For example, does someone focus more on obtaining one or a few primary goods, while ignoring others? A person who wants autonomy and mastery but who doesn't take relatedness into account may end up having few friends and no partner. Does that make sense?

A third flaw is when his attempts to attain goods are in conflict with one another. For example, if that person desires excellent health and functioning, but tries to attain the primary good of happiness by smoking and excessive drinking, his behavior creates a conflict.

Finally, some flaws involve capacity. If someone wants to find a suitable partner but does not have the skills or the confidence needed to develop and maintain a relationship, it is going to be very difficult to attain the goal of relatedness. Also, if the person has no way of meeting potential partners, this, too, creates a problem with "capacity," one that is external to, or outside of, the person.

What flaws can you imagine in your own good lives plan?

Client: *Well, a few minutes ago I was talking about how I want to feel at home in my own town again, get a job, and be able to go to church with my head held high. As I'm listening to you talk, I'm thinking that those goals may not be possible for a long time. Everyone in that town knows what I did. Being in that town might also* *make it more difficult to find work to support myself. That means two conflicts. Frankly, I'm not sure being in that town again would really be all that much like being a part of a community; it wouldn't be the same thing I've been hoping for. It might be better if I found some way to settle in another town that's not too far away so that I could still visit. I need to be in a place where I can work on all these things. I'm going to have enough trouble living with myself, to be honest with you.*

Introducing the Good Lives Model: Relationships among Primary Goods, Secondary Goods, Flaws, and Offending

Lastly, a discussion needs to take place about goods, good lives plans, and flaws and their relationships to offending and to self-regulation. This discussion is intended to be an introductory one, as these topics are addressed in greater detail when the offense progression exercise (see chapter 10) is conducted.

Therapist: *We've been talking about your hopes involving community, agency, and spirituality. We've also talked about relatedness. I wonder how these primary goods fit in with your offense? What was your good life plan then, and how was it flawed or what problems did you have?*

Client: *I've been thinking about that a lot lately. The things that are valuable to me haven't changed. I've always valued my community, my self-reliance within it, and my involvement in church. That hasn't changed. That's always going to be the same, although, as I said before, I'm going to have to consider a new area where I can live. I can think of a couple of things to answer your question, though. The first is that I haven't valued what you call relatedness anywhere near as much as I should have. If I had, I wouldn't have sexually assaulted my wife's sister. I know I said before that I would focus on relatedness after I got settled into a new community and job, but that may have been a mistake. Not taking care of my relationships—not valuing them—caused a lot of harm to my wife and her sister. That's kind of funny given that I'm actually very religious. I mean, there are so many Bible teachings about that.*

The other thing is that my plan went wrong when I tried to get happiness and pleasure in a really awful way. Drinking as much as I was doing and coming on to my sister-in-law—that kind of pleasure ruined all those other goods that are important to me. I need a new life. I was tempted to say that I just need to go to church more, but that's not it. My life was out of balance. There are better ways to get happiness, and I intend to do it by re-building my relationships.

Therapist: *You've really been giving this some thought. As you continue to think about your good life plan, it will also be important to take into account the other*

primary goods, such as knowledge and creativity. I wonder where those fit into your past, your offending, your present, and your future? Perhaps we can discuss these the next time we meet.
Client: *That sounds good.*

Recall that the pre-treatment evaluation includes assessment of primary and secondary goods, flaws in the client's good life plan, and the relationship of goods to offending. In conducting the above therapeutic exercises, the therapist should be alert to any missing information as well as to any additional information from what was obtained in the initial assessment. Then the therapist can proceed accordingly. In conducting this part of treatment, a therapist may also want to use individual exercises (i.e., "homework") designed to assist a client to reflect on these constructs in greater detail. Once all elements of the Good Lives Model have been sufficiently addressed in treatment, the therapist may wish to provide a handout of primary and secondary goods with their definitions.

Example: Goods Exercise

1. *Please list the things that are important right now in your life.*
2. *Indicate the ways you go about getting these things. Please include both criminal and non-criminal ways.*
3. *What works well for you and what does not?*
4. *When things go wrong getting these things, what happens? Be specific.*
5. *Please list things that used to be important in your life but that you do not focus on in your life now.*
6. *Why did these things become less important to you?*
7. *What things are related to your sexual offending and other criminal behavior?*

Introducing Self-Regulation and Offense Pathways

When introducing self-regulation theory and its relationship to offending and offense pathways, therapists should focus on the individual differences that exist between the goals of each client and his strategies and abilities to exercise control over his behavior. Therapists should provide some general information pertaining to offense-related goals (as well as to be able to contrast those goals with good lives goals in order to avoid confusion). Therapists can help clients understand how their goals—healthy and unhealthy ones—are established and on what values, beliefs, and schemas they are based. General information pertaining to establishing strategies to achieve goals, including both offense-related goals and primary goods, should be provided, as well as basic information on self-regulation failure. The aim is to introduce the notion that the client tried to achieve his goals via a pathway that led to offending rather than by choosing a pathway to the goal that was not harmful. This dichotomy is addressed more fully in treatment through the development of a client's relevant life history and offense progression, as described in chapters 9 and 10, respectively. The therapist may introduce the constructs of self-regulation and pathways as follows:

> **Therapist:** *We've spoken some about the things that are important to you in your life. Part of treatment is also to understand your offense and how you came to offend. As you know, people can engage in sexual abuse for a variety of reasons. Some people may engage in sexual behavior with children to meet non-sexual needs (for example, because they don't feel they will ever be attractive to an adult), while others may have an erotic preference for children. Very often, the people engaging in these behaviors have a number of ways of looking at the world that make it easier to give themselves permission to have sex with children even though they know it's wrong and against the law. This justification can include attitudes and beliefs that work together to form a kind of theory about the world called a* schema.
>
> *Also, people can have different goals when they are offending. Some people offend because they either didn't know how to prevent it or because they tried to prevent it but weren't successful because they tried the wrong strategies. In other words, they haven't been able to regulate or control their behavior. When the offense is over, they may regret having done it. On the other hand, some people are quite deliberate in their offenses and indeed that offense is a goal that they set for themselves. These people have few problems regulating their behavior, but their schemas are such that, unless they take steps to re-evaluate their goals in life, they could very well hurt others and end up back in prison.*
>
> *In relation to the goods people seek in life, it often happens that people offend as a way of attaining one or more of these goods, even though the offense may make the attainment of other goods impossible. I wonder what thoughts you have about what I've said.*
>
> **Danny:** *I really think I have a lot of the attitudes and beliefs you're talking about, and I also have a real problem because I am very attracted to children. That means there are a lot of things I haven't done with my life that I should have. I've known all along that my life has been out of whack for a while, but I've felt powerless when I get in the wrong situation. When I get into a bad state, especially, I end up thinking more and more about children. I just can't seem to do anything about it. I try to ignore how I feel, but when things are really bad, I just forget about everything else that's important to me. I know that when I offend I really don't want to, but I also end up feeling powerful again, at least for a little while.*

In the above example, the therapist has introduced the concept of self-regulation and the different pathways an individual follows to offending. In addition, the primary good of agency has been uncovered as both very important to the client and as instrumental in the offense progression. Also, the notion of cognitive schemas that support offending has been introduced.

Addressing Specific Treatment Targets throughout Treatment

Chapter 1 described common targets addressed in treatment that are based on current research that shows those targets' relationships to sexual offending and the risk to re-offend. When addressing these topics, the goal is always to reinforce and strengthen a client's existing skills and to develop new skills and capacities, in the context of his good life/self-regulation plan. As mentioned above, the therapist needs to focus on developing and assisting the client to meet positive approach goals and conjointly needs to encourage the client's personal fulfillment through achieving human goods that are important to him.

Addressing treatment targets using the integrated GLM/SRM-R involves linking risk factors or criminogenic needs to the primary goods with which they are associated and imparting the necessary skills, strategies and opportunities to attain these goods in ways other than through sexual offending (Ward, Gannon, and Yates, 2008; Ward et al., 2006, 2007; Ward, Vess, Collie, and Gannon, 2006; Yates, in press). In addition, standard treatment techniques for managing risk are also included. Approaching each of these treatment targets within the GLM/SRM-R framework is described below.

Sexual Self-Regulation/Deviant Sexual Fantasy, Arousal, and Interests

As described previously, problems with sexual self-regulation represent a significant risk factor for sexual offending and include such problems as preoccupation with sexual activity and sexual stimuli, deviant sexual interests and/or fantasy, and the use of sexual activity to cope with negative mood states (e.g., Hanson et al., 2007). Very different dynamics may be present in clients who have problems with sexual self-regulation, however, and different primary goods may be implicated in those clients' offending as well as different flaws in their good lives plans.

Problems with sexual self-regulation may result from early experiences such as witnessing or being subjected to sexual abuse that led to the belief that children are capable of consenting to sexual activity and/or that sex may be pleasurable or educational for them. As a result of such experiences, the individual may value the primary good of happiness (under which is subsumed sexual pleasure) but may lack knowledge, in this case, the knowledge that children are unable to consent to sexual activity. Additionally, the individual may also place too much emphasis on the good of happiness via sexual pleasure and may minimize other goods in his good life plan, thus indicating the flaw of lack of scope in the plan. For other individuals, problems with sexual self-regulation may result from a desire or need for, or a history of pairing and reinforcement of, sexual activity accompanied by aggression or violence. Such an individual may even hold a preference for violent sexuality over consensual activity. In such a case, this risk factor may be linked with attaining the primary good of excellence in agency by using violence (the flaw of means).

As can be seen in these examples, a relatively direct relationship can exist between the value placed on, or the absence of, a particular primary good and sexual offending. In each case, offending is used as a way to attain the good. By contrast, the relationship between goods and offending can also be more indirect. For example, an individual who highly values relatedness and who has suffered the loss of a highly valued intimate relationship may attempt to re-acquire this relationship through various inappropriate means, ultimately offending while depressed and intoxicated (which also represents a problem in trying to obtain the primary good of inner peace through substance use). Such an offense represents a series of events during which there is a "cascade" effect resulting in eventually committing an offense.

Case Example: Jason

Jason's father sexually abused him from infancy until his placement in foster care at the age of 14. Jason vividly recounted how his father would force him to have sex with his younger sister while he watched. Jason stated that he genuinely thought that this was normal behavior until he turned 12 years old. At that time, he realized that this was not something that brothers and sisters do, and that sex was supposed to occur between adults. When asked how he responded to this revelation, Jason stated, "I kept on going. I wasn't going to stop." Jason's behavior warranted his placement in increasingly restrictive foster homes until he was arrested for an incident in which he broke into a neighbor's house late at night and sexually assaulted her. He was 16 years old at that time. He was placed in a detention center where he attempted to set fires, break into staff members' cars, and sexually assault a staff member who had fallen asleep. Now 36, Jason has a long history of criminal behavior. He has never experienced a long-term relationship, and others perceive him as having a very shallow range of affect and an arrogant interpersonal style. Jason is frequently impulsive and easily irritated. He views the world as a hostile and punitive place where men have to fight to get even, and women are deceitful and unknowable. He spends much of his free time viewing on-line pornography and masturbating to violent themes. He has told previous interviewers that he has used pornography routinely to cope with stress. He also enjoys reading true crime novels, noting that it is "cool" how well-organized some of the world's better-known offenders have been.

Jason possesses a number of sexual scripts related to sexual offending, which include that it is acceptable and even desirable to have sex with others when they are unwilling or unable to consent. Possessing schemas related to the world being a dangerous place in which only the aggressive survive, Jason also copes with the stresses of daily life by masturbating. His experiences to gain a sense of mastery have been almost exclusively centered on antisocial activity, including both covert (e.g., fire setting) and overt (e.g., sexually abusing his sister; attempting to assault a staff person as she slept) behavior. Jason pursues knowledge by reading about other criminals and appears to find creativity in perpetrating diverse crimes. He has pursued the goods of inner peace and pleasure through masturbating at rates well above average, and appears to have undervalued community and relatedness. He utilizes explicit self-regulation strategies to achieve his goals, although there is also some evidence of impulsivity. Jason's good life plan is flawed by its lack of scope (evident in his restrictive focus on happiness (pleasure) and autonomy). His primary goods of happiness and relatedness are in clear conflict, because the means by which he attains the former severely limit his ability to attain the latter (e.g., his frequent contacts with the legal system inhibit his ability to attain happiness and relatedness). Furthermore, possessing the schemas that he does makes it more difficult to perceive himself as a member of a meaningful community, and he further displays a lack of knowledge about the many perspectives on masculinity that one might hold, as well as about the world and his place in it. Clearly, much of Jason's initial treatment experience will focus on raising awareness of the lack of scope in his good life plan, and the conflict between Jason's attempts to attain primary goods.

A primary focus of Jason's treatment will be on sexual and general self-regulation. Clinicians working with Jason will first want to know what he has sought to achieve through sexual offending and his use of pornography. They will ask such questions as

- What did he hope to achieve, and what were the related primary goods?

- How can he attain these same goods in the future?

- What skills and attitudes toward sexuality will he require in order to be successful?

- How can he acquire them?

- In what ways can he use his treatment group as a venue to rehearse these skills?

- How can he use his peers in group treatment to provide feedback on his attempts to enact these skills in daily life?

- As he begins to embark on a new good life plan, what flaws might occur (e.g., means, scope, conflict, or capacity)?

- How will he develop the external conditions and environments where he has access to sexual outlets and romantic partners that are consistent with his good life plan?

- With further exploration of his sexual scripts, what behavioral methods might also be at his disposal? (These methods could include cognitive methods such as thought-stopping, or sexual arousal reconditioning, for example.)

Cognition

As described previously, treatment-targeting cognition focuses on multiple areas, including cognitive distortions, cognitive schemas and implicit theories, and meta-cognition. Treatment typically focuses on cognitive distortions (i.e., specific statements that justify or rationalize offending), which may represent the products or expression of cognitive schemas (i.e., larger structures representing attitudes and through which social information is processed and understood). Meta-cognition involves being able to "think about thinking" (Wells, 2000; Wells and Matthews, 1994, 1996) and to be able to conduct self-monitoring (Heidt and Marx, 2003; Leahy, 2001).

As with other treatment targets, distorted cognition and schemas can be linked to acquiring primary goods. And although potentially harmful, such cognition may, in fact, serve an adaptive function for clients in the context of their lives (Marshall et al., 1999; Yates et al., 2000). For example, individuals who hold the view that the world is a dangerous place may have developed this view because this was, in fact, true for them in their lives. Their lives may have involved abuse or neglect, leading to the belief that other people are primarily hostile and rejecting individuals who inflict pain and suffering. As a result, these individuals may react aggressively toward others in order to protect themselves. They are also likely to hold offense-related approach goals as a result of these beliefs. In terms of primary goods, such clients may lack knowledge (e.g., that there are individuals who are genuinely caring and who will not harm them) and may over-value the good of excellence in agency in order to assert themselves before they are harmed.

In treatment, in addition to the use of schema therapy (Young, 1999) and to assisting clients to process and evaluate social information differently, a goal within the GLM/SRM-R approach would be to focus on increasing knowledge and understanding that developing different views can facilitate obtaining other important goals in life. In addition to an offender learning how to challenge his own cognitive distortions and schemas, he will learn how to change by improving his emotional world, such as through experiencing greater enjoyment or enhancing his relationships by becoming able to view others differently and to re-evaluate the truth of his core beliefs (i.e., developing his internal capacity). Acquiring these skills is also, therefore, linked to the primary goods of relatedness and inner peace. Such individuals may desire to establish relationships with others; however, their belief systems are likely to alienate others and to result in chronically unsatisfying personal and intimate relationships. Treatment can contribute to change in this area, however, via a therapist who is genuinely interested in the client and via treatment that is explicitly designed to benefit the client. This approach speaks both to increasing motivation as well as to forming satisfying relationships that contribute to attaining a good life.

Case Example: Jason

Therapist: Jason, I've heard you say a few times that it's a dangerous world out there, and that it's crucial that others respect you. What's that all about?

Jason: I don't know about where you grew up, but where I'm from, if you don't have the respect of others, you're not going to live very long. Other people are going to challenge you, and if you don't rise to the occasion, you could get hurt. That's why I don't take disrespect from anybody.

Therapist: So aggressively defending your honor is part of where you come from. It's a matter of survival.

Jason: That's right. No one seems to understand that here, but that's right.

Therapist: In fact, it's not just a way you think, it's a way you look at the world and interact with it.

Jason: Yeah.

Therapist: And it's like that everywhere.

Jason: Well no, I don't mean everywhere. I imagine it was different where you grew up.

Therapist: Maybe. If I'm hearing you right, this is reality in some places and not others.

Jason: Okay. What's your point?

Therapist: Only that if it's one way in one situation and another way in other situations, you may be able manage things differently depending on where you find yourself.

Jason: Well, people better respect me, that's all I've got to say.

Therapist: Others need to be flexible to your needs but not the other way around.

Jason: Okay, I see what you mean. Maybe I need to think about looking at things differently if I'm going to make it out there once I'm released.

Therapist: If we go back to our primary goods, it's almost like you've lacked knowledge, because you were too busy trying to survive your circumstances, and you've placed so much emphasis on agency—again, in order to survive—that you wouldn't be able to develop new ways of fitting into the world, even if you wanted to.

Jason: I see what you mean, and there isn't anything I can't do if I put my mind to it.

Therapist: And that's the kind of confidence that gets you through hard times. So in the past, your push toward autonomy and agency has been based on limited knowledge, through nobody's fault. Where does examining how you think about things fit into your future?

Jason: Well, I don't know if that will work—it didn't before—but I guess I have no choice but give it a try.

In this situation, the therapist is eliciting from Jason his own acknowledgement that different perspectives exist in a variety of areas, rather than telling Jason that he must think differently. The schemas that one develops in response to childhood adversity can be very different from schemas developed by others who have had different life experiences. For example, respect may be given and received differently. In addition, cognitive flexibility in interactions with others is critical to attaining primary goods. Once the client begins to consider that other ways of viewing the world are possible, this subtle change in perspective will continue throughout treatment in an attempt to alter his pre-established schemas.

Social Functioning, Attachment, Intimacy, and Relationships

Sexual offenders appear to be especially prone to experiencing difficulties in the areas of relationships, intimacy, and social competency. Dynamic risk factors in this area include intimacy problems, hostility toward women, and emotional identification with children. In addition to addressing these attitudes, clients may also experience a sense of inadequacy and low self-esteem (problems achieving the good of inner peace) that contribute to offending in some cases. In terms of the GLM/SRM-R approach, the primary goods associated with social competency include relatedness and community, as well as inner peace and agency, which offenders may attempt to seek via inappropriate means. In the case of seeking those goods via sex with children, for example, the individuals' goals are acceptable, but the means they use to achieve these are harmful.

In treatment, the aim is to instill the capabilities (both internal and external) to develop and maintain the kind of relationships that will enhance well-being and that are consistent with individuals' good lives plans. That is, treatment in this area must be respectful of individual clients' desires to establish specific relationships. For example, if an individual does not wish to be involved at this time in his life in an intimate relationship, such a romantic connection cannot be a goal of treatment, although the skills to establish healthy relationships (i.e., internal capacity) in the future will be included in treatment for any future relationships. In addition, one aim of treatment is to help establish external capacity—those conditions outside the individual that are necessary to implement this aspect of the good life plan. Developing external capacity involves assisting clients to access opportunities to develop friendships with others and to attain a sense of connectedness to particular (pro-social) groups. This particular good is not typically included in traditional treatment, which often tends to take the stance that offenders cannot be trusted in relationships with others. In some jurisdictions, actively helping clients to access such opportunities will represent a challenge, given the clients' restrictions on movement and associations with others and the tendency of therapists and other members of the treatment team to not become involved in such goods promotion. In such cases, the therapist will need to be creative in order to assist clients in the establishment and pursuance of realistic opportunities and goals in this area.

Addressing social functioning also involves developing and reinforcing such skills as communication and assertiveness. It is essential that the therapist recognize and reinforce these skills, even when the client expresses himself in ways that may contradict treatment or the therapist's objectives.

Case Example: Jason

> **Therapist:** *Jason, last time we discussed how some parts of the world, such as where you grew up, can be dangerous, while others can be less so. We talked about the way you've come to look at the world as a response to the circumstances you were in when you were younger, where it was important to gain respect from other*

men, and in which women often seemed deceitful and unknowable or secretive. We talked about how surviving your own upbringing meant that you developed systems of maintaining autonomy and agency, but often without full knowledge of the world beyond your personal experience. I wonder if we can now discuss your relationships with others.

Jason: *That's fine with me.*

Therapist: *How do these beliefs about men, women, respect, distrust, and danger all come together in your interactions with others? It's like you've had a roadmap of the world that has guided the way you think. It's been based on your experience of the world and—thankfully—not the entire world. Yet it is a roadmap just the same. How do you think this roadmap of thoughts and attitudes has guided your relationships with other people?*

Jason: *Well, it might have been different if I had had different parents and lived a few neighborhoods away. All my life, it's been about getting what I can when I can find it. That goes for sex, respect, happiness, pleasure. I can accept that I need to find better ways to find pleasure and happiness, and I think I also need to gain a better knowledge about the world out there so that I can actually be a part of a community where I'm not always looking over my shoulder. I think I need to make some plans for how I'm going to have relationships in the future, but to be honest, I'm not interested in having any right now. I need to take care of me.*

Therapist: *You've been giving this some thought. You're saying that you're committed to making changes in how you relate to the world, how you seek pleasure, and how you gain knowledge. You believe you need to make changes in your relationships, even though you don't want a close relationship right now.*

Jason: *That's right. I just want to get along everywhere; I don't want to have to get all caught up in a complex relationship. Not right now. Maybe someday.*

Therapist: *So you might not want to be a committed partner right now, but for you it's time to start thinking about being a committed partner-in-waiting.*

Jason: *Yeah!*

Therapist: *A lot of times, being able to get along with others involves understanding where they're coming from. This isn't the same as feeling happy for them or sad for them. Instead, it's about being able to really understand how things look and feel for them.*

Jason: *Empathy.*

Therapist: *That's what a lot of people call it.*

Jason: *I'm actually not too bad at that, believe it or not. When I was growing up, if I didn't know what my father was thinking, he might kill me. I had to be really careful. I'm not such a bad judge of people and situations.*

> ***Therapist:*** *You've got solid experience that you can build on. The difference is that back then you had less knowledge, and you didn't have access to other people that you could be with, or groups of people, like social clubs, that you could join.*
>
> ***Jason:*** *That's right. It was a tough world. Now I know more. I'm also learning that everyone around me had a lot of the same goals, those primary goods, and that they weren't doing such a great job of getting them either. It's really messed up, but that's how it was.*
>
> ***Therapist:*** *It's hard coming to terms with that.*
>
> ***Jason:*** *Yeah.*
>
> ***Therapist:*** *What do you think you're going to do about how you relate to others?*
>
> ***Jason:*** *I think I need a plan for how I can stop my thinking for a second so I can understand where people are coming from. And I need to be able to help them do the same. And it seems like I need to think more about how it can be different in some places, like where you grew up.*

In this example, the clinician is attempting to elicit an understanding from Jason about the manner in which his schemas have contributed to his interpersonal style and his relationships with others. Jason is able to understand that his experience of the world is just one of many perspectives a person can have. By coming to understand that all humans seek primary goods, he can begin to plan for how he might function more effectively by seeking knowledge, relatedness, and community. In learning to pursue those goods, he is also exercising his creativity in a healthier direction. As opposed to many treatment programs, where the goal is solely to develop empathy for the victims of one's offenses, Jason's first steps are to function effectively in his social environment, and to interact empathically with others and to be able to take their perspective in a general way. Jason is beginning to understand better that all human beings seek intimacy, friendship, love, caring, and support. This new awareness comes with the realization that his family and childhood experiences were more adverse than he had realized, as well as the understanding that other situations and people might not be as dangerous or hostile as those he experienced as a child.

Emotion Regulation

To address this risk factor, treatment typically aims to help clients to manage mood states and stress by predicting and identifying the accompanying emotional states and then by developing skills to cope with them. While the regulation of emotion is included in treatment within the GLM/SRM-R approach, this area is also linked to the primary good of inner peace—the inherent need of individuals to have emotional equilibrium in life and to be free from emotional distress. Emotion regulation is also linked to styles of self-regulation. Thus, in addition to developing emotion management skills, the goal of working on this primary good is to assist clients to establish equilibrium as a baseline in their lives as well as to be able to manage themselves during times of distress. By establishing such a baseline, there is a greater chance that self-regulation will remain intact during times of stress. Equilibrium is accomplished, in part, through a good life plan that reflects what is important to the client, thereby assisting him to develop the capacity to attain overall satisfaction with his life, and helping him to develop and utilize effective self-regulation skills and strategies. Although coping skills are imparted, treatment goes beyond teaching an individual to identify or recognize emotional states and how to cope with them. Treatment also helps the client to implement a satisfactory good life plan so that overall emotional equilibrium can be achieved on a regular basis.

Typically, group therapy is particularly helpful in this area. The emotional support and encouragement of peers who have experienced similar problems cannot be underestimated. As mentioned earlier, meta-cognition (thinking about one's own thought processes) can be helpful to clients as they develop their abilities to self-monitor and self-regulate their internal worlds. Sometimes this process involves the clinician not just asking, "How did you feel about that?" Instead, the question can be, "How do you feel about feeling that way?" or "How do you feel about thinking that way?"

Let's return to Jason, this time in a group therapy session.

Case Example: Jason

Jason: *I had an argument with Scott over there. It was over something stupid, a game of cards we were playing after we were working on our treatment assignments.*
Therapist: *What happened?*
Jason: *Well, it started with the treatment assignment. He gave me some feedback about my homework that I thought made no sense, and I told him so. He told me I just didn't understand. We put away the assignments and played some cards. I told him what he had said before was disrespectful. He said that disrespect is a big treatment issue for me. I blew my cool, but I walked away. I did curse him out, however. Sorry, Scott.*
Scott: *That's all right.*
Therapist: *So almost without knowing what was happening, it was like some of the same things from your past happened all over again.*
Jason: *Yeah.*
Donnie: *Believe me, we've all been there. Jason, I've really been there. These things*

just happen. That's where living the change can happen. It's one thing to talk about it and another thing to do it. We all talk about agency. The question for me is whether I can really live my life when I'm angry. I've been really working hard at trying to see through the anger, to tell myself I'm aware that I'm angry. Being aware that I'm angry gives me just enough opportunity to take a breath and remember that I've got agency, power, and skills to do what I need to do and to not throw anything away by acting angrily. That way, I'm also working on my goals of creativity and life.

Jason: *It's harder than it looks, that's all I've got to say* [smiles slightly]. *Thanks.*
Scott: *Let's try again later. But maybe this time, if you think I'm being disrespectful you can just ask instead of holding onto it until you blow, okay?*
Jason: *Okay.*

In this situation, the therapist is using open-ended questions and reflection to elicit Jason's account of how his attempts at self-regulation were unsuccessful. Rather than moralize or educate, the therapist is allowing the group to provide supportive feedback. In this way, it is Jason himself, as well as other clients, who are arguing for change and not the therapist, an approach that will be more effective in ultimately making changes.

General Self-Regulation

Problems with general self-regulation are associated with risk among many different types of offenders, including sexual offenders. Self-regulation includes such factors as impulsivity, negative emotionality, hostility, and deficits in problem-solving (e.g., Hanson et al., 2007). More broadly, self-regulation involves the capacity to set goals and to be able to engage in actions to achieve these goals, both over time and in various circumstances. Problems with self-regulation can interfere with attaining primary goods across multiple areas of clients' good lives plans. For example, impulsivity can prevent clients from attaining important relationships, work, connections with community, and so forth. Thus, while such techniques as anger management, assertiveness, impulse regulation, and problem-solving should be imparted in treatment, approaching general self-regulation within the GLM/SRM-R framework involves assisting clients to identify the ways self-regulation problems can interfere with attaining goals, both in general and explicitly with respect to their goals. Clients learning problem-solving skills in treatment should actively practice and rehearse using these skills to attain valued goods and to implement effective self-regulation. For example, a client who desires to establish an intimate relationship should be assisted to rehearse using these skills to meet others and to work toward developing and maintaining healthy, fulfilling relationships.

Ancillary treatment that involves mindfulness, reflection, and meditation is gaining currency in the literature on psychotherapy. Many treatment programs in prison settings have turned to these kinds of activities as a means of promoting general self-regulation. Such practices can help clients acquire, rehearse, and enact cognitive and other problem-solving skills in daily life.

Case Example: Jason

Jason: I have been working very hard on my problem-solving skills. I've used these just about every day in order to cope with stress. I haven't looked at any pornography in two weeks, and I'm meditating instead of masturbating when I feel uptight. I'm doing these things so that I can practice keeping my act together while I work on goals around agency, happiness, and inner peace. Moving away from coping with things only with sex is actually making me happier, even though it is hard to do sometimes. But, it seems like I have all kinds of ways to cope inside me that I didn't know about before. Plus, that whole world of pornography just seems dangerous to me, now. I've come too far to go back now.

Therapist: You've been finding your own good reasons to keep going with this process. The time you devote to yourself with reflection and meditation has meaning. If I'm hearing you correctly, that world of pornography is too much like the one you grew up in, where people are selfish and danger lurks everywhere.

Jason: That's exactly right. I used to think that meditation and stuff like it were boring, but now I know it isn't. But even if it is, I think a little boredom isn't such a bad thing. Now, when I'm playing cards with Scott and I think he's getting on my case, it's like I can look at all my thinking like a train that's going by. I'm aware that part of that train is my old belief about needing to fight to get even. I've now got enough self-respect that I can step back from my initial response. I don't need to worry about what Scott is saying in the moment. I'm big enough in my own mind that I can just be with Scott and work it out.

In this situation, the therapist is offering a summarizing statement that reflects Jason's own efforts at improving his general self-regulation. In doing so, the therapist is acknowledging and reinforcing Jason's gains in treatment, demonstrating an understanding of Jason's statements and efforts, and encouraging further discussion. Jason responds well to this approach, and describes his efforts more clearly. Jason is able to describe how he is replacing unhealthy general and sexual self-regulation habits that can increase risk (e.g., masturbating when he "feels uptight") with more adaptive ones that he can apply in diverse situations. Critical to this brief interaction is that it is Jason himself who is finding out what works for him, rather than having the therapist dictate to him what must be changed and how.

Victim Awareness and Empathy

Although understanding the experiences of the people an offender has harmed is not a factor shown in research to be associated with the risk to offend, many treatment programs include a component on developing awareness and empathy for victims. This component often takes the form of activities such as lectures about the short- and long-term effects of sexual abuse on victims and the writing of letters of apology to the victim(s) of one's offenses (though the letters are typically not sent to the victim). These letters are usually evaluated by the therapist and other treatment participants to assess clients' levels of empathy. Clients may also be subjected to victims' accounts of abuse and its impacts. On the one hand, when offenders come to a deeper understanding of how their actions have affected others, it can be a long-term process that yields lasting gains. On the other hand, the impact and effectiveness of teaching offenders the impact of their actions can have a very different outcome when the therapist has the intent of inducing distress and guilt. Not only does that latter approach offer little therapeutic value, it can have a detrimental impact on the clients. These types of exercises run the risk of provoking feelings of guilt, shame, and self-denigration for the clients, as well as moral condemnation on the part of the therapist and other clients. Eliciting such responses on the part of a client is unhelpful and unlikely to contribute to treatment change, as well as contradictory to the GLM/SRM-R approach. Shame-based education can threaten the primary good of inner peace as well as self-regulation by creating powerful negative emotional states in the clients. It is not that offenders should not experience empathy or take responsibility for the harm caused to others, but within the GLM/SRM-R framework, empathy is approached very differently.

Whereas many traditional treatment programs develop victim empathy through apology letters and the like, a process that can ultimately benefit victims by returning responsibility for the abuse to the offender, the GLM/SRM-R approach first establishes what a better life would be like. As the client develops his own good life plan that includes exploration of such goods as inner peace, relatedness, life, and knowledge, he can begin to understand others' perspectives and to put himself in their position (i.e., relating to others in more empathic ways). This process allows him to empathize better with all people with whom he has had negative interactions, and not just the victims of his sexual abuse. Possessing an understanding that all humans share the same basic primary goods can enable the client to better understand at a cognitive level what others may be experiencing and, in many cases, to develop an affective response for how he should proceed. This last point deserves further exploration. Where many victim empathy exercises seem to emphasize experiencing the distress of those one has harmed, this technique is not always how empathy actually works effectively. Empathy includes cognitive skills such as the decoding of another person's actions or statements and the identifying of that person's internal experiences. For example, the empathic mother of a newborn baby does not need to experience hunger to know that it is time to feed her baby; rather, she needs merely to understand the signs that her baby is hungry. Likewise, an empathic understanding of one's partner can include singing "happy birthday" at the appropriate time even though one does not enjoy singing; the singer understands that his partner will value the experience. The key elements to remember are the person's ability to identify and decode another's internal state and to become moved to respond to it. A tearful apology or acceptance of responsibility is not the same as empathy.

Furthermore, many programs appear to approach empathy as though it were an enduring trait to build into clients' personalities, rather than a fluctuating state that varies based on personal, psychological, and situational factors. Anyone in a long-term relationship who has argued with his or her partner knows that it is easy not to experience empathy from time to time, depending on the situation. Empathy is also dependent on the person involved. Many people experience greater empathy for individuals about whom they care than they do for strangers or individuals whom they dislike. For these reasons, the GLM/SRM-R promotes perspective-taking and overall empathic relatedness to others as a means of attaining primary goods and reducing risk; victim empathy is a natural component within this greater endeavor.

Case Example: Jason

> *Therapist:* Hi, Jason, how was your week?
> *Jason:* Well, no more arguments with Scott. In fact, we've been getting along really well. We've actually been talking a lot about our lives and what we're going to do when we get out of here. I have to admit, the week has flown right past!
> *Therapist:* So you've been finding friendship where this wouldn't have seemed possible just a year ago.
> *Jason:* Yes. I'm trying to put the pieces together. I'm taking good care of myself, exercising a lot, and I'm trying to actively take the perspective of everyone around me,

> *including the judge who sent me here. I guess with my record he didn't have much of a choice. I mean, here's a defiant guy who wants everyone else to get along with him rather than the other way around. I bet he's seen a lot of that in the courtroom. I have to admit that doing this work is helping me with my own good life plan.*
>
> **Therapist:** *That can't be easy, taking a long, hard look at your behavior.*
>
> **Jason:** *Well, actually it is. What's really hard, though, is thinking about the people I've hurt along the way. I'll come straight to the point: Where I came from it only counts as harmful if you knock someone out or leave them in a pool of blood. The argument over homework with Scott has got me thinking. If I'd punched him, that would have threatened both of our plans for our lives. I'd be in trouble, and he'd be second-guessing treatment. Likewise, all these people I hurt—just imagine what that did to their lives. If it's true that they want the same basic things that I do, then they might be developing the same thoughts and beliefs that I did when that stuff happened to me. That's really messed up; I don't even know what to think. I want to apologize or try to help them, but maybe the best thing I can do is change. Donnie says maybe I should go through others to see if I should apologize. Scott says I shouldn't even presume that those people would want that. In AA, I keep hearing about making amends. I'm really confused.*

In this example, Jason is describing his efforts at attaining a number of primary goods, although he does not use that term. He describes his efforts in seeking to attain relatedness and agency. In doing so, he is also demonstrating an emerging ability to relate to others empathically, to take their perspective, and to understand how his behavior has harmed them. Importantly, the therapist responds to Jason's statements with a reinforcing empathic response, thus both modeling empathy to Jason and other group members as well as providing positive reinforcement for the changes Jason has made. This approach is very different from asking Jason to write an assignment about how others (including victims) might think or feel in various situations, and it is also likely to be more effective.

Relapse Prevention and Release Preparation

As discussed previously, multiple problems exist with the traditional relapse prevention approach. It is possible that some of the goals of RP may fit with certain offenders. This specifically includes those who follow an avoidant-passive pathway. It may help, in some situations, to assist with managing risk, such as through monitoring access to potential victims. Within the GLM/SRM-R approach, traditional relapse prevention is minimized and the self-regulation pathways model takes precedence.

As indicated previously, one fundamental goal of the GLM is to assist clients with developing good lives plans that include important goods and active strategies to achieve what is important to them in life—allowing them to live fulfilling lives. Thus, instead of framing this part of treatment as avoiding or managing risk, it is approached as putting into place the elements of one's life that will lead to fulfillment and psychological well-being. Similarly, one important goal of the SRM-R is to develop the capacity and strategies, and to strengthen existing skills, both to manage risk and to achieve positive goals. Since self-regulation is individualized to each person and different clients follow different pathways to offending, the "one size fits all" RP approach is insufficient to achieve these treatment goals.

While developing a relapse prevention plan is relatively simple, developing an integrated good lives/self-regulation plan is far more complex. Developing a risk management plan involves predominantly identifying high-risk situations and implementing strategies to avoid or cope with these. By contrast, developing a good lives plan that addresses self-regulation both broadly and in the context of offense pathways and progression involves numerous key elements. For example, not only must situations that potentially pose a risk be identified, but specific means, strategies, and capacities to implement clients' good lives plans must be identified and included in the management plan (see chapter 12). Follow-up maintenance treatment and supervision must also include the monitoring and implementing of the good lives/self-regulation plans (see chapter 13). Furthermore, meta-cognitive skills will be required on the part of clients in order that they can identify when both the good lives and risk management plans are being implemented effectively and when these may be threatened or in jeopardy of not playing out as planned. In addition, plans must contain positive approach goals toward which clients can work; they cannot focus solely on avoidance, escape, and risk management.

Thus, for example, developing such plans can be particularly difficult for clients who have followed an avoidant pathway, because their plans will require the continued enactment of self-regulation skills to manage risky situations (thereby preventing re-offending) as well as the pursuit of primary goods through approach goals. These clients will need to be buffered against the loss of control and cognitive deconstruction that occur when they are unable to achieve their goals or when they are under conditions of stress and need to use specific, additional strategies to achieve their goals. Conversely, for clients who have followed an approach pathway, it may be more important to emphasize continuing the enactment of skills and plans that focus on attaining a balanced and self-determined life.

For all clients, it will be useful to compile a list of "warning signs" so that others can recognize and provide help should clients start to have difficulty implementing their plans. These warning signs should include signs that the good lives plan may be threatened as well as warning signs of an increasing risk to re-offend. In addition, a list of "effectiveness signs" should also be included that allows clients and their service providers to know when plans to achieve a good life and to manage risk are being implemented effectively.

Case Example: Jason

Jason: [to his treatment group] *I'll be released back to my community before too long. I have a big plan that I have written down, but here are the main points. I obviously want a life where I can attain all 10 of the primary goods we've discussed in treatment. I am going to be sure to spend at least two 20-minute periods of each day in quiet reflection on my life and the lives of others. That will be one of the most important risk management strategies that I use. At this time, this meditation and reflection is about my meaning and purpose in life. You all know that I want the goal of relatedness, and I'm going to work on that outside the bounds of any kind of steady relationship. I just want the connections that come from being with my friends. I'm going to use the knowledge I've gained in treatment to study more about meditation and maybe take some classes in psychology, but I need to make sure I have a job first in order to pay for the classes—I need to have the means. I'm kind of interested to learn more about how people work. I'm going to join a couple of social groups to try to meet the needs of relatedness, knowledge, and community. There are health clubs and hiking club in the area, and that would be a good way to keep the perspective that there are other ways to live besides in neighborhoods like the ones where I grew up. That, along with finding work, will help with my agency and my life. I need to keep exercising and stay healthy; I've learned that health has a lot to do with how I'm feeling. That brings me inner peace. Doing all these things is also how I'm going to be creative because I don't care much about art or poetry or music or anything like that.*

The driving force under all of this is that I'm now 37 years old. Forty is just around the corner. I am committed to spending these years as a man who is approaching 40 years old. Remembering that my identity is that of a man approaching middle age is also a risk-management strategy. I don't want adversarial relationships; those are for young men in trouble. I don't want computers and porn and all that stuff, I only want the communication that computers are sometimes good for. The rest is just flashy stuff that appeals to young men in trouble. That might have to wait, though, because I am going to have restrictions on using a computer because of my history. But, I'll wait and from now on, I'm a strong man in middle age. That's me. If I get the opportunity to help my community or those I've harmed, I'll take it, but I'm convinced that a quiet life is a good one, and that happiness and pleasure come from everywhere. Entertainment just isn't the same thing as happiness and pleasure, although the right kinds of entertainment can help.

I believe I can understand where my supervising agent is coming from. He's a little younger than I am, and he's seen a lot of crime scenes and criminals. A big part of my job will be to remain patient with all the rules I'll be under. I can do that. I've learned in treatment that following little rules is as important as following big ones. If my agent starts acting like he's nothing more than a gun and a badge, I'll remember that he comes from his own neighborhood and has his own schemas. And if he's a good guy, I'll remember that we have in common the primary good of community, and that he is just trying to do what is right for the community that he is a part of.

I know that all sounds optimistic. The most important thing will be that I keep reflecting and being aware of how I feel. I've been pretty quick to anger most of my life, but can change direction quickly now, as well. My self-regulation pathway in the past was often impulsive and opportunistic. To others, my offending would have appeared to come from "out of the blue." Anyone who sees me get angry and stay angry will know that I need help because I might be on the road back to thinking positively about offending. I don't want that. Another danger point will be if I don't have any contact with any of my friends or if I'm not getting out to do activities in the community. That will mean that I'm not communicating with others as much as I should. Isolating myself is what I did when I was offending. That is no longer an option, and I'll need to watch for it and let others help me if they see I am starting to do that again.

Clearly, Jason has come a long way in treatment, and he serves as an exemplar. However, the key points are that he is working toward goals in his life as much or more than he is avoiding offending and related high-risk situations. It will be useful to have additional detail on his specific strategies. To that end, addressing self-regulation in treatment and developing a good life plan that achieves the goals described here is described in more detail in chapters 11 and 12, respectively.

Maintenance and Supervision

Maintenance is an essential part of treatment that assists clients to integrate and entrench progress made during more formal treatment. Those using the GLM/SRM-R who are involved in the supervision and community support of clients will need to be familiar with the key elements of their self-regulation pathways and good lives/self-regulation plans. These elements are as important to community supervision as they are to treatment.

Case Example: Jason

Agent: Hi, Jason, how are things going for you?

Jason: Not too bad. I have a lead on a job, and thanks to the resources you sent me, I'll be able to move into a new apartment in three weeks. It's not the house I'd like to own someday, but I need to be realistic.

Agent: Good for you. You're obviously committed to following through on the court's directions. You're also implementing your plans for getting what you want out of life.

Jason: Yeah. The only thing is that I started to get into an argument with my brother. He wanted to watch a violent movie after dinner last night and I told him I couldn't be a part of that. He looked at me like I was crazy and said the treatment program had turned me into a robot. I can't even tell you what went through my mind. I almost walked out. I couldn't believe my own brother wouldn't take this seriously.

Agent: So it happened really quickly. Here's your brother supporting you, but not getting how important it is for you to stay away from violence.

Jason: It's just all too new to me. Maybe I can look at something like that again, but I am having a really hard time with all this.

Agent: And your brother understands, but only up to a point.

Jason: That's exactly it. I suppose to him, I must seem crazy. I just have to understand where he's coming from. I just couldn't explain it to him. I'll tell you, though; it was a close call for me.

Agent: You're having close calls—that's to be expected—and what's more, what's really important, is that you're trying not to react—and succeeding—and also that you're willing to come and talk to me about it. That was part of your action plan. What treatment goal is that related to?

Jason: Right now, inner peace, but I sure want to maintain my autonomy, that's for sure. And giving in to my brother and getting into an argument with him wouldn't *have helped me get that autonomy at all. It's also about relatedness. I want him to be my brother now and to support me that I'm coming up on middle age and am no longer a kid.*

Agent: *These are all good things and show that you are working on your plans. I also remember that getting into arguments and feeling like others don't understand is risky for you. How did you handle the situation? What did you do?*

Jason: *Well, I reminded myself of my bigger goals—you know how in treatment they teach you not to lose focus. I was able to monitor myself, and I could feel the bad emotions, like anger, coming back. So, I took a few deep breaths first of all, just to relax. It was like a little bit of mini-meditation, and my brother didn't even notice. Then, I told my brother that I really did want to spend time with him, which I know is important to him, so I asked him if we could play cards instead. He still didn't really seem to understand, but he said that was okay and so that's what we did.*

Agent: *Jason, those are some excellent strategies, and they seemed to have worked, both to keep your focus on your goals and to manage how you were feeling.*

Jason: *That's it! It was hard but I'm really proud that I was able to do it.*

There is no reason why the various aspects of community supervision cannot work together as they do in this case. In fact, increasing numbers of supervising agents are becoming versed in motivational interviewing skills (Miller and Rollnick, 2002) in order to deliver a more balanced range of services that benefit the offender and community safety alike. As the above example shows, there is also no reason why supervising agents cannot work in support of good lives plans and reinforce positive gains when these are evident. After all, an offender who is working toward a more fulfilling life has few reasons to engage in crime.

SUMMARY

This chapter has described important steps for treatment, including methods for introducing and exploring material specific to the GLM/SRM-R. It has also provided a focus on those treatment areas that are important targets for change, within the framework of the GLM/SRM-R. It is essential that treatment using the GLM/SRM-R focus on approach goals—that is, those goals concerned with realizing a desired situation—rather than solely or predominantly focusing on avoidance goals, those concerned with avoiding an undesirable outcome. Within the model, treatment also must aim to assist clients' to attain good lives as well as to manage risk. The next chapter focuses more closely on offense progression.

CHAPTER 9

Offense Progression I: Personal History

Treatment commonly uses an exercise such as a personal history or "autobiography" to enable clients to uncover, examine, and begin to understand their backgrounds and lifestyle characteristics that made them vulnerable or that predisposed to offend and/or that opened them to various other problems in life. Such an exercise, typically conducted early in treatment, also allows participants to practice and become comfortable with disclosing personal information in treatment and to begin to take responsibility for their actions. When conducted in a group setting, the exercise allows participants to assist each other in examining the influence of their own personal history on their offending behavior and life problems. Such an exercise also enables the therapist to confirm previous evaluation results, critical life events, the influence of these events on future events, behavior, attitudes, and the like, and clients' perceptions of various life events and how they view the world and people in it. Reviewing clients' relevant personal histories and development can also provide useful information about clients' strengths and resiliencies.

As with other chapters in this book, a step-by-step guide to conducting this exercise with clients is not provided. Rather, the focus here is on integrating key constructs from the Self-Regulation-Revised and Good Lives models into established techniques. As indicated previously, the aim is to assist therapists to adapt cognitive-behavioral treatment and to augment this treatment with current models. That said, some key notions essential to this technique are described in this chapter.

Constructing a personal history or autobiography typically begins with early events in the individual's life, including childhood experiences, family functioning, experiences in school, relationships within the family, and so forth. The second major section of the personal history exercise typically relates to sexual development, including the onset of sexual arousal, early sexual activity and preferences, and early sexual experiences—which may be consensual or may be experiences in which the individual was a victim of sexual abuse. Care should be taken, however, because the individual may not always define the latter as abusive. For this reason, the therapist will want to ask questions using specific behavioral indicators (e.g., "Tell me about the first time that you had intercourse") instead of with vague or emotionally-laden language (e.g., "Were you ever sexually abused?"). In a similar fashion, the presence and nature of intimate relationships are explored, with the aim of understanding patterns in areas such as the individual's history, preferences (for example, short-term versus long-term relationships), ability to develop and maintain intimate relationships, views and beliefs surrounding intimacy and intimate partners, and attachment styles. Personal history disclosures also include such issues as education and employment functioning as an adult, problems such as substance abuse, current social support and social relationships, and criminal history or other criminal behavior in which the individual has engaged.

Typically in treatment, clients construct a first "draft" of this exercise on an individual basis using structured guides. The individual next presents his "life story" to other treatment participants (when treatment is conducted in a group format). The therapist and other participants typically ask questions and provide feedback to the client providing the disclosure, and this feedback, in conjunction with information from other sources such as assessment, set the stage or background for understanding the client's sexual offending behavior specifically (see chapter 10).

As can be seen from this very brief description, the purpose of conducting a personal history disclosure is to allow the individual, the therapist, and other members of the treatment group to gain a comprehensive understanding of the background factors that have influenced sexual offending behavior and other life areas, as well as the factors that make the client vulnerable to sexual offending. Assembling and relating these personal elements requires a skillful balancing act on the part of the therapist. Moving too quickly through this exercise can overlook important elements of dynamic risk and leave the client feeling misunderstood. Unfortunately, many treatment programs allow this exercise to be open-ended, unnecessarily detailed, and inclusive of irrelevant events—indeed a full "autobiography" of the individual's life. Conducted in this manner, the time allocated to this exercise can become excessive, particularly when developmental and offense information and history are available from other (sometimes more reliable) sources, such as official court documentation and pre-treatment assessments. Prolonging this exercise can also be frustrating to other treatment participants (as well as to the therapist), and can result in wasting precious resources. Thus, we recommend that this exercise focus on relevant events and that it be time-limited, particularly since no specific research indicates that the act of disclosure in and of itself results in any subsequent behavior or attitude change. In fact, authors such as Jenkins (1990) and Yates et al. (2000) urge caution not to allow clients to mistake studying their personal history for actual treatment progress. That said, it is important that the personal history exercise allows both the individual and the therapist to gain a relatively complete understanding of the individual's historical functioning, and that this knowledge then be incorporated to allow a better understanding of the multiple influences on development, as well as self-regulation and good lives components. For that reason, the task of the clinician is to keep the exercise relatively brief and to balance the demands of time and the need for the experience to be productive and relevant to the client and his peers in group therapy.

Examining Background Factors

As indicated, the purpose of examining background factors is twofold and involves understanding clients and their goals, including how each client's goals developed and changed over time. In short, this first objective is to gain an understanding of those elements that, for an individual client, are desired and are, in their view, essential to a good, well-balanced life. In addition, the objective is to understand the multiple influences that initiate and maintain sexual offending behavior.

Numerous theories have been proposed to explain the causes of, or predisposing factors for, sexual offending. Currently, it is acknowledged that multiple factors predispose a given individual to offend sexually, and these factors lead to offending in an interactive or integrated manner (Beech and Ward, 2004; Finkelhor, 1984; Hanson and Harris, 2000, 2001; Marshall and Barbaree, 1990; Thornton, 2002; Ward and Beech, 2006; Yates, Hucker, and Kingston, 2007). Predisposing factors currently identified that may influence the development and maintenance of sexual offending include: genetic predispositions; neuropsychological and neurobiological factors; adverse developmental experiences, such as abuse or attachment problems; psychological characteristics, such as attitudes supportive of sexual assault; deviant sexual interests or preferences; general and sexual self-regulation deficits; social and cultural structures and processes; and, contextual or situational factors. In short, because sexual offending results from a number of different causal factors, the aim of evaluating background factors during treatment is to identify these predisposing factors for individual clients so a clinical case conceptualization and treatment plan can be developed and so treatment can proceed to address relevant factors that require attention.

In addition to the above, unlike in other treatment approaches, within the integrated GLM/SRM-R framework, this exercise explicitly includes clients' good lives plans, how these plans may have changed over time, and how flaws and obstacles have developed over time that have resulted in a life that is less than satisfactory and that has led to problems and to sexual offending.

Personal History—Self-Regulation and Good Lives

In using this exercise as it is presented here, the therapist should be familiar with both the GLM and SRM-R described previously and elsewhere (see chapter 3) and should have conducted prior assessment pertaining to the self-regulation pathway, good lives, risk, and other factors implicated in offending and other pertinent life areas and problems (see part III of this book).

Within the integrated GLM/SRM-R approach, this exercise focuses on two areas: (a) Phase I of the SRM-R, *Preconditions to Offending*; and, (b) uncovering clients' good lives plans and changes to these plans over time. Thus, the purpose of the personal history or autobiography exercise integrated within the GLM/SRM-R approach to treatment is to assist participants to examine *relevant* historical, developmental, and personal characteristics and events that have influenced both offending behavior and the attainment of a good life. Specifically, the exercise serves to examine background events (Ward et al., 2004, 2006; Yates and Ward, 2008), some of which may be problematic and some of which may be adaptive and/or effective. These events may have

1. predisposed the individual to specific life problems;

2. led to the development of specific styles of interacting with others and the world;

3. resulted in particular modes of thinking;

4. contributed to the development of attitudes supportive of offending;

5. contributed to the offender's lack of capacity to regulate his behavior, mood, and cognition (i.e., his self-regulation style);

6. contributed to the development of the good lives plan and the specific goods valued by individual clients;

7. resulted in problems in implementing a good lives plan (i.e., the flaws of scope, coherence/conflict, means, and capacity);

8. resulted in the development of dynamic risk factors for sexual offending;

9. resulted in the development of associations between good lives goals and risk factors;

10. led to offending; and

11. led to problems attaining a good life.

Within the integrated GLM/SRM-R approach, the purpose of this exercise is also to allow participants to uncover and examine strengths and interests in specific life areas, thereby permitting a positive focus to the exercise and allowing for the later development in treatment of a more adaptive good lives plan (see chapter 12). For example, an individual may be particularly good at learning how things function mechanically, which may later contribute to the development of positive goals such as employment plans.

It is important to stress that this exercise must be focused and, ideally, time-limited so as not to become an unfocussed "life history" that includes unimportant or irrelevant experiences and events. Typically, participants are provided with guidelines, workbooks, or "homework" exercises that they use to focus on relevant life areas and on the development of a "first draft," which they later present to the therapist and to other treatment participants (when treatment is conducted in a group setting). The client then revises and refines the autobiography based on feedback from the therapist and other group members in treatment. While treatment can proceed in this manner, it must be stressed that the utility of such an exercise (designed to raise awareness of historical events and their impact on current functioning) has not been demonstrated to change behavioral and cognitive patterns or to lead to the development of new skills. As such, it is recommended that this exercise be viewed as an awareness-raising activity and an activity to allow the client to become comfortable with disclosure in treatment, rather than one designed to invoke cognitive or behavioral change.

Steps in Constructing an Integrated Personal History

Depending on the timeframe a therapist has for this exercise, it can be informative to first ask clients to prepare an informal personal history on their own time of the elements that they think are important to know. In itself, this assignment can produce information about how clients understand their lives. For example, if they discuss their lives at home exclusively, with little mention of their time at school, the absence of such information can be an avenue for further inquiry. Again, the purpose is not to produce a long period of contemplation. An open-ended first attempt, however, can certainly yield information about clients' motivations, abilities, and values.

Key components of a relevant personal history will include clients' levels of functioning in their daily lives and at the time of their offending. For example, as the exercise unfolds, both the therapist and the client should become aware of dynamic risk factors that were evident in the client's general functioning and in the offense progression. Because this exercise takes place prior to formal exploration of the offense progression, some dynamic risk information may not be included, but its appearance in treatment can inform further inquiry. It is noted, however, that pre-treatment assessment in this area should be relatively comprehensive and should inform this process. Likewise, the clinician and client can explore what primary goods the client was seeking to attain at various times within his life, including at the time of offending, as well as what good life plan flaws have existed at various times throughout the client's life.

Relevant personal histories can focus on areas of life such as

- relevant family background circumstances;
- relevant birth circumstances;
- health-related experiences;
- educational experiences;
- interpersonal experiences;
- work experiences;
- military experiences;
- sexual and romantic experiences (using behavioral terms, as indicated above); and
- early good lives plans and ideas.

A good personal history will include positive and negative experiences in most areas. It is not necessary for clients to write out these autobiographies, although putting the stories on paper can be helpful to clients as they organize their thoughts. Ultimately, clients should present their autobiography verbally in a group setting.

It can be useful to provide a list of primary goods and dynamic risk factors as handouts for discussion or for written work. Questions for exploration can include the following:

- How did this factor or primary good play a role in your life generally?

- How did this factor or primary good play a role in the period of time leading up to your offense(s)?

- How did this factor or primary good play a role in the offense itself?

As noted above, the clinician and client will explore these questions in much greater depth during exploration of the offense phases.

Presenting the Personal History in Treatment

As noted earlier, the client presents the relevant personal history in a group therapy session. It can be most effective when the clinicians prepare the group to

- initially respond only with observations about the positive aspects of the client's presentation;
- ask clarifying questions about the material presented; and
- ask open-ended questions to explore aspects of the autobiography itself. The point is to provide clarification and expansion, and not to confront the client.

It is important that the climate of the presentation remain positive and supportive. In addition to the purpose of exploring and understanding the predisposing factors to offending, the exercise is also preparatory for the more difficult disclosure and change work that lies ahead in treatment. As such, a treatment environment that is conducive to disclosure and change, and to the development of the working alliance and group cohesion and support, is essential.

Many clinicians believe that nothing short of full disclosure of all past crimes is acceptable in an autobiography. As a result, they may feel that this exercise overlooks important elements and may, therefore, be less effective than an exhaustive autobiography. It is important to remember, however, that this exercise takes place for the benefit of the client and not the therapist. No research exists that demonstrates that only full disclosure reduces risk. Clinicians will, therefore, want to remember that many opportunities exist throughout the treatment process to establish the therapeutic context where disclosure, exploration, and change can take place.

Getting Past the Basics

Sexual offender treatment providers serve a diverse population. Many clients will use an autobiography for the intended purpose. Others will require redirection in order to stay focused. Some clients will have difficulty moving beyond providing basic information into exploring how they have tried to attain primary goods throughout their lives. Under these circumstances, the therapist can explore certain areas as a means of bridging concrete events and the client's underlying intention.

- **Yearnings:** When the client was young, what did he long for? What was missing from his life? What were his hopes and dreams about his life when he was younger? Sometimes this information can be accessed by such questions as, "When you couldn't get to sleep at night, what kinds of things were on your mind?" This question can be a vehicle to draw out the discrepancy between where a client is and where he wants to be in his life.

- **Escape fantasies:** When times are hard, what would the client rather be doing and where would he rather be? This can be a rapid pathway to the discussion of primary and instrumental goods (for example, a statement like, *"Some days I wish I could just go back to the farm I used to visit. I really miss working with my hands all day"*, can lead to further discussions of primary goods such as excellence at work and play, excellence in agency, knowledge, and other goods the client values).

- **Animals:** Many sexual offenders describe disastrous attempts at relationships with other human beings. However, it is common that they recall being particularly close to a pet, good with farm animals, etc. Exploring these relationships can also provide excellent avenues into discussions of primary goods such as relatedness, inner peace, creativity, and happiness, etc.

- **Locations:** Likewise, many people identify strongly with places they have been. Where would they most like to be in this world and why? What primary goods do they believe they could more easily attain there?

The following provides an example of an abbreviated version of relevant personal history. A complete version may contain additional information.

Case Example: Donnie's Autobiography

Donnie: I actually spent my first years not far from here in a little town further west of the city than we are now. I don't have any memories of my dad at all. He died in an accident on Route 11 late on a Saturday night when I was about 3 years old. I have no idea if he'd been drinking. My mother told me that after that, whenever I saw a motorcycle, I would say that Dad was home. I don't really know what happened with my mom, either. Things were really tough, I guess. She sent me to her older brother's house to live. She kept my sister at home, though. I guess there's a lot I don't know and don't really understand about those days. She was as nice as could be. I remember her crying when she dropped me off at my uncle's place.

My uncle lived a good three hours north of here, and I went there when I was about 7 years old. He had a little farm that he worked nights and weekends, and he worked repairing trucks during the day. Insane hours—he was out by four in the morning, and back home roaring drunk by the time I got home after school. I don't know how he managed it all, and I guess he really didn't.

Anyway, my uncle was the first guy who abused me. He would take me upstairs and just do all kinds of awful sexual things to me. I won't get into the details, but it was weird. He was the only person who was a constant in my life, and he—that place—was my whole life for a long time. I knew that we weren't like other families, I knew that he wasn't like other uncles, and I knew that I wasn't like the other kids in school. I got picked on a lot by the others, and I was miserable. It took a good three years before I had any friends. The school thought something was wrong; I remember they made me see a psychologist who gave me some weird tests, but that didn't help at all. They didn't know what was going on.

Finally, I made friends with another kid. His dad was sexual with him, too. It didn't take too long to figure that out. I went over to his place and I could see his father doing the same stuff to him that my uncle did to me. This might sound creepy, but I just watched for a few minutes and then I ran away. My friend, Billy, and I would go fishing and walking down the train tracks and that sort of thing. He was the first and only friend I had for a long, long time. We did sexual things with each other, and I think that's how I got so interested in watching other people. Billy and I were really close, and I guess I never felt better than when we were having fun off someplace in the woods outside of town. Those were good times. It wasn't until later that I realized just how different I was from others.

Eventually, my uncle went off to prison, and Billy's family moved away. My uncle got arrested for molesting other kids in the neighborhood. I didn't know about any of that, although he had done some things that made me wonder. I think Billy's dad got into some kind of trouble and wanted to get away. I heard that their entire family died in a fire. The whole house burned down with them in it, even the dog. I loved that dog. Things have never been the same for me since.

I actually started doing a little better in school; I'm not sure why. But I made some changes. I kept my eyes open a lot more and started taking better care of myself. It was clear to me that the world can be a very strange and unpredictable place. I decided that I would always expect the worst, keep my eyes open, hope for the best, and never give up.

I also molested a couple of young girls in the neighborhood and never got caught. The main thing for me, though, was that I got fascinated by trying to look at other peoples' bodies—especially kids—when they didn't know I was doing it. I developed all kinds of creative ways of doing this. I joined a couple of sports teams so that I could shower with the other guys, and I took long walks through different neighborhoods trying to look in windows. At different times of year, I had to do this differently because of when it was light or dark. I usually brought a gym bag and some clothes so that if anyone asked questions I could tell them I had some reason to be in the area. Mostly what I liked was just looking at bodies. Any bodies would do, although I really liked little kids. Male, female, it didn't matter.

By that time, I was about 15 years old. High school wasn't all that bad. I could fit in by not fitting in. What I mean is that I didn't want to be the freak that attracted all the attention. That was too dangerous. I had given up on fitting in a long time before that. So I just made myself look unconcerned by anything, and that way I kind of fit in at a distance. I developed a whole world for myself. I stopped looking into windows when I was a teenager. Nowadays, I look at a lot of porn on the Internet, but only adult-oriented.

I've worked at the paper plant since I left high school. I don't know what else to say. You do your job, you get paid, and it's all good. It's a job. Some days are better than others, and sometimes I've taken nonsense from other guys. I've worked it so I can spend most of my time doing the loading and, that way, I don't have to spend too much time with the other guys. They just know I'm dependable, and we all look out for each other. It's a good group of guys, mostly.

After Billy was gone, I decided that all people are like fire. People are beautiful, but they're also dangerous. It's best not to get too close. I developed the "fire" approach to other people: great to look at, but don't get too close. People and fire can burn you. Every time I've gotten close to people, it's been like fire. There was my mom. She couldn't be too close to me. Then there was my uncle, and when I got too close to him, he took advantage of me. Then there was Billy. That couldn't last, and then he even died in a fire. How can anyone be safe in this world? So that's how I decided that the best way to be connected and still protected was to keep my distance. So I spent a lot of time when I was younger finding really creative ways to understand people, follow them, and most of all, watch them. Nowadays, I just watch people; I don't go out of my way to do it. I would love to find a wife and settle down some day, but that just hasn't been an option, and I've never met anyone I could be really close to.

I knew before I got arrested that I had gone way too far when I molested that young kid named Billy. Same name—funny, huh? He lived across the street, and I used to look at him out the window all the time. I couldn't believe when his parents built him a tree house in their side yard. I could watch him play most days—his birthday party, his sister's birthday party, family barbecues, and everything.

I absolutely knew I shouldn't go near him, but I did. The economy's been tough on the paper industry. A lot of guys have been laid off. Things are tense. I haven't known what to expect. I kept watching him and wanting him. I tried brushing it off, telling myself to knock it off. But the next thing I knew I was getting him into my place to play video games. All I know is that I never for a moment wanted to hurt anyone. The only reason I'm telling you this is because I want to put out this fire.

When you talk about the things in life that everyone wants, here's what I'm thinking. Yes, I want them all, but mostly I want inner peace and happiness. I'm 26 years old, and I think it's time to find out more about my meaning and purpose in life. I'm not too worried about my health, but I know that the life I've been living is no good. It's time I find a way to be better at my work, in my time by myself, and my time with others. This program talks about creativity and knowledge, and I've spent too much of my time in those areas focused on sex and getting away with things. I know a thing or two about hard work, and it's time I start focusing on other people. The only thing is that I really don't know how to do that without screwing something up. I guess I also want to know about my family, but that could take a while.

When you talk about risks, I think I need to find some way to get to know other people. Now you have to admit that how I've gotten to know people without them knowing me shows some creativity. Just the same, it's time for other people to know me, and I don't know how to make that happen. These risk factors about lack of intimate relationships are right on the money. I also need to find other ways of dealing with stress because I'm like a burning building. If I don't start doing something soon, there's no telling what's going to happen.

At this point in his treatment, given the information provided, Donnie presents as having followed an avoidant-active pathway to offending. Despite apparent insight, he possesses few skills for coping with the stresses of life. Donnie lacks emotionally intimate relationships, and has been unsuccessful at self-regulating his sexual arousal. His self-regulation style has focused more on avoiding problems than addressing them directly. There is some question as to whether his use of pornography might not have simply made his efforts to self-regulate worse.

Donnie obtains low-moderate scores on actuarial measures. His unrelated male victim and the absence of a long-term partner indicate an elevated risk. The fact that this is his first officially recorded offense is also a noteworthy indicator. His avoidant personality style (including a lack of emotionally intimate relationships and deficient attempts at self-regulation) indicate moderate levels of dynamic risk.

Donnie's good life plan has focused primarily on resolving conflicts associated with inner peace, happiness, relatedness, agency, and community. By his own account, he has valued these goods highly, but has lacked the necessary means to attain them more fully. His attempts to attain the goals of agency and inner peace in the wake of an adverse childhood have placed him at some distance from attaining the goal of community. His earlier pursuits of creativity and knowledge have appeared primarily in the context of voyeuristic activities. From Donnie's account, he has not spent much effort thinking about the broader goods of life, including spirituality. Finally, Donnie's heartbreaking childhood has resulted in cognitive schemas related to friendship, relatedness, and community that will clearly remain the focus of treatment efforts for some time.

Donnie presents for treatment as highly motivated to change. He has a clear overlap between his good life plan and the dynamic risk factors that have contributed to his offending. He will require careful attention from his clinicians. Given his largely avoidant personality style, he will be at some risk to revert to historical interpersonal functioning in the absence of a supportive therapeutic environment.

Autobiographies are as diverse as the offender population. However, they can be an excellent starting point for finding the nexus between dynamic risk and the broader good lives plans of sexual offenders. Although relatively brief, Donnie's autobiography is thorough and comprehensive, and allows the therapist to understand what Donnie values in life, the flaws in Donnie's good life plan, his risk factors, and the self-regulation style, both overall and with respect to offending, specifically.

Summary

This chapter has described an approach to conducting a relevant personal history exercise that enables clients to explore and understand their backgrounds and lifestyle characteristics that made them vulnerable or that predisposed them to offend and/or that opened them to various other problems in life. The exercise is based on the

10-phase SRM-R as integrated with the GLM. Autobiographies need not be an overly exhaustive exercise, although they should be meaningful to the client and provide an opportunity for the therapist and client to explore relevant dynamic risk factors. Crucial to this work, however, is that this exercise explicitly includes clients' good lives plans, how these plans may have changed over time, and how flaws, obstacles, and self-regulation styles have developed over time, resulting in a life that is less than satisfactory and that has led to problems and to sexual offending.

CHAPTER 10

Offense Progression II: Offense Disclosure

Treatment commonly uses an exercise such as disclosure of offending behavior or an "offense cycle" to determine cognitive, emotional, and behavioral patterns of offending, to enable clients to examine and understand factors associated specifically with offending behavior, and to help clients to take responsibility for their actions in offending. Such an exercise also allows clients to receive feedback from the therapist and other group members on motivations and dynamics of offending behavior. From here, clients can refine and augment their understanding and perceptions of offending.

Within the integrated GLM/SRM-R framework, this exercise does not follow a cyclical model, but utilizes the 10-phase Self-Regulation Model (Yates and Ward, 2008; see chapter 3) to examine offense pathways in detail. The cycle model is overly simplistic and does not sufficiently address the dynamics of offending or differences in self-regulation. It also changes over time with repeated offending. Finally, it varies in offense patterns that are evident between and among offenders, or inclusion of elements from the Good Lives Model.

Phase 1 (preconditions to offending) was examined through the personal history exercise described in the previous chapter. The present chapter deals with Phases 2 though 10 of the SRM-R and comprises a detailed examination of offending beginning with offense-specific precursors through to post-offense evaluations. These phases include

- the life event that triggers the offense progression;
- the desire in response to life event;
- goal establishment;
- selection of strategies to achieve goals;

- opportunity to achieve goals;
- pre-offense behaviors;
- commission of sexual offense;
- post-offense evaluation; and
- future intentions with respect to offending and adjustments to good lives plan.

In using this exercise, the therapist should be familiar with both the GLM and SRM-R and should have conducted prior assessment pertaining to self-regulation pathway, good lives, risk, other factors implicated in offending, and other pertinent life areas and problems (see chapters 4, 5, and 6).

When conducting such a disclosure exercise, one challenge in treatment is to remain focused on the objective of the exercise: to understand the offense pathway and its progression, the goals associated with offending, and the cognitive, affective, and behavioral patterns within the progression. Treatment providers and other group members can become overly focused on activities such as admitting all details of each offense the client has committed, which can distract the participants and result in everyone focusing on irrelevant or peripheral aspects of offending. Often this detail-driven approach means that more important elements of the offense progression might be ignored and the end result will be an incomplete understanding of the offense pathway, patterns, and dynamics. It is, therefore, important to examine all phases of the offense progression and to avoid focusing solely or predominantly on those phases associated in time with the commission of the offense (i.e., Phases 5 through 8). As with other treatment exercises, although assessment will have given the therapist a comprehensive understanding of the client, it is essential that he or she remains flexible and open to new information that may arise during the offense disclosure. In particular, the therapist needs to be alert for approach goals associated with primary goods alongside the detection of risk factors.

Another challenge is to ensure links between the offense progression or between the progression and the development of new skills and behaviors in treatment. All too often, treatment focuses on raising awareness of offending behavior, but stops short of developing sufficient skills and strategies to help the offender to pursue personal goals or manage behavior and risk. Simply raising awareness without concurrent skill development is unlikely to lead to changes in behavior, either in the short-term or over the long-term. For this reason, the offense progression exercise within the GLM/SRM-R approach has the dual purpose of both understanding the offense pathway and the dynamics and building strategies to manage behavior later in treatment. The offense progression should be revisited periodically throughout treatment in order to augment awareness when specific treatment targets, such as cognition or sexual arousal, are addressed later. The offense progression exercise should also be used in the later development of the good lives/self-regulation plan (see chapter 12).

Within the integrated GLM/SRM-R, this exercise focuses on Phases 2 through 10 of the offense progression. The goals are to develop an understanding of:

- (Phase 2) the progression of offending from its inception (the life event that triggers the progression) through to its conclusion and post-offense events and responses;

- (Phase 3) the influence of predisposing background factors on the offense progression;

- (Phase 4) events that, for individual clients, trigger offending-related behaviors and pre-offense elements that pose a risk, such as offense-supportive attitudes, problematic good lives plans, and cognitive schemas;

- (Phase 5) individuals' cognitive, affective, and behavioral responses to the various events that occur throughout the offense progression;

- (Phase 6) dynamic risk factors evident in the offense progression and any associated primary goods;

- (Phase 7) the self-regulation pathway(s) followed in offending and the primary and secondary goods evident in the offense;

- (Phase 8) post-offense dynamics and responses that result in reinforcement for behavior and the formulation of future intentions with respect to offending;

- (Phase 9) the relationship between offending and the good lives plan and its goals, problems, and influence on offending behavior; and

- (Phase 10) particular strengths, skills, and strategies evident in the offense progression that may be further refined and developed in treatment.

As with the previous personal history exercise in chapter 9, it is important to stress that the offense progression exercise must not only be comprehensive, but also focused, relevant, and, ideally, time-limited. Typically, participants receive guidelines, workbooks, or homework that enable them to focus on specific behaviors and risk factors. They use these to develop a first "draft" that they present later to the therapist and other treatment participants. The offense progression is then revised and refined based on feedback received from others. Proceeding in such a manner is likely effective, as individuals do not often fully understand all of the elements of the offense progression, particularly at the early stages of treatment.

In conducting this exercise, it is essential that participants' disclosures be linked to prior evaluation results, such as assessment of dynamic risk factors, sexual and personal history, psychological functioning, primary goods, and so forth. If clients have previously reviewed their own personal risk factors, this process will facilitate the development of the offense progression and the disclosure exercise. The result is comprehensive and inclusive of all relevant factors associated with offending and life problems, but the process presupposes that clinicians have conducted the comprehensive pre-treatment assessment, which is an essential element of treatment.

It is also stressed here that clients do not need to develop a separate offense progression for each offense they have committed; offenses that are similar in nature, including undetected offenses, may be included in one exercise when patterns are similar across multiple offenses. Of note, however, offenders following more than one pathway to offending may demonstrate some variability in their offense progressions. Therefore, they may need to develop different offense progressions for different types of sexual offenses. Typically, the exercise begins with the most recent sexual offense and incorporates other offenses as the exercise progresses. It is not necessary to include all details of all offenses, as the objective is to understand behavioral and other patterns across offenses. Doing a step-by-step write-up allows for determination of other offense pathways that may have been followed at different times during clients' offending history, and the process can allow for better detection of patterns that run across offenses. For example, individuals with lengthy offense histories may have followed one pathway early in their offending career, but later may have switched to a different offense pathway. The SRM-R proposes that offenders may have initially followed avoidant pathways early in their history, but followed approach pathways more recently. Conversely, individuals who previously received treatment may have switched from an approach pathway to an avoidant pathway, albeit unsuccessfully.

Since assessment is also ideally based on objectively gathered information (e.g., collateral, police, and court documents), therapists should be alert to missing information in the offender's self-report of the offense progression. Supportive challenging by the therapist and other treatment participants can augment the client's report of offending behavior and dynamics.

Below are described the steps involved in conducting the offense progression exercise. At the end of this exercise, therapists and their clients integrate information obtained through disclosure with existing information (e.g., information derived from evaluation), which helps to establish a pathway to offending for each participant. Those pathways are then compared to pre-treatment assessment findings with regard to each pathway followed by individual clients.

LIFE EVENT (PHASE 2)

Using the integrated GLM/SRM-R approach, development of an offense progression commences with examination of the life event(s) that triggered the offense. This event may be major or minor in nature and will be individualized and personal to each offender.

Depending on the individual, the life event may be more proximal or distal to offending, although typically, the focus at this phase is on more distant, earlier triggers in the offense progression. More distal factors represent general vulnerability factors and are included in the relevant personal history disclosure (see chapter 9). In addition, more proximal or acute factors occur later in the offense progression (see Phase 6 of the progression).

Multiple life events may trigger the offense progression for an individual offender, and so all of these events should be included in the analysis of this phase. In addition, for individuals with diverse offense histories, different life events may be associated with different specific offense instances and, possibly, with different offense pathways. Again, each should be examined during this phase, with additional offense progressions generated as required and appropriate.

In examining this phase, life events are defined broadly, and can include events external to the individual, as well internal cognitive and affective states (e.g., depression, arousal). Furthermore, these events can be longer-term events or more transitory, short-term events. Again, each should be examined. The key objective at this stage of this exercise is to understand and raise awareness with respect to events that initiate the offense progression, while also building on individual vulnerabilities, tendencies, and core values identified in the personal history of Phase I. In addition to offense-inducing life events, examination of this phase of the offense progression also includes evaluation of evident primary goods that are associated with offending via problems or flaws in the good lives plan.

Therapists should probe the client's narrative, as appropriate and required, in order to establish the life event(s). Official offense information may also provide useful information.

> *Therapist:* If you think back to when you first had the thought of offending, or perhaps even earlier, what would you say triggered the progression of events that later led to the offense?
>
> *Client:* I would say it started when I first saw the boy in the park.
>
> *Therapist:* I expect that was a trigger, though I'm wondering if there might have been something going on before you went to the park—something much earlier. For example, what had happened that made you decide to go the park in the first place?
>
> *Client:* Nothing much, really. I was just sitting around home feeling bored, and I decided to go out for a walk.
>
> *Therapist:* Why were you bored?
>
> *Client:* I wasn't working and didn't feel like staying at home. I really wanted to work, but I hadn't been able to find a job, which meant I also couldn't go anywhere because I didn't have any money.

In this example, the life event that triggered the offense progression, based on available information, was boredom, which may be linked to unemployment, which is, therefore, also a life event that triggered the offense progression. Going to the park and seeing the boy represents a more acute trigger later in the offense progression.

In this example, three primary goods may be operative in the offense progression (although these goods require confirmation): excellence in play and work, mastery, and inner peace. Specifically, it appears as though the client highly values work, the lack of which resulted in boredom and financial distress with which he may have been unable to cope, all of which appear to be associated with the life event that triggered offending. Although confirmation is required, problems with internal capacity and the means to attain goods are possible but evident flaws in the clients' good life plan.

Desire in Response to Life Event (Phase 3)

The life event that occurs in Phase 2 triggers perceptions, attributions, associations, affect, cognitive schemas, attitudes, and implicit theories in response to the event. The life event may also activate memories of previous offending. These responses are likely to be relatively automatic. The offender's perceptions of the life event, as well as the interpersonal context in which the event occurred, influence the information to which an individual attends and that he processes as well as the meaning associated with the event. The individual's self-perceptions also guide his subsequent behavior and goal establishment.

Within the integrated GLM/SRM-R framework, various desires and higher order goals may be triggered as a function of the life event, its interaction with the individual's prior experiences, and his overall tendencies and vulnerability factors (all of which were established in Phase 1 and during assessment). Examining this phase of the offense progression raises awareness about each of these responses and their influence on subsequent events as related to sexual offending, the attainment of primary goods, the context of the specific life event, the individual's broader self-regulation capacity, and the predisposing factors.

The desire that emerges at this phase may be non-sexual, sexually deviant, sexual (but not deviant), or appropriate, depending upon the individual and the context. For example, the life event may trigger the desire for sexual activity, which is an appropriate desire on its own but one that ultimately results in a sexual offense due to predisposing factors, such as its association with aggression in a given individual. Alternatively, the life event and its interpretation may result in anger or hostility, leading to a desire for retaliation or to alleviate or express emotion. Those emotional responses manifest later in the offense progression as sexual aggression. This kind of angry reaction would occur among offenders for whom violent and sexual behaviors are cognitively and behaviorally linked. Finally, the desire triggered by the life event may be, in fact, a non-sexual and appropriate desire, as in those cases in which the individual seeks to obtain primary goods in response to the life event. That is, the life event may trigger the desire to regain such states as autonomy, relatedness, or intimacy, thus re-establishing equilibrium in the client's good life plan. Intimacy may be a goal the offender ultimately expects to gain via offending. It is also possible that all three desires may be simultaneously present to varying degrees, again depending on the individual and the context. Thus, according to the GLM, direct and indirect pathways to offending involve primary goods and their associated secondary goods (Ward and Maruna, 2007). A direct pathway occurs when an offender's pursuit of a primary good ultimately results in the commission of a sexual offense (e.g., seeking intimacy through sex with a child), whereas the indirect pathway has a cascading or downstream effect when problems such as lifestyle imbalance result in disinhibition and subsequent sexual offending (e.g., overwork, poor stress control, relationship disruption, etc.). At this stage, sexual and/or aggressive fantasy may be present, in addition to covert or overt rehearsal of offending.

In implementing this section of the offense progression, desires, responses, and goals are also linked to dynamic risk factors identified during assessment and to later treatment targets. Perceptions, attributions, associations, affect, cognitive schemas, attitudes, and implicit theories, both general and specific to sexual offending, are also examined and evaluated. Thus, the goals in this phase are to

1. determine the clients' responses to the life event that allows the offense progression to continue;

2. evaluate the impact of these responses on subsequent behavior;

3. understand offense-specific scripts, schemas, implicit theories, etc.;

4. understand clients' general tendencies or predispositions with respect to cognitive and behavioral scripts, schemas, values, attitudes, etc.;

5. understand the accompanying emotional states and clients' abilities to tolerate these states;

6. understand clients' responses with respect to the implementation of their good lives plan and its associated flaws;

7. evaluate clients' abilities to self-regulate in response to life events; and

8. link responses to dynamic risk factors identified through assessment in order to raise awareness and so the factors may be targeted for change in treatment.

The following case study provides an example to illustrate each of these points.

Case Example: John

John is a 45-year-old man convicted for child molestation on three occasions. During Phase 1 of the offense progression, he reported that he experienced a strict upbringing by his parents, that he grew up feeling inadequate, and that he felt he was never able to do anything right. Although he tried hard in school, he was not academically inclined and did not get good grades, for which he was often criticized by his father. As an adult, he has always been employed, however, and has in fact been employed in the same job for 19 years. He has had very few intimate adult relationships, although he reports interest in adult females and expresses an interest in having a long-term relationship.

During his offense disclosure, John revealed that several months prior to offending, he had made a significant mistake at work. Although his supervisor was understanding, John was very critical of his own performance. John believes that because his parents were so critical of him, he is particularly sensitive to failure and is also somewhat of a perfectionist, reporting that it is important that he do the best he can at everything. At the time of his offense progression, he focused on his work, trying to "make up for things." Although he worked extra hours and asked for extra work, causing him to eventually stop going out with his friends, he did not feel better.

In this example, making a mistake at work is identified as the life event. This life event was interpreted in view of the client's predisposing tendency to view himself overly critically, resulting in the desire at Phase 2 to make up for having made the mistake and the behavior of working extra hours. Neither choice resolved either the immediate problem or John's longstanding feelings of inadequacy. His choices indicate that John prioritizes the primary good of mastery at work, and always strives for excellence. This situation also resulted in John's reduced engagement with pleasurable activities. In terms of affective responses, he experienced negative emotions in response to such events and he appeared to lack the capacity to tolerate and manage those states. This example illustrates a non-sexual response to an event and a more distal life event that initiates the offense progression.

As stated above, based on available information thus far, John appears to value the primary good of excellence in work, which is also implicated in his offending. The capacity to attain inner peace, linked to the dynamic risk factor of general self-regulation (the regulation of emotions and possibly problem-solving) also appears associated with John's offending, as well as possibly relatedness and intimacy goods (and deficits). Sufficient information regarding this primary good and risk factor is currently lacking, however, and the topic will need to be explored further.

Consider the following example:

Case Example: Nelson

Nelson is a 28-year-old man convicted for one count of rape, which he committed against his common-law marital partner. During Phase 1 of the offense progression, Nelson indicated that he had had a difficult childhood in which he was "always getting into trouble." That trouble included truancy from school, poor peer groups, minor juvenile delinquency, suspensions from school, living in several different foster homes, and finally moving out on his own at the age of 16. Nelson has had difficulty retaining employment, indicating that he becomes frustrated and quits jobs "without thinking." Although his sexual history (confirmed via collateral information) was uneventful and seemed developmentally appropriate, as an adult, he has tended to have predominantly short-term relationships characterized

> *by dominating and controlling his partners. His current relationship is by far his longest; he and his partner were together for three years prior to the offense (they have since separated).*
>
> *During his offense disclosure, Nelson revealed that, several days prior to offending, he began to think his partner was cheating on him, and he worried that she was going to leave him for someone else. Nelson reported that he was fearful of being alone again and that he did not believe his partner could manage life "on her own." On the night of the offense, Nelson and his partner were engaged in a heated argument. When she tried to leave the house, Nelson said that he "freaked out" and grabbed her to stop her from leaving. When she protested, he physically and sexually assaulted her.*

In this example, the life event occurred several days prior to offending, when Nelson initially became suspicious of his partner and felt that his relationship was threatened. The argument on the night of the offense represents a separate, more acute event (Phase 6) and does not comprise the life event that initially triggered the offense progression, because the first threat to the relationship (real or perceived) occurred several days prior to the offense. It was that event which activated cognitive and affective schemas regarding relationships and that threatened Nelson's good life plan. This example also illustrates the importance of examining the precise nature and timing of events that initially set the offense progression in motion at early stages.

In this example, the life event was interpreted in view of Nelson's cognitive schemas surrounding relationships. His schemas appear to reflect both a fear of losing relationships and a tendency to control his partners, thereby suggesting a partner abuse dynamic that would require additional exploration.

Based on available information thus far, Nelson appears to value the primary goods of agency and relatedness (specifically, intimate relationships). Agency and relatedness are also implicated in his offending. The capacity to attain the good of inner peace, linked to the dynamic risk factor of general self-regulation (emotion regulation, impulsivity, and, potentially, problem-solving deficits) also appears linked to Nelson's offending, as well as possibly sexual self-regulation and intimacy deficits.

This example includes a more proximal life event that initiates the offense progression, as is evident from the relatively rapid progression from initiation to offending. This example also shows a non-sexual—although likely hostile and aggressive—desire in response to the life event (i.e., the desire to sustain his relationship, even by control), as well as the possibility of offending as a way to re-establish a primary good that is threatened (the potential loss of relatedness as a result of the loss of the current relationship).

Goal Establishment (Phase 4)

Within the integrated GLM/SRM-R, at Phase 4 of the offense progression, the individual establishes goals in response to the desire triggered by the life event, again based on predisposing factors and personal history. Both offense-specific goals and broader goals related to the attainment of primary goods are included. These goods are linked to the desires (Phase 3) triggered in response to the life event (Phase 2) that initiates the offense sequence. Also at this phase, the individual considers the appropriateness or acceptability of his desires and what, if anything, he will do about it, along with his ability to tolerate the emotional states that are associated with the desire(s) that were activated in Phase 3.

Thus, in examining this stage of the offense progression exercise, the objectives are to

1. determine the goals the individual establishes with respect to the desire(s) activated in response to the life event. This process specifically includes offense-related goals;

2. categorize goals such that the offense pathway can be later determined;

3. determine whether goals in service of implementing the good lives plan are also established or evident (e.g., are in service of re-acquiring primary goods that are threatened by the life event) and are something the individual desires;

4. link goals to dynamic risk factors;

5. integrate information obtained with previous assessment findings and other available information; and

6. determine changes in goals and/or the individual's ways of achieving goals that will be targeted in treatment.

With respect to offending, two goals need to be considered:

- ***Offense-related avoidance goals***, in which the individual desires to prevent or refrain from offending at this early stage in the offense progression, and which cause anxiety or distress at the possibility that offending will occur; and

- ***Offense-related approach goals***, in which the individual does not desire to avoid offending, and which support progressing to later offending.

Attempts to acquire primary goods are also considered at this phase.

In examining all goals, the therapist focuses on what a client reports that he was trying to achieve at this stage in the offense progression. For example:

> ***Therapist:*** *So far, we have established that the event that triggered the offense progression was your jealousy and your thoughts that your partner might leave you. You said this resulted in a desire that she stay with you. Would you say that this was your goal, at least at the beginning?*
>
> ***Nelson:*** *Yes.*
>
> ***Therapist:*** *Often, in situations like this, people often also have other goals. What would you say were your other goals in this situation?*
>
> ***Nelson:*** *I wanted to find out if she had been seeing someone else.*
>
> ***Therapist:*** *Anything else? How were you feeling at the time?*
>
> ***Nelson:*** *I was feeling angry at her and felt that she was disrespecting me.*
>
> ***Therapist:*** *So would it be accurate to say that your goal might also have been to show her how angry you were, and maybe also to teach her to respect you, or, in other words, to not disrespect you?*
>
> ***Nelson:*** *I wanted to show her that she just could not do that to me.*

In this example, multiple goals are evident, representing predominantly approach goals. Specifically, Nelson reported that he wanted to re-acquire the intimate relationship or, alternatively, to avoid the loss of the relationship (the primary good of relatedness) and to re-gain a sense of agency (as indicated by the desire to gain "respect" and control over the situation). Nelson also had the offense-related approach goal of expressing his anger toward his partner. In this example, it is clear that, at this stage, Nelson does not desire to avoid offending, that his goals will allow him to continue advancing through the offense progression, and that he likely followed an approach pathway to offending.

Links to dynamic risk factors are also evident, including offense-supportive cognitive schemas, intimacy deficits, and problems with self-regulation and emotion management.

STRATEGY SELECTION (PHASE 5)

Once an individual has established a goal with respect to the desire(s) activated in response to the life event, he selects the specific strategies or methods that will be used to attain these goals. These strategies may be selected relatively automatically, may ultimately be effective or ineffective in meeting the goal, and may represent passive or active efforts to meet the goal.

In the integrated GLM/SRM-R, the strategies examined at this phase include strategies aimed at achieving the offense-related goal as well as those selected to obtain primary and secondary good lives goals. Thus, in examining this stage of the offense progression exercise, the objectives are to:

1. determine the strategies the individual implemented or attempted in order to achieve the goals established in Phase 4;

2. evaluate whether the strategies were active or passive in nature;

3. categorize strategies in order to combine them with goals and determine an offense pathway;

4. link strategies to dynamic risk factors;

5. link strategies to broader tendencies the client manifests with respect to achieving various life and offense goals;

6. integrate information obtained through previous assessment findings and other available information; and

7. determine what treatment interventions are required in order to develop self-regulation skills, manage risk to offend, and attain and maintain goals appropriately.

It is important to stress that strategy selection may not necessarily be explicit, but may occur relatively automatically as a function of habitual action and entrenched cognitive and behavioral scripts. For some individuals, strategy selection will be impulsive, while for others strategy selection may be very explicit and strategies carefully chosen.

Consider the following example:

Case Example: Ron

Ron is a 36-year-old man convicted of sexual offenses against his daughter. During Phase 2 of the offense progression, he reported that the life event that initiated the offense sequence was his wife's illness. He reported that she was very sick and, as a result, was unable to meet his needs, including his sexual needs. His daughter was doing most of the housework and was taking care of him. He was aware that he had started to think about his daughter in a sexual way, which he found very distressing. Because he worried that he might ultimately "do something" about these thoughts, he attempted to stay away from his daughter and to not be alone with her. He tried working extra hours, going out with friends, or inviting his brother and his family to his home. He also tried to suppress the sexual thoughts he was having about his daughter. Although these strategies were initially effective, he was ultimately unsuccessful when a significant opportunity to meet his needs presented itself, at which time he acted on these thoughts on two occasions.

In this example, Ron established an avoidance goal at Phase 4 of the offense progression, as indicated by his desire to avoid acting on his sexual thoughts about his daughter and his distress and anxiety associated with the possibility that he would act on these urges. Once he had established this goal, he implemented several active strategies to avoid offending, including staying away from home, avoiding being alone with his daughter, and actively attempting to suppress sexual fantasies about his daughter.

The available information does not indicate that Ron had any clear goal of attaining certain primary goods, although the good of happiness does seem to be salient and relevant, as does relatedness. The dynamics underlying Ron's offending require additional evaluation.

Although verification from assessment and other phases of the offense progression is needed, available information thus far suggests that Ron followed the *avoidant-active pathway* to offending.

In addition to understanding goals, strategies, and offense pathways, information obtained in this phase is also used to determine treatment targets and interventions to develop risk management and self-regulation skills and the client's good life plan. In addition, strengths are also examined here. In this example, Ron was initially successful in avoiding offending. Thus, in exploring this phase of offending, therapists should also evaluate what pre-existing skills and strategies someone like Ron already possesses, which could then assist in risk management and self-regulation in the future. Such pre-existing strengths and skills will be reinforced in treatment and built into the good lives/self-regulation plan developed later in treatment.

OPPORTUNITY TO ACHIEVE GOALS (PHASE 6)

Treatment traditionally examines high-risk situations, which are typically external circumstances that pose a risk for sexual offending. Indeed, the construct of high-risk situations was built into the original SRM. The revised GLM/SRM-R expanded this phase to include not only opportunities or risks to offend, but also the opportunity to achieve all goals established at prior phases. This assessment acknowledges that some goals and their accompanying strategies may be appropriate, non-sexual, or non-deviant in nature, and may also represent efforts to attain primary human goods. Thus, at this phase, the individual may indeed encounter a high-risk situation, such as access to a potential victim. Alternatively, the situation may represent the opportunity to achieve pro-social goals or the potential to re-establish the good lives plan. The model also acknowledges that the opportunity may not be necessarily external and that individual perceptions, cognition, affect, and the like with respect to the opportunity are also important.

Encountering the opportunity to achieve goals results from the actions, responses, appraisals, and planning throughout previous phases in the offense progression. Responses to encountering this opportunity will vary by offense pathway and individual goals established in Phase 4.

For an individual with an offense-related avoidance goal, encountering a situation that places him at risk to offend will represent failure in achieving his initial goal, since the situation signals that he has been unsuccessful in avoiding offending, which is now more imminent. The individual is likely to experience negative affect and low self-efficacy, and his goals linked to offending behavior are then activated. The individual also narrows his focus, and information processing reverts to a more basic, habitual, or immediate level. Cognitive deconstruction, loss of control, and disengagement of self-monitoring may also occur, resulting in self-regulation failure.

Conversely, for an individual with an offense-related approach goal, this phase represents a success experience as he is closer to attaining his initial goal. For these individuals, this phase is also likely to be associated with positive affect and anticipation of offending as a way to achieve the goal. The individual focuses on proximal planning to achieve immediate goals in the situation, and self-efficacy is expected to be high.

For both avoidant and approach pathways, the presence of a potential victim increases the salience of offense-related goals, thus reducing the focus on longer term or higher level goals, such as avoiding offending or maintaining the good lives plan.

Individuals may concurrently experience anticipation with respect to achieving the primary goods. As such, affect and expectations may be mixed, regardless of the pathway involved. For example, an individual who is focused on attaining non-deviant sexual pleasure (subsumed within the primary good of happiness), and who holds an avoidance goal with respect to offending (e.g., with a child), may experience both a sense of goal failure upon encountering the opportunity to obtain sexual pleasure with a child as well as anticipation of attaining gratification and/or the primary good.

In implementing this phase of the offense progression exercise, therapists examine the situation in relation to the preceding phases (i.e., with respect to goals previously established, strategies selected, covert and overt planning, etc.), as well as the cognitive, affect, and behavioral processes that are evoked at this phase in response to the opportunity that is presented. Attention is paid to habitual and automatic actions and cognitive and behavioral scripts and schemas.

In investigating this stage of the offense progression exercise, the objectives are to

1. determine the specific situation that resulted from previous offense progression phases and in which the opportunity to achieve offense-related and good lives goals was presented;

2. assess clients' cognitive, affective, and behavioral responses when the opportunity arose;

3. link opportunities to dynamic risk factors and earmark implications for capability building, flaws in the good lives plan, and reduction of risk;

4. link responses to opportunities and to dynamic risk factors;

5. link responses to broader tendencies clients manifest with respect to achieving various offense-related and other life goals (e.g., a tendency toward impulsivity, loss of control, cognitive deconstruction, or antisocial attitudes);

6. integrate information obtained with previous assessment findings and other available information;

7. determine what interventions are required in treatment in order to develop self-regulation skills, competencies for effective goods attainment, manage risk to offend, and attain and maintain appropriate goals;

8. determine what interventions are required in order to assist clients to attain and

maintain primary goods and to differentiate between appropriately attaining these goods and obtaining these goods via offending; and

9. determine external interventions that may be required for community supervision (e.g., victim access restrictions) to reduce risk.

In examining the opportunity to offend, it is important to emphasize that therapists do not focus solely on the external situation, but they also consider clients' interpretations and responses to the opportunity or event. While therapists will identify specific risk situations that clients will need to avoid or manage, it is not possible to account for all possible situations that could pose a risk. As such, in addition to identifying situations that pose a risk, this part of the exercise aims to assess clients' entrenched or habitual self-regulation styles and other tendencies, in order to effect broader change in treatment.

PRE-OFFENSE BEHAVIORS (PHASE 7)

Engaging in pre-offense behaviors results from goals, responses, and planning during previous phases of the offense progression. At this stage, the individual has encountered the opportunity to offend and is now engaging in behaviors that represent immediate precursors to offending, such as actively grooming a victim or otherwise seeking victim access, planning offending, or engaging in deviant sexual fantasy or rehearsal. As with previous phases, the individual may be attempting to achieve either or both an offense-related or a good lives goal, and, therefore, analysis proceeds accordingly.

Behavior and responses at this phase will vary by offense pathway. For example, individuals initially holding offense-avoidance goals may switch temporarily to an approach goal as a result of becoming disinhibited and focusing on anticipation, immediate gratification, and lower level, more immediate goals. Planning that was previously covert may become more overt or direct. Individuals with offense-related approach goals will continue to strive toward meeting these goals, with some demonstrating impulsivity in offending and others demonstrating an explicit plan to offend. The individual may experience increased sexual arousal and anticipation at this phase in the offense progression, as well as positive affect and low victim empathy or perspective-taking.

At this stage, it is also important to evaluate what the individual did to overcome inhibitors to sexual aggression (as well as perhaps other forms of aggression and violence), and to gain victim compliance. Also relevant is whether the individual engaged in activities, such as sexual fantasy or pornography use, that may have served to increase arousal. Similarly, therapists should also be alert to any evidence that the individual was able to implement some self-control, as such strategies will represent strengths on which treatment can build. Developing an understanding of self-regulation functioning at this phase is essential. Therapists at this phase should also be alert to information that suggests specific targets for intervention, such as the presence of cognitive distortions and schemas or deviant sexual interests, any of which can be changed in treatment.

COMMISSION OF SEXUAL OFFENSE (PHASE 8)

The behaviors, goals, planning, and other elements from previous phases culminate in the commission of the sexual offense. The aim of examining this phase is to understand the precise nature of the offense and to integrate the individual's understanding with available information, such as official documentation. It is important to note here that the aim is not necessarily to insist that the client admit all the details of offending. Some discrepancy between the clients' version and official versions of the offense is likely, which may or may not need to be addressed, depending upon the scope of the differences. Supportive challenging by the therapist and other group members can aid in resolving significant discrepancies and in assisting clients to expand their understanding of the nature of the offense. This challenging can be done either during the offense disclosure exercise or during a subsequent, revised disclosure, after the client has had the opportunity to reflect on feedback and to learn more about their cognition, behavior, and affect during offending (e.g., via treatment modules that address these specific factors).

As in Phase 7, this part of the offense progression exercise also examines the ways in which the individual overcame inhibitors to aggression and gained victim compliance. Particularly important are the individual's cognitive distortions and attributions of responsibility for offending, as well as the previously examined links to cognitive schemas and implicit theories, which represent general tendencies (e.g., self-regulation, deviant sexual arousal/interest) and allow the individual to proceed with offending in the situation.

Ward and colleagues (2004) have suggested that variability will exist in an individual's focus during this phase of offending. Specifically, individuals may have a *self-focus*, a *mutual focus*, or a *victim focus*. Individuals with a self-focus tend to make statements at this phase of the offense progression that reflect a lack of consideration of the victim's perspective. For example, "I was aroused and started to masturbate, and threatened him if he told anyone." Individuals with a mutual focus will describe the event as beneficial or pleasurable for both the offender and the victim. For example,

"When I first touched him, he didn't say 'No' and seemed to be enjoying it as much as me, so I continued." Lastly, individuals taking a victim focus regard the offense as primarily benefitting the victim, and are likely to make statements pertaining this experience of pleasure: for example, "I didn't hurt her and was thinking that she enjoyed it as much as I did when it happened to me before."

Understanding the focus taken by the individual in the commission of the offense provides information for specific interventions that can be taken in treatment, such as increasing clients' understanding of the victim's perspective.

Consider the following example:

Case Example: Sam

Sam is a 32-year-old man convicted for three counts of rape that he committed against a stranger. Sam also has a non-sexual criminal history, including assault and theft, arising from his membership in a Maori gang. In examining his offense progression, it became evident that he actively approached offending as a result of his inability to control his emotional states (specifically anger) and that he held hostile attitudes toward women, which were reinforced by other gang members. Prior to the commission of the offense, Sam had experienced several major disappointments, the most notable of which was his inability to return to school, which had been his main goal in life. At Phase 5 in the offense progression, Sam went to a strip club, actively seeking what he called "company" and "companionship." He approached one of the dancers, who immediately rejected him, stating that she did not wish to spend any time with him. Sam became enraged and began watching her, waiting for her to finish her shift. When she left the club, he followed her to the parking lot. He stated that his intentions were to "convince her to go home" with him. She attempted to walk away from him in order to return to the club, whereupon he grabbed her, pulled her to a field in the back of the building, and raped her. Sam stated that he felt both in and out of control—specifically, that he felt he was finally regaining a sense of personal power in his life, at least at that moment, but also that he couldn't stop his attack because he just could not cope with his anger and hatred toward all the women in his life who had rejected him, along with all the other things that had gone wrong. Although he acknowledged that he had injured the victim considerably, he felt that, as a stripper, she was likely "accustomed to rough sex" and that she probably enjoyed some of it as well.

In this example, Sam actively held offense-supportive approach goals, which were activated at Phase 4 of the offense progression. Although he may not have intended to offend when he initially set out, upon being rejected, offense-supportive schemas were activated, and he actively selected strategies to achieve the offense-related approach goal at Phase 5. His planning was more explicit with respect to setting up the opportunity to offend and achieve goals (Phase 6), which appear to include sexual offending, attainment of sexual gratification, reduction of negative emotional arousal through the use of sexual aggression, and the regaining of a sense of control and personal agency. Sam predominantly indicated a self-focus during the commission of the offense, although his attitude suggests he had a potential mutual focus, as well. In addition, the offense pathway contains elements of both an approach-automatic pathway (as evidenced by the situational activation of cognitive scripts and schemas) and an approach-explicit pathway (as indicated by some elements of planning). Additional information on other phases of the offense progression is needed in order to definitively establish the offense pathway. Lastly, primary goods, dynamic risk factors, and preconditions to offending (Phase 1) include agency, inner peace, knowledge, mastery, happiness, community, general and sexual self-regulation, attitudes, intimacy deficits, association with criminal peers, and use of sex as a strategy to cope with negative mood states, although the presence of this last strategy needs to be confirmed. These factors all appear to result from Sam's problematic developmental and background history, prior relationship history, and association with criminal gang members.

Post-Offense Evaluation and Adjustment of Good Lives Plan (Phase 9)

Some models of the offense progression have placed insufficient focus on events that occur after offending and on the individual's responses to the offense after its commission. The original SRM included two post-offense phases that have been expanded in the integrated GLM/SRM-R.

At this phase of the offense progression, the individual evaluates his behavior and goal attainment, assessing the immediate outcome(s) of offending, attributing responsibility for offending, and determining the "role" played by the victim in offending. The individual also evaluates his cognition and emotion associated with offending. Individuals following avoidant pathways are expected to experience predominantly negative emotions and will describe shame and guilt associated with committing the offense. Individuals following the avoidant-passive pathway specifically are likely to experience shame and a sense of personal failure, while individuals following the avoidant-active pathway are more likely to experience a sense of guilt and to regard themselves as being "weak." Offenders following approach pathways are expected to experience predominantly positive affect and are likely to evaluate the offense in terms of success in achieving offense-related goals. Lastly, all individuals may experience a sense of success or positive affect if the offense resulted in their attainment of a good lives goal. That is, while they may experience negative affect and guilt or shame at having committed a sexual offense, they may also report experiencing a gratification and a sense of success because a goal such as intimacy (the primary good of relatedness) was also obtained via offending.

Let's continue with the example of Ron:

Case Example: Ron

Thirty-six-year-old Ron was convicted for sexual offenses against his daughter, reporting during Phase 2 of the offense progression that his wife's illness was the life event that initiated the offense. During her illness, his daughter took on many of her mother's tasks, and he started to think about his daughter in a sexual way. Despite his attempts to avoid acting on these thoughts, he ultimately failed.

Following the offense, Ron felt extremely guilty and ashamed about his behavior. He reported that he knew it was wrong and believed that he was a "monster" and that there must be something seriously wrong with him to have offended against his daughter. Upon further examination in treatment, however, Ron admitted that he also felt a sense of gratification. Specifically, he stated, "Though I felt horrible, I also felt really satisfied. Part of it was that I hadn't had sex for so long and masturbating just didn't do it for me anymore. I know that sounds really twisted, but if I'm being honest, that was how I felt—satisfied and loved. I just wanted my wife to love me again. I sometimes think that part of me might have been getting back at her for not being there for me."

In this example, Ron, following an avoidant-active pathway, felt guilty following the commission of the offense. However, he also indicated that, through offending, the primary goods of happiness (sexual pleasure), relatedness (intimacy), and agency (regaining some control by punishing his wife), were also obtained.

This example also illustrates an important enhancement of this phase within the revised GLM/SRM-R. In addition to acknowledging primary goods and the possibility that these are attained via offending, even among individuals with offense-avoidant goals, it also illustrates the concept of positive reinforcement for offending. This revised model includes a more explicit focus on reinforcement for behavior (both positive and negative) than previous models (Yates and Ward, 2008). Basic behavioral principles of reinforcement (Pavlov, 1927; Skinner, 1938) and social learning models (e.g., Bandura, 1986) indicate that behavior that is reinforced becomes entrenched in the individual's repertoire over time, and that such reinforcement functions to maintain the behavior and increase the frequency with which it occurs. Such reinforcement includes both positive reinforcement for behavior in the form of rewards or positive consequences associated with behavior (such as sexual or other gratification), as well as negative reinforcement in the form of removal of an aversive stimulus (such as the alleviation of negative emotional states). Thus, it is important to understand the nature of the reinforcement that individuals experience immediately after offending such that, in treatment, these reinforcement contingencies can be altered. The goal of altering these contingencies is to have offending no longer be reinforcing, so the individual becomes able to achieve reinforcement for attaining goals via other, non-offending behaviors. Ultimately, reinforcement for attaining goals and primary goods without offending will also assist the individual in implementing his self-regulation/good life plan.

Lastly, depending on the outcome and perceptions of offending behavior, the individual may adjust his good life plan. Some individuals may conclude that they lack the ability to attain certain goods and, hence, abandon them. Conversely, others may conclude that offending is a successful way to achieve goods and so they may adjust the methods by which they attain them (i.e., via offending rather than via pro-social behavior). Thus, in examining this phase of the offense progression, individuals and their therapists also seek to identify any such changes the individual has undergone as a function of offending.

In summary, in examining this stage of the offense progression exercise, the objectives are to

1. understand clients' cognitive and emotional responses immediately following the commission of the offense;

2. determine clients' attributions of responsibility, such as the "role" they attribute to victims, their understanding of victims' perspectives and experiences, how in control of their behavior they feel, etc.;

3. establish the reinforcement contingencies (for both offense-related and goods acquisition) after the offense, which serve to reinforce and maintain offending behavior;

4. examine any reinforcement contingencies that could serve to extinguish future offending;

5. understand the extent to which clients perceive that they met attained goods via offending, and the influence this is likely to have on reinforcement contingencies;

6. determine any immediate adjustments individuals made to their good lives plans immediately following offending; and

7. understand the degree of responsibility for offending taken by clients and/or denial and minimization of offending, both currently and immediately following the commission of the offense.

Future Intentions and Adjustments to Good Lives Plan (Phase 10)

After evaluating their behavior immediately following an offense, individuals formulate longer term goals and intentions with respect to sexual offending and goal attainment in the future. Their intentions are also influenced by reinforcement for behavior, as well as the type of offense pathway and other general tendencies, such as cognitive schemas, implicit theories, and sexual deviance or interest.

Some individuals may decide to alter their behavior in the future so as to avoid offending, while others may alter their attitudes to be more in favor of future offending. If the individual concludes, based on this evaluation, that offending was a successful and acceptable means to achieve goals, he is likely to be more positive with respect to considering offending in the future. Depending on the offense pathway, he may also integrate the offense experience and devise or refine offense strategies to attain goals in the future via offending. Conversely, if the individual concludes that his behavior was unacceptable, negative, or not reinforcing, he may resolve to resist offending in the future, thus renewing his avoidant goal.

With respect to pathways, individuals following an avoidant pathway may attempt to re-assert control and may resolve not to offend in the future. Without intervention, however, those individuals lack the skills or opportunities to achieve this goal, and so will be likely to offend again. Alternatively, individuals following avoidant pathways may abandon the offense-related avoidance goal and adopt an approach goal with respect to offending, thus over time switching to an approach pathway. Without intervention, individuals following an approach pathway are likely to focus on the reinforcement they received for offending and how offending led them to achieve their goals. In the case of the approach-explicit pathway, those individuals may actively learn from the offense experience and may refine their strategies to ensure continued or better success in future offending.

It is important to note that this assessment and an offender's formulation of future intentions may not necessarily represent explicit decision-making, but may be more automatic in nature. In addition, in establishing longer-term intentions, individuals attend to aspects of the offense, and they process information in a selective manner so as to support decisions and attitudes as well as to minimize cognitive dissonance when it has occurred. Thus, for example, an individual who was unsuccessful in meeting his goal of avoiding offending and who resolves to re-assert control over his behavior, may selectively ignore information about his loss of control and the cognitive deconstruction that occurred during offending, a process that will prevent him from learning how the offending occurred or how to prevent a recurrence. In integrating the offense experience, individuals incorporate the offense experience into existing attitudes and schemas or, alternatively, alter these attitudes or scripts. It is, therefore, important when analyzing the offense progression, to attend to such changes that occur over time as a function of offending.

Lastly, as in Phase 9, individuals may make adjustments to their good lives plans at this phase in the offense progression, although these adjustments represent longer-term or broader changes than those in Phase 9. For example, if the individual has evaluated offending as a reasonable and acceptable means to achieve goods, he may, at this phase, incorporate offending as a means to achieve goals in the future. Other individuals who evaluate the offense experience as an unacceptable means to achieve such goods may simply abandon the good, concluding that they will stop attempting to meet this need. For example:

> *"The first time I offended, I told myself that I would never do that again. It was a terrible experience. The second time, I really wanted sex and lost control. I knew then that I just had to stop thinking about sex if I wasn't going to do this again. The third time I did it, I just gave up. Obviously, there is just something wrong with me, and this is just the way I am."*

As indicated in this brief excerpt, the reinforcement contingencies in Phase 9 of the offense progression changed during the second offense instance, with sexual gratification likely to have reinforced the client's behavior. An avoidant goal is evident early in offending, which is evolving to an approach goal following the commission of the third offense. Thus, it is evident that longer-term goals and intentions with respect to offending have been reformulated over time, in this case to reflect abandonment of the avoidance goal and the adoption of an approach pathway to offending.

Summary

This chapter provides a detailed method of examining the offense progression in a step-by-step fashion that allows for understanding and evaluating of offense pathway and the route that clients followed to offending. This evaluation begins with identifying a life event that initiates the progression, through to post-offense evaluations, information processing, and the formulation of future goals and intentions with respect to offending and goal attainment. This exercise, which may be conducted through an offense disclosure treatment activity, is designed to build on an understanding of clients' predispositions for offending as examined in Phase 1 (see chapter 9) and to assist clients to understand and change the dynamics of their offending behavior. The examination of individuals' own offense progression or progressions includes the GLM and elements incorporated into the SRM-R, and seeks to provide a full understanding of all elements of offending. These elements are then integrated with risk factors and the other processes active in sexual offending, such that a complete understanding of offending is possible, setting the stage for targeted change and skill development in problematic areas.

CHAPTER 11

Self-Regulation Pathway Treatment Methods

Chapter 3, describing the Self-Regulation Model of the offense process, noted that this model has been revised in order to be fully integrated with the Good Lives Model (i.e., the SRM-R; Yates and Ward, 2008). This revision allows for an understanding of the relationship between individuals' good lives plans and sexual offending, which was not included in the original SRM. Such elements as important goods and goals come explicitly into focus in order to identify and understand factors that predispose individuals to commit sexual offenses and that play a role in the progression to offending itself.

Self-regulation is a complex process through which individuals evaluate various situations and establish goals and strategies. Applied to the sexual offense process, these goals and strategies combine to reflect distinct pathways to offending (Ward and Hudson, 1998; Yates and Kingston, 2005; Yates et al., 2009). Because self-regulation varies across these pathways, different treatment approaches and methods are required for each pathway. This chapter outlines methods to apply when considering both how the individual goes about offending and how he seeks to acquire primary goods in his life (Yates and Ward, 2008). Readers may wish to review Ward et al. (2006) for additional information regarding treatment within each offense pathway.

Avoidant-Passive Pathway

Recall that the avoidant-passive pathway is associated with under-regulation. When following this pathway to offending, the individual's goal is to avoid sexual offending—an inhibitory goal associated with anxiety and fear that the undesired outcome (in this case, sexual offending) will occur. Despite this goal, however, the individual does not have the skills needed to prevent offending, and so does not implement any active strategies to achieve this overarching goal. At best, he may simply try to ignore or deny urges and desires as they arise during the offense progression and, therefore, his efforts to avoid offending are passive. When it becomes evident that sexual offending is likely to occur, he experiences disinhibition, a loss of control, and cognitive deconstruction. He then abandons his higher order goal and pursues offending. In following this pathway, such individuals commonly have low self-efficacy expectations about their ability to avoid offending. They will most likely experience negative emotional states associated with offending behavior, lack coping and, possibly, general self-regulation skills, and negatively evaluate the experience after offending.

Generally, by virtue of holding an avoidance goal with respect to offending, individuals following an avoidant-passive pathway will share the therapist's goal to cease sexual offending and prevent re-offending. As such, they are likely to be amenable to treatment designed to assist them to achieve their goals, and are unlikely to be resistant to the idea of change. In treatment generally the first step, therefore, is to establish mutually agreed-upon goals building on this pre-existing motivation. In addition, this goal should be explicitly reinforced by the therapist, as it represents a positive starting point in treatment and allows clients to develop ownership over their treatment plans.

Therapists at this point in the treatment process can use motivational enhancement techniques to assist their clients to prepare for change. For example, in order to begin the process of goal development, a therapist can take care to develop a clear understanding of the difference between a client's current status and where the client would like to be in his life. This process can include eliciting the client's thoughts on what he would like to accomplish with self-regulation (including, for example, coping with disinhibition and loss of control) and how he might better set and maintain goals for himself. These discussions can involve the use of reflective statements and summaries. They might also involve developing an understanding of "old me" and "future me." For example, the therapist might guide the client in the direction of how, in the past, he has lost control of himself easily and how, in the future, he can possess more skills for attaining the good things that life has to offer.

Also essential at this stage is that the therapist be fully supportive of the client's sense of self-efficacy. It can be easy for therapists to offer advice and information that the client will experience as unhelpful. Therapists will likely be more effective by exploring and reflecting back to a client the ways in which he has been successful in his life, including in areas of self-regulation and goal maintenance. In so doing, a client can better apply his own strengths to the challenges he faces. As tempting as it can be for therapists to set goals, clients almost always find the goals they set for themselves to be more desirable than those goals that others set for them.

Motivation and treatment engagement are also likely to be enhanced by identifying the primary goods most important to each client and linking those goods to the treatment plan. It is important that *what* a client was seeking to attain via offending, with respect to goods, is validated and regarded by the therapist as acceptable, even though the means were not.

> *Jacob:* I had been admiring that boy for months. I thought we had a special connection, and I was sure that I could make our connection even better.
>
> *Therapist:* You really value your relationships with others.
>
> *Jacob:* Yeah, even though I knew it wasn't right. I still wanted it.
>
> *Therapist:* So, on one hand, you felt that this was someone you could connect to, but on the other hand, you knew it could get you into serious trouble.
>
> *Jacob:* Absolutely.
>
> *Therapist:* And there are some aspects of connecting with this young boy that seemed right at the time. So what did you do and what happened?
>
> *Jacob:* I don't even know. It's like I went blank. I tried to ignore him, but I couldn't do it. I just gave in to temptation. I figured that if I wanted it that much, he might enjoy it, too. I went outside and talked to him and invited him to play games. I wasn't sure what would happen, but I figured I could give it a try. I thought since he didn't say "No" that he was okay with it. The more we played, the better it seemed, and I guess I stopped worrying about it. I don't even know what I could have done differently.
>
> *Therapist:* You were having a good time.
>
> *Jacob:* Yeah.
>
> *Therapist:* So it's important to you to have ways to enjoy yourself and be connected to others.
>
> *Jacob:* But not like this. All this has ruined my life. I don't know how I'll ever have fun or spend time with others again.
>
> *Therapist:* It's a mystery to you how you might find ways to be independent and able to be connected to others—or even have fun—now that this has happened, and you'll be facing community restrictions.
>
> *Jacob:* Yeah. If you or anyone else has any ideas, I'd welcome them.
>
> *Therapist:* You're looking for ways to have a good life—one that doesn't involve offending—and you're not sure how to get there. And sometimes, it seems like you have a goal, but you lose sight of it in the situation. You don't want to offend, but

> in the moment, you forget this and don't really do anything to make sure you keep this goal in mind.
>
> **Jacob:** That's exactly it! I don't want to do it, and I try to just ignore the situation, but that doesn't seem to work. It seems to be that way with me all the time, whenever I have a problem. I want to do something, but I just don't know what to do other than to ignore the situation and hope it gets better.
>
> **Therapist:** That's really tough. But if I also heard you correctly, you're willing to try new ideas.
>
> **Jacob:** Yes, absolutely!
>
> **Therapist:** Can I make a suggestion?
>
> **Jacob:** Yes.
>
> **Therapist:** How about if, between now and next week, you keep track of all the times you feel stressed out, lonely, or anxious. Then, write down how you coped with those times. You can pay special attention to whether you coped by trying to avoid the situation or the feelings you had, by reacting to the emotions you experienced but not doing anything about the situation itself, or by doing something directly about the situation.
>
> **Jacob:** I'll give it a try. Maybe I can learn something about what I can do when I start feeling bad.
>
> **Therapist:** That's the idea. And when you're done, bring the list to the treatment group next week and see what the others have to say. Many of them will have been through similar experiences and have some good ideas.
>
> **Jacob:** Okay.

Treatment for offenders following the avoidant-passive pathway typically begins with raising awareness of the entirety of the offense progression (from its inception to post-offending), those goods an individual was seeking to acquire through offending, and the absence of strategies to achieve his goal to prevent offending. In terms of primary goods, an individual following the avoidant-passive pathway lacks knowledge about the offense progression and its precursors, and does not know what effective actions he can take to prevent offending. It is also necessary to raise awareness about the fact that he loses control and abandons the offense-avoidance goal when faced with offending, and that he seeks to obtain primary goods through the offense progression. He needs to come to understand how not taking action throughout the offense progression leads to both offending and to not meeting his goal (i.e., avoiding offending), as well as to possibly preventing him from attaining primary goods in the future.

Once his awareness is raised, treatment addresses the development of the necessary skills to prevent future offending, to manage risk, to develop more effective self-regulation in life generally, to obtain goods, and to effectively implement his good life plan. Awareness of vulnerability factors that place a client at risk to offend may also require attention.

The client's skills to prevent offending need to be developed and rehearsed in key problem areas. Also, the client needs to develop skills to manage his individual risk factors. Specifically, he must develop the ability to cope with the desire to offend and/or to obtain primary goods by offending, along with the ability to manage the loss of control that occurs when offense-related desires or a desire to attain goods via offending emerges. He must also learn to retain his higher level avoidance goal and focus on achieving positive goals in life, so that he does not abandon his efforts to avoid offending when faced with the possibility to offend. Understanding how offending can interfere with attaining life goals and is not consistent with his own goals (i.e., creating cognitive dissonance) can help to implement his good life plan. Specific skills pertaining to meta-cognition, self-monitoring, cognitive restructuring, managing negative emotional states, and impulse control—targeted to specific risk factors—will also be needed. In addition, the client will need to develop risk management strategies to avoid or escape high-risk situations, particularly while he is learning skills and until these skills become well entrenched through rehearsal and practice.

With regard to more general functioning, it helps to know the origin of self-regulation deficits and whether they represent a client's usual ways of dealing with events, stressors, and problems that arise in his life. For example, if self-regulation problems result from a sense of inadequacy, helplessness, or powerlessness, treatment should focus on what the client can do in his life to gain a sense of agency and autonomy and to help him gain self-confidence and self-efficacy. Thus, one goal of treatment with individuals following this pathway may be to increase self-regulation in multiple areas of their lives beyond offending behavior. This method should also aid in managing risk factors. For example, the self-regulation strategies learned to address risk areas such as problems with sexual self-regulation, impulsivity, or problem-solving can also become self-management strategies to address problems in life more generally. Lastly, this method also involves enhancing clients' ability to cope more generally in life when they are unable to attain goods and meet goals.

Self-regulation and implementation of the good lives plan can also be enhanced by reinforcing positive approach goals and developing clients' capacity to attain valued goods. Thus, it is essential that both the therapist and each client be able to distinguish between an individual's goals and the means he uses to attain them. That is, the primary goods that are important to a client and that he seeks to attain should be reinforced. It must constantly be recognized, both internally and in discussions between the therapist and the client, that it is the *means* that are problematic and not the *goals*. For example, if a client has offended against a child because the client was seeking intimacy or hoping to increase his sense of self-worth, the therapist must validate these goals as acceptable and common to people in general. Treatment, therefore, needs to focus on alternative methods to gain intimacy, the building of existing skills, and the imparting of new skills in order for clients to develop appropriate relationships. It is also essential to create opportunities to attain goods, both by rehearsal and reinforcement of skills and progress and by developing external opportunities to attain valued goods. These skills also address risk factors, although when done effectively, an appropriate good life plan should eventually decrease the need for specific coping skills to manage risk factors.

Case Example: Don

Let's return to Don, mentioned in chapter 5. Recall that Don is a young man of 21 years. He entered a new treatment program following re-offense after involvement in a previous treatment program. At age 15, he used bribes to persuade his sister to agree to engage in sexual intercourse. He was sent to a residential program, where he only partially engaged in treatment. Don's therapists were concerned that he had difficulty acknowledging his role in his abusive actions. Don turned 18 years old before completing this program and has lived with his mother ever since. Don now spends much of his time at home. He has few friends and drinks six to eight bottles of beer per day. When he feels stressed, he tends not to do anything about it except to wait until it passes.

Don's current offense involved a visit by his sister. Don began to experience sexual arousal toward her during her visit. At first, he tried to ignore it, but the more he tried not to think about it, the more it was at the front of his mind. He told himself that if she actively said "No," he would stop. As his impulsive attempts to initiate sex progressed, however, he became increasingly aroused and could not cope with the fact that his sister did not want to comply. She became clearly distressed, but by this point Don was focused only on doing what he wanted. In recounting this offense, Don expressed confusion and self-hatred. He attributes his behavior to the fact that he was bored and "probably spent too much time around pornography."

Throughout his assessment and the earliest phases of treatment, Don expressed guilt and shame regarding his actions. A risk assessment found that his actuarial risk was relatively low due to the absence of static risk factors. For example, the victim of his offense was related to him, and he has no violent or non-contact offenses. He is young, however, and has not lived in a stable relationship. Dynamic risk indicators include intimacy deficits and deficits in both sexual and general self-regulation. Alcohol abuse is also problematic (although it is noted that chronic alcohol use is not a risk factor in and of itself).

Primary goods implicated in Don's offenses include happiness/pleasure, inner peace, and relatedness. His good life plan is severely limited due to a lack of scope (in that Don does not include many primary goods in his plan and seems to have little idea how to attain other goods). His plan is also limited by a lack of means, for example, by staying home, drinking, and hoping that his urges would go away. So there is little likelihood that he can make meaningful progress in any good life plan. Finally, his attempts to find pleasure and relatedness are in conflict when they involve his sister.

Treatment will focus on raising Don's awareness of primary goods and how he has sought to attain these goods throughout his life and in his offenses. He can use the personal history exercise to this end (chapter 9), and also can explore the factors that contributed to offending at each phase of the offense progression (chapter 10). Don and his therapist will also wish to explore his thought patterns, attitudes, and schemas and assess how those factors have contributed to his daily functioning and to his offenses. Treatment can further focus on acquiring and rehearsing cognitive and behavioral skills to respond to situations that produce negative affect. Don's therapist will continue to provide ongoing support for his goal of preventing re-offending, and will emphasize the development of skills to achieve this goal so that Don does not abandon his offense-related avoidance goal for an approach goal when stressed. However, it is important to note that treatment should go beyond teaching Don how to manage his urges. It should also focus on developing a plan for a more satisfying and fulfilling life. This approach includes teaching Don to become more reflective on his life and his abilities to function successfully using effective self-regulation skills and strategies.

Avoidant-Active Pathway

Recall that the avoidant-active pathway is associated with mis-regulation. When following this pathway to offending, the individual's goal is to avoid sexual offending—an inhibitory goal associated with anxiety and fear that the undesired outcome (in this case, sexual offending) will occur. Individuals who follow this pathway actively implement strategies to avoid offending, with the expectation that the strategies will be effective. As such, they are able to plan, monitor, and evaluate their own behavior, and may generally have adequate self-regulation skills or at least will have these skills, in certain situations. The strategies they use, however, will be ineffective in preventing offending. In fact, paradoxically, these attempted strategies may actually increase their risk to offend. For example, an individual who uses alcohol to cope with negative emotional states associated with the desire to offend may increase his risk via alcohol's disinhibiting effects. Similarly, an offender who masturbates to deviant sexual fantasies as an alternative to acting on these fantasies may actually increase his risk to offend through pairing deviant arousal with sexual gratification and receiving reinforcement in the process. In terms of primary goods, these individuals lack knowledge of the required skills and strategies to prevent offending. When it becomes evident that sexual offending is likely to occur, individuals following this pathway often experience anxiety, disinhibition, a loss of control, cognitive dissonance, and cognitive deconstruction. At this point, they abandon the avoidance goal and pursue gratification through offending. In following this pathway, these individuals initially experience high self-efficacy expectations about their ability to avoid offending, although this decreases when they become aware that they are unable to avoid offending. The pathway generally is associated with negative emotional states connected to offending behavior, and a negative self-evaluation after offending.

As with offenders following the avoidant-passive pathway, treatment for offenders following the avoidant-active pathway typically starts with raising awareness of the offense progression from its inception to post-offending. For individuals following the avoidant-active pathway, however, treatment focuses specifically on raising awareness that the strategies they use in their attempts to avoid offending (Phase 4 of the offense progression) are ineffective. Thus, the therapist at this stage needs to guide clients to understand how their attempts to avoid offending have been ineffective in the past, and to help clients to understand the reasons why these strategies have not been effective in achieving this goal (i.e., mis-regulation). This raising of awareness also focuses on how, when faced with the possibility of offending, ineffective strategies result in negative emotional states. Those states include anxiety, which comes with an offender's awareness that he is about to fail in achieving the avoidance goal, loss of control, and reduced self-efficacy in the face of offending. Raising awareness will help clients to understand how they have abandoned their avoidance goals and adopted approach goals, albeit temporarily, with respect to offending. If the offender's strategies also serve to increase risk, therapy needs to addresses the client's awareness of that increase and its accompanying risk. As such, treatment needs to focus on reinforcing existing strategies that *are* effective, including ones based on situations during which clients have been successful in avoiding offending. Treatment also needs to help clients build and rehearse new skills that will be effective, as well as helping to extinguish ineffective strategies.

As with all clients, regardless of the offense pathway they have followed, treatment raises awareness of the primary goods the clients were seeking to attain through offending. Unlike the avoidant-passive pathway, however, the focus with clients following an avoidant-active pathway is predominantly to show them that ineffective strategies to offending not only prevent them from achieving their positive goals and implementing their good lives plans, but also can lead to a return to offending.

Once clients learn to recognize their patterns of implementing ineffective strategies, treatment needs to address the development of any necessary skills and strategies to avoid offending in the future, to manage risk, to develop more effective self-regulation in life generally, and to obtain goods and implement their good lives plans effectively.

Preventing offending involves developing and rehearsing skills in key problem areas and developing strategies to manage specific risk factors. In particular, clients must develop the ability to cope with the desire to offend and to manage the loss of control that occurs when offense-related desires or the desire to attain primary goods via offending emerges. In addition, they must develop strategies to retain their higher level avoidance goals and keep their focus on achieving positive goals in life so that they do not abandon their efforts to prevent offending. Clients also benefit by understanding how offending can interfere with attaining life goals, how it is not consistent with their goals (i.e., it creates cognitive dissonance), and how it can impede implementing their good lives plans.

As evidenced by their ability to detect when offending is possible and to implement strategies in an attempt to prevent offending, clients following the avoidant-active pathway already possesses some capabilities, but specific additional skills—such as self-monitoring—may be required. Thus, the therapist must explicitly reinforce any existing capacity for individuals following the avoidant-active pathway, yet at the same time the therapist needs to help the client develop strategies that will be more effective in preventing offending. Clients will also need to strengthen such skills as cognitive restructuring, impulse control, and the effective management of negative emotional states. They will additionally need to develop risk management strategies to avoid or escape situations that present a risk for offending, particularly while they are initially learning and reinforcing these skills through rehearsal and practice. Such self-monitoring builds on each client's existing self-regulation capacity to observe and understand when he is at risk to offend.

With regard to more general functioning, it may be helpful to know the origin of each client's mis-regulation tendencies and whether these inclinations reflect how he commonly deals with various events and problems that arise in his life. For example, does the client experience difficulty with problem-solving skills more generally in life? Does he typically lose control in the face of problems, stressors, or life circumstances that he is unable to manage effectively? If so, such factors can point to more general problems with self-regulation, which will need to be addressed in treatment by increasing self-regulation skills in multiple areas of his life beyond his offending behavior.

With the avoidant-active pathway, self-regulation and implementation of the good lives plan can also be enhanced by reinforcing positive approach goals and developing a client's capacity to attain valued goods. It is essential that both therapist and client are able to distinguish between the individual's goals and the means he uses to attain these. The therapist must be able to reinforce the client's valued goods and goals in life, in addition to his existing strengths. Treatment should focus on alternative methods to achieve goals and, particularly with the avoidant-active pathway, build on existing skills to intervene when problems arise. It is also essential to create opportunities to attain goods, both by rehearsing and reinforcing skills and progress and by developing external opportunities to attain valued goods. These skills also address risk factors, although implementing a good lives plan that is fulfilling should ultimately decrease the need for specific coping skills to manage risk factors.

Case Example: Ken

Recall Ken from chapter 5. Deeply religious, he spent much of his life attempting to convince himself that he had no sexual interest in males. He briefly married a woman at the age of 21 and became active in his church. Ken knew he was in a position of authority and so, when he felt attracted to boys, immediately reminded himself of the importance of his role and immersed himself further in church activities. Nonetheless, he offended against a 14-year-old boy in the church choir.

In his treatment program, Ken blamed his offense on a lack of religious observance. Within weeks of his reintegration into the community, his family made it clear they wanted only minimal contact with him. His peers at church seemed distant, and he grew increasingly lonely. He found himself attracted to young men in the area around the church and felt that he had no one with whom he could talk openly. Ken became attracted to a young man, molested him, and sank into self-loathing upon detection.

Ken's actuarial risk is in the moderate range. He has a prior offense and unrelated male victims. He has not lived with a partner in a long-term relationship, although he was married briefly. Dynamic risk factors include a lack of emotionally intimate relationships, emotional congruence with those who are significantly younger than he is, and deficits in sexual self-regulation, including possibly deviant sexual preference. These dynamic risk factors elevate his assessed level of risk. In addition, his attempts to avoid offending are ineffective and likely make matters worse.

Primary goods implicated in Ken's offending include spirituality, relatedness, and inner peace. His good life plan, in which these primary goods play a central role, has been flawed by a limited scope, as well as by his problems with the means he uses to attain goods. There also are many primary goods he has not sought to attain (e.g., knowledge with respect to self-regulation and the creativity required to improve his life and to prevent re-offending). Furthermore, he has lacked the means to attain the primary goods in his life in ways that do not involve sexual abuse. It will be worthwhile to explore in treatment how his goals related to spirituality have created a conflict with the other goals in his life. Ken relies on spirituality to solve problems in his life rather than a more balanced good life plan.

Treatment with Ken will focus on examining the factors that have made him vulnerable to offending. The therapist will work with him to explore his historical attempts to attain primary goods, and will help him to develop an understanding of the flaws within his good life plan. As in Don's case earlier, the therapist will also actively support Ken's goal to not re-offend. Ken and his therapist will explore the strategies Ken has selected to avoid offending in the past and assess specifically how these strategies represent misregulation. Although Ken has skills that enable him to regulate and manage many areas of his life, treatment will focus particularly on how he can acquire and rehearse new skills for preventing re-offending specific to his sexual behavior. In examining the later phases of his offenses, Ken will also explore his historical responses to offending (e.g., believing that he simply needs to become more devout in his faith). Throughout treatment, the therapist will ensure that Ken is working to develop a more balanced good life plan so that many of his efforts at avoiding re-offending are themselves instrumental to attaining primary goods. For example, Ken may wish to attain the primary goods of knowledge and life in ways that ensure new forms of relatedness to others (e.g., going back to school or joining adult-oriented clubs or organizations in the community).

APPROACH-AUTOMATIC PATHWAY

Recall from chapter 3 that the approach-automatic pathway is an under-regulated or disinhibition pathway that involves a desirable offense-related goal. That is, when following this pathway, individuals hold an approach goal with respect to offending and attaining primary goods via offending. Their attitudes may also explicitly support offensive behavior, and they may offend impulsively. This pathway is further characterized by failure to control behavior as well as by relatively rapid and automatic responses to situational cues in the environment, which are based on well-entrenched cognitive scripts that support and facilitate sexual offending. Common cognitive scripts may include a sense of sexual entitlement, hostile or stereotyped attitudes (e.g., toward women), general hostility or suspicion, or beliefs that sexual activity with children is acceptable.

When following this pathway, these individuals do not attempt to avoid offending, but rather act to meet their needs in a specific situation in an impulsive or unregulated manner. Any planning on the individual's part is relatively rudimentary and unsophisticated. These individuals are likely unaware of the situational cues that trigger offending or their responses to these cues. Individuals following this pathway may experience either positive or negative emotional states during the offense progression, depending upon the individual and the circumstances. However, positive affective states indicate progress in achieving goals and, thus, motivate the individual to move forward in the offense progression. His post-offense evaluation is typically positive, as the approach goal has been achieved.

Treatment of an individual who follows the approach-automatic pathway begins with raising awareness of the cognitive scripts and implicit theories he holds, as well as examining how these elements tend to generalize to his life overall and to his offending behavior specifically. The focus includes fostering awareness that the individual holds an approach goal with respect to offending. Raising awareness of the offense progression is especially essential, given that offending unfolds relatively automatically based on cognitive scripts and responses to cues of which the individual may be unaware. He may indicate that offending "just happened," which may be his perception, particularly if he tends to be impulsive in setting goals and making decisions during offending or in life generally. The offense progression exercises described in chapters 9 and 10 will help clients following this pathway to understand the steps, decisions, and planning they use during offending, how they use these automatically—responding to cues in the situation and their environment—and what the source of cognitive schemas is that direct their behavior.

In raising awareness of offense-supportive schemas and implicit theories, it is important that clients understand the origin and content of these scripts. For example, based on each client's background and vulnerability factors, does he view the world as a dangerous place and, thus, feel a need for retribution in life? Is this view associated with an over-reliance on the primary good of agency or problems with the means he uses or his capacity to attain agency or inner peace? The aim in exploring this area is to help each client understand his cognitive schemas and how those belief systems influence his interpretation of life events, his offending and the implementation of his good life plan. It is likely that these schemas influence the client's functioning in multiple areas of his life, such as his relationships or his work.

Once awareness has been raised, treatment for clients following the approach-automatic pathway involves altering their cognitive schemas, often through the use of schema therapy (Young, 1999). Because these schemas are likely longstanding and entrenched, treatment may require significant time to alter them, and the therapist must be careful to reinforce progress in the change process. Because the issues that form the foundation of these scripts (especially those coming from early in a client's development) are substantial, it is important to recognize that it may be difficult for a client to let them go, as they likely form a significant part of the client's personal identity. Furthermore, these responses will be difficult to change because a client's behavioral responses are well-entrenched and because, due to those responses, the client may have a history of successfully meeting his goals and attaining primary goods, which, in turn, reinforces the client's schemas.

> *Aidan:* You know, I just don't worry all that much about these things. If other people don't like the way I behave, they can tell me. They don't have to go to the police. And if they still don't like things, well then that's on them. I'm just living my life.
> *Therapist:* You really just want to be free to live your life as you please.
> *Aidan:* Now you're getting it!
> *Therapist:* And the real problem is that the law won't give you a break. And they send you here.
> *Aidan:* Well, I'm mostly here because they sent me here.
> *Therapist:* So most of you is here because it's hard to see any choice in the matter, and some of you—a little part—is here for other reasons.
> *Aidan:* Well, actually I figure I can always learn something, and if it keeps me out of trouble, then why not come here.
> *Therapist:* Let me see if I have this right. You really want to be free to live your life the way you see fit, and at the same time there's a part of you that wants to stay out of trouble.
> *Aidan:* Yeah.
> *Therapist:* And then there's the expectation for you to be in treatment. You're not here because of your free will; you're here because you want to get your freedom back.

Aidan: Yeah.

Therapist: In your world, it's you fighting for freedom. It's not about working with others to find out—for yourself—how to build the freedom that's available to you.

Aidan: There are a lot of things you don't know about my world.

Therapist: You need to work with people who can understand your world before you can consider changing it. That makes a lot of sense. Given everything else you've got going on—your happiness, your pleasure, your freedom, your autonomy, your life—what do you think you might do about being in this treatment program?

Aidan: I can give it a shot. It can't hurt to try.

Therapist: You want to get something for your effort. You might be able to look at the world differently.

Aidan: I'm willing to try.

Therapist: You said there were things I didn't know about your world. Tell me a little about that. What's it like in your world?

Aidan: Where I've lived, you have to fight back or people will walk all over you. In fact, there are many more people who are out there breaking the law than there are who get caught. That's pretty crazy. So I've never had the luxury of waiting for things to be fair. I've had to fight back at every turn.

Therapist: It sounds like that's worked well for you a lot of the time.

Aidan: That's right.

Therapist: And what other people call impulsive may actually be about you trying to maintain some independence, some autonomy, some control over your situation.

Aidan: I never really thought of it that way, but that's true. The world is a dangerous place, and unless I'm prepared to get what's coming to me or stand up and fight for myself, there's no telling what would happen.

Therapist: So you actually have a set of skills that have helped you out and that maybe kept you alive when you were growing up. How are things different for you now?

Aidan: Well, I'm here, aren't I? I think it's safe to say that some of the things I do don't work out all the time.

Therapist: So you have one way of understanding and responding to the world, but it doesn't work when you're in other parts of the world.

Aidan: Yeah.

Therapist: It's like you grew up with one set of beliefs and attitudes—a whole way of thinking—and yet it doesn't work elsewhere. In fact, it <u>more</u> than doesn't work; it landed you here.

Aidan: Yes. Do you think there's something I can do about that? I want to be able to go places in my hometown where it isn't like entering a whole new country with different customs and laws and things.

Therapist: I think we can help with that. I've seen a lot of people explore their beliefs and thought patterns very successfully. But, you are the final expert on yourself, so we would need to know more about how this all works for you. I've got complete confidence, however, that when you are ready to really look at your life and the world differently, nothing will be able to stop you. One of the things that happens with all people when they have a set of beliefs about the world is that their beliefs influence how they receive the information that comes at them from outside. Our minds have to work this way because there is just too much information out there for us to understand all at once. Think about all the activity in the world. Without a way to make sense of it, it would be chaos in our minds. But, there are side effects to this response mechanism of ours. When we believe certain things about the world and ourselves and others, we tend to pay attention to information that is consistent with these ways of thinking, and we ignore information that isn't consistent. Does this make sense? Can you think of a time when you did this, and recall what happened?

Aidan: That makes perfect sense. I never thought about it that way. I do remember this one time when my brother borrowed my car without asking me. I was really pissed off because he should have known I had somewhere to go. He's always doing stuff like that—he just doesn't think! We got into a big fight when he got back. But what I didn't know was that my mother had told him that I wasn't working that day—she didn't know I had picked up an extra shift—and she had told him that I wouldn't mind. Plus, he had to go to meet with his probation officer or else he would get in trouble, which I also didn't know. I guess you could say I assumed he was just being his usual self, but I was wrong. Is that the kind of thing you mean? That maybe it was my mind that thought he was stupid, so I just made assumptions that weren't even true, and I didn't think of what other reasons there could be for him taking my car?

Therapist: Yes, it is. That's a very good example. And it sounds like you understand the idea and that you are able, when you try, to think about things differently. And I'm also hearing you say that you think it's really time to do something and to maybe start to look at the world a little differently. Is that right?

Aidan: Well, I guess I have to, but yes, I think it is time.

Therapist:. Great. Can I make a suggestion, then?

Aidan: Sure.

Therapist: How about if you keep a journal of the things you do for the next week.

> *Each day, take two things that really capture your attention. Write down what those are, and then write down what went through your mind. It doesn't have to be good or bad; just write down what went through your mind. Next, write down how you felt about the situation, and then write down what you did in response. Then—here's the harder part—think about other things that might be going on in the situation. It doesn't matter if they're true or not. Just write down all the ideas you can come up with—just brainstorm. This is like an exercise for the mind, like when you do physical exercise, and it helps the mind to expand itself. Since you want to look at things differently, I think this might help. Then you can talk about these things in group, and the other guys might have ideas on how you can look at things differently, and how you can respond differently. How does that sound?*
>
> **Aidan:** *Like I said before, I'm willing to give it a try. I have to do something about this "might makes right" attitude of mine.*

In order to manage risk and successfully implement clients' good lives plans, treatment will also focus on increasing meta-cognitive control so clients can become aware of when they are at risk to have cognitive schemas activated, and then can direct their reactions and responses better. This increased awareness will allow them to become more alert to their risk levels and their reliance on entrenched scripts. Because treatment aims to change these cognitive scripts, it will also help clients to understand when they are reverting to previous schemas and, in turn, to respond to situational cues and life events based on newly developed scripts that involve better self-regulation and pro-social goals. Building an increased self-awareness will likely require considerable effort and practice on the client's part, as well as some patience on the part of both the therapist and the client. Therefore, it will be important for the client to focus on his goals in life and to recognize how offending can interfere with achieving those goals and implementing his good life plan. The process needs to involve the resolution of the conflict between primary goods and the means used to attain them. It will also be necessary for clients to develop specific skills to manage under-regulation and impulsivity.

Lastly, clients who follow an approach-automatic pathway will need help in developing an avoidance goal with respect to offending. It is essential, however, that treatment not rely on this goal exclusively, given the difficulties associated with maintaining avoidance goals, as described previously. Thus, clients will need to develop and rehearse specific strategies for attaining primary goods and meeting positive approach goals—such as acquiring a sense of agency and autonomy—without needing to achieve retribution against others.

Case Example: Jay

Recall Jay, from chapter 5, who grew up in a home where his father dealt drugs and abused his mother. Jay developed few emotional ties to others and came to view the world as a place where one has to have fun when opportunities arise. He viewed authorities as hostile, controlling, and unpredictable. Jay eventually landed in a juvenile detention center where he forced sex onto younger teens during staff shift changes and while the overnight staff slept. Jay did not overtly plan his assaults during these times. Instead, he indicated that something "just came over" him; he saw opportunities when they presented themselves. Jay was regarded as a "tough guy" and the others looked up to him, which made him feel superior and worthwhile. His attitude toward these assaults was that the behavior itself was pleasurable and worth the risks.

Jay also held a general belief that women could not be trusted to tell the truth, particularly in sexual matters, and that, because he thought that the woman against whom he had offended had flirted with him, it made little difference to him that he had assaulted her, because, in his view, "she owed him." He had actually not had any particular plans to assault anyone the evening described in chapter 5. Jay viewed his actions of the evening favorably, as they involved sex and alcohol. To others, however, Jay's assault seemed to come from "out of the blue."

Jay's behavior in prison was frustrating to others, as he seemed unperturbed by his actions, attempted to flirt indelicately with staff members, and became involved in illicit sexual activities, among other rule violations.

Jay's actuarial risk level is in the moderate range. He has prior offenses. His unrelated victims include some strangers. He has not lived in a stable relationship. Dynamic risk factors include antisocial attitudes and beliefs, impulsivity and other self-regulation deficits. Jay possesses schemas related to the world being a dangerous place where "might makes right," and women are adversarial and unknowable.

Jay's good life plan has focused on pleasure and autonomy/agency. He has wanted to function autonomously and act as he wishes. These primary goods are implicated in his offending behavior. His plan lacks scope in that he has undervalued primary goods such as relatedness, knowledge, and spirituality and has over-valued pleasure and agency. His attempts to gain pleasure, however, have frequently resulted in a significant loss of autonomy (e.g., because it lands him in prison), thus representing a conflict between these two goods. Furthermore, his impulsivity appears related to problems with his capacity to attain the good of agency. Although impulsivity enables him to function autonomously, it also leads to others depriving him of his liberty.

Jay's treatment will focus on raising awareness of the conflict between autonomy and pleasure, and will also explore the role of other primary goods in his life. The therapist will need to ensure that Jay recognizes that offending does not help him to achieve his goals in life. By appealing to Jay's self-interest, the therapist gains a better chance that treatment will have value for Jay. Treatment will also focus on Jay's longstanding responses to the world and the people within it (i.e., his schemas). Highlighting the discrepancy between Jay's attitudes and beliefs versus alternative means of understanding his life and surroundings will be important in the first stages of Jay's treatment. This comparison will likely require the use of considerable open-ended questions and reflection, rather than education (which risks building resistance). Jay will also benefit from exploring other ways to attain agency and pleasure. Much of this work will involve the therapist highlighting the differences between Jay's current and future desired states. Jay will require considerable motivational enhancement, as he currently sees few reasons to stop offending. As a result, the therapist will wish to validate Jay's desire to attain primary goods while exploring with him how many of his attempts have not produced desirable, long-term results. This approach differs from treatment in the avoidance pathways, where the therapist validates the client's goal of preventing re-offense. In addition, an avoidance goal will need to be developed for clients like Jay.

Approach-Explicit Pathway

Recall from chapter 3 that the approach-explicit pathway is an acquisitional or appetitive pathway characterized by a goal that explicitly supports offending and intact self-regulation. Individuals following this pathway consciously and explicitly plan their offenses and implement well-developed strategies to achieve anti-social goals. They hold values and attitudes that explicitly support sexual offending, and they act on the basis of these well-entrenched beliefs and cognitive schemas. Following this pathway often creates a direct route between some of the primary goods offenders value and their offending behavior. For example, these individuals may actively and directly seek the good of relatedness (e.g., in the form of sexual pleasure) through sex with a child, or the good of agency through sexual domination or other abuse, goals, and activities that they believe are legitimate and acceptable.

Individuals following this pathway do not desire or attempt to prevent sexual offending and do not offend as a result of problems with self-regulation or a lack of coping or self-regulation skills. Rather, they explicitly plan their offenses using effective strategies to achieve their goals. Although they may have some deficits in functioning or skills, such as establishing intimate or other relationships, these deficits do not represent the primary dynamic in sexual offending. Rather, offense goals are associated with core beliefs—such as sexual entitlement or the view that sexual aggression is acceptable—which support sexual offending and which are the predominant motivation for offending. Cognitive distortions may or may not be evident in these clients' verbalizations—distortions and justifications may simply be unnecessary to excuse offending behavior because these clients simply believe that their behavior is acceptable and, as such, does not require justification. These offenders tend to experience positive emotional states during offending, and the post-offense evaluation is typically positive because they have achieved their goal.

The focus of treatment for offenders following the approach-explicit pathway includes understanding and changing core beliefs and schemas both in general and in relation to offending. Goals associated with offending behavior must be specifically changed to avoidance goals. This alteration requires understanding exactly what goods the individual seeks via sexual offending as well as how offending benefits him. The therapist also needs to determine what capabilities, resources, and opportunities such offenders will need in order to attain valued goods and goals in socially acceptable ways such that others are not harmed. Because treatment involves changing well-established beliefs and schemas, it is essential to have a therapeutic atmosphere that is conducive to disclosing intentional harmful behavior, as well as its origin in the individual's development. The latter will likely present greater difficulty than the former, as individuals following this pathway are likely to be fully disclosive of all factual information as they do not need self-protective mechanisms (Ward et al., 2004). Thus, these clients need to be encouraged, through motivational enhancement techniques, to disclose offensive core beliefs, attitudes, and sexually deviant cognition, schemas, and behavior, disclosures that are likely to be more difficult than simply confessing facts about offending. These clients are unlikely to regard their behavior as problematic, and so may benefit from motivational techniques for individuals at the pre-contemplative stage of change (DiClemente, 1991; Prochaska and DiClemente, 1982). They are also likely to benefit from intervention that encourages them to work toward their goals and to act in their own interests (although obviously through pro-social means). This intervention can be facilitated by focusing on the primary goods that are most important to them and that appear to be associated with, and that may direct, offending. The process may be a particularly difficult task for the therapist, as the primary goods and goals must be validated and reinforced throughout. Thus, the therapist will need to ensure that he or she is able to focus on the problematic means by which these clients meet these goals.

Palmer: I can fantasize about kids just sitting here in a room. I did it all the time in my treatment groups before. I would look at the sun coming in the window and just imagine what it would look like on their soft skin.

Therapist: So when things like that are going on, it's easy to find happiness and pleasure in a sexual fantasy.

Palmer: Yes. And almost no one would ever know, except for the other guys who feel the same way.

Therapist: Sometimes the only people who understand you are the other clients in the program.

Palmer: Yeah.

Therapist: In fact, your sexuality is amazing. You can think about happiness and pleasure in circumstances that make others miserable. When you get challenged, you have an entire world to which you can retreat.

Palmer: Well, I'm not so sure that's a good thing. It keeps getting me into trouble. I failed two programs before this. It seems like this is who I am; I was born to it.

Therapist: As strong and pleasurable as your attraction is to young people, you still have a concern that there are other areas of your life that are not reaching their full destiny.

Palmer: I'm not getting out of here any faster.

Therapist: So some days your sexuality is about creativity and happiness, and other days it seems to keep you back.

Palmer: Even I have to admit I have my doubts.

Therapist: If I'm understanding you correctly, you've had strong beliefs that sex with children is acceptable to you even though it's not acceptable to most others. You've felt this so strongly that you've been able to fantasize about children even when you've been sitting in treatment groups. For you, sex with children is something that you've approached explicitly and not avoided unless it was too risky at the moment. This part of your life is not something you've been contemplating changing. And at the same time, you're aware that there are other areas of your life—important areas like your autonomy, inner peace, and other kinds of happiness and pleasure—that you're not getting to live because of the realities associated with offending. Did I get that right?

Palmer: Yes.

Therapist: So what do you think you might do?

Palmer: Well, I'm willing to look at other ways to live my life to catch up on what I've been missing. I'm willing to look at my beliefs because I've been so stubborn about them in the past. I'm willing to set some goals in those areas you've referred to, like *trying to feel peaceful most times, and living life in a way that's going to keep me from coming back here. But I also don't want to lose what I get out of my life, now.*

Therapist: *That is a lot right there, and it shows you've been exploring what's valuable and important to you in your life. You just mentioned that you're stubborn. What's that about?*

Palmer: *Well, in the past, when I've set my mind to something, I've always been able to accomplish it. No one's going to stop me.*

Therapist: *You have quite a track record for when you're dedicated to something. What does that say about these other areas of your life?*

Palmer: *It says that when I'm ready to make serious changes, nothing and no one is going to stop me. The only thing is that I have to do them for myself and not because someone else makes me.*

Therapist: *The whole rest of the world has told you to change, but they can't do it for you. Only you can do it, and you have to want to.*

Palmer: *Yes.*

Therapist: *Which of those areas—autonomy, inner peace, happiness/pleasure—do you want to make a change in for yourself the most?*

Palmer: *I need to find new ways to enjoy myself. I haven't had that lately. I'm willing to make some goals in that area.*

Therapist: *Given the restrictions on your life, that might involve joining up with others in some activities you've never tried before. What would that be like?*

Palmer: *I'm willing to give it a try. I just can't promise that I'll like everything, but I'm willing to give it a try.*

Therapist: *How about if we set up a plan for the new activities you can try here in the prison in the next week, and you come back to group and report on it? That way, your peers who will have seen you through some of this can give you feedback and offer more ideas. Remember that this kind of treatment program is all about what works for you, but the other men in group might have ideas that neither you nor I will have thought of. How does that fit for you?*

Palmer: *Okay. I can do that. I <u>will</u> do that.*

Treatment of offenders following the approach-explicit pathway begins with examining and understanding the developmental and historical events that have led them to explicitly support offending behavior. Treatment helps these clients to understand precisely what needs they have attempted to meet, and those they have met, through their offending—such as agency or sexual pleasure. In this early phase of treatment, one goal is to help clients to identify the relationships between these early experiences and then to motivate them to contemplate the notion that they can achieve the same goals without harming others. It will be essential that the clients' primary goods are validated and reinforced, and that they also contemplate the notion that offending may interfere with other life goals and may not be in their best interests. For example, these clients may place considerable value on the primary good of agency, which is reinforced as important and worth pursuing but which is impeded by arrest, incarceration, court mandates, supervision, and the like. The good lives approach can aid these clients specifically because it directly appeals to the clients' self interest in ways that are likely to increase their motivation to engage in the challenging process of change.

Once clients achieve a degree of awareness in the above areas, and are able to identify offense-supportive attitudes and their origins as well as the goods they seek to attain via offending, treatment proceeds to develop the specific means, capacity, and opportunities to implement the clients' good lives plans without harming others. Additionally, as was the case with the approach-automatic pathway, approaches such as schema therapy and meta-cognitive monitoring and control will be of significant value in altering schemas and core beliefs that support offending.

Once attitude change has begun and pro-social means to achieve goals have been established, treatment helps clients to develop and practice meta-cognitive techniques (Wells, 2000; Wells and Matthews, 1994, 1996) that will assist with achieving treatment goals, as well as entrenching new cognitive and behavioral responses and scripts. An example of this process is the client who strongly values a sense of personal agency but who has previously successfully attained agency via retribution and retaliation. Through this approach, such a client is helped to conduct a cost-benefit analysis and to reframe those means into pro-social goals that are in his own interest, thus developing alternative ways to think about attaining agency and autonomy. This process is likely to be most effective when the therapist is able to shape responses and use positive reinforcement for successive approximations of honest disclosure, attitude change, changes to core beliefs and scripts, and positive movement toward appropriate means of acquiring primary goods.

Case Example: William

Recall William from chapter 5, who made frequent trips to the Orient to sexually assault children. He gained access to these children by becoming a teacher through the Peace Corps and other charitable organizations.

William believed strongly that sex with children, under the right conditions, was a matter of love and mentorship, outside the bounds of what a government should decide on behalf of its citizens. William was eventually apprehended after molesting a number of children in his capacity as a substitute teacher. At times, he has expressed considerable pride in avoiding detection for as long as he did.

William scores in the moderate range on actuarial measures of risk. Although his offending behavior has been prolific, the current arrest is his first offense of record. He does not have any other criminal history. However, he has offended against unrelated boys as well as girls, and has no history of living in a long-term relationship. Dynamic risk factors include sexual preoccupation, emotional congruence with children, and attitudes tolerant of sexual abuse.

Primary goods implicated in William's good life plan and offending include happiness/pleasure, relatedness, inner peace, creativity, and excellence at play and work. Flaws in his good life plan include his lack of capacity to attain these goods outside the realm of offending, means used to attain goods, and the fact that sexual activity with children creates conflicts with his attainment of other goods.

William's treatment will focus on raising his awareness of flaws in his good life plan and on his development of alternative means to attain primary goods in more acceptable ways. Treatment for William will emphasize that the primary good he sought through offending was acceptable and desirable, even though the methods through which he attempted to attain it were not. A primary focus will include developing William's understanding of the difference between how he has attained goods in the past and potential alternatives he might pursue that do not create conflicts with himself, the law, and others. To accomplish this, William and his therapist will spend considerable time exploring his offense-related schemas and values. As with Jay, the therapist will validate William's attempts to attain primary goods in ways that do not involve offending. Because William will initially see few reasons to stop offending when he begins to explore his life, he will require significant motivational enhancement, along with cognitive restructuring and the development of new cognitive schemas.

SUMMARY

This chapter has described specific methods to apply when considering both how an individual goes about offending and how he seeks to acquire primary goods in his life, based on an offense pathway. Because self-regulation varies across these pathways, different treatment approaches and methods are required for each pathway. Regardless of the offense pathway a client has followed, treatment using the GLM/SRM-R raises awareness of the primary goods the client was seeking to attain through offending.

However, each pathway requires its own area of emphasis. Ultimately, preventing offending involves developing and rehearsing skills in key problem areas and developing strategies to manage specific risk factors. Differential treatment according to the chosen pathway can ensure that the client and therapist are working in the most effective direction.

CHAPTER 12

Developing an Integrated Good Lives/Self-Regulation Plan

Thus far in treatment, therapeutic activities have taken place that target altering risk factors, acquiring primary goods, developing skills and strategies to both manage risk and achieve goals in life, and other relevant factors. Typically, near the end of treatment, these relevant factors and skills are brought together in a relapse prevention plan in which clients delineate the situations that pose a risk and the actions they will take to reduce or eliminate risk in these circumstances. The plan may also describe external conditions to be imposed as part of supervision and living in the community. Problems inherent with this approach include that it tends to be negative and avoidance-based in orientation, and that it focuses solely on risk and problem areas. Most importantly, this approach fails to address the difficulties found in sustaining avoidance goals over the long-term, the reliance on building a plan that includes only one self-regulation pathway to offending, and the lack of focus on attaining psychological well-being and a satisfying life.

The GLM/SRM-R treatment approach does not include a relapse prevention plan, but instead includes an *integrated good lives/self-regulation plan*. In addition to substantive differences, the difference in terminology avoids a negative orientation. In other words, by its very nature, a relapse prevention plan implies problems, avoidance, and risk. By contrast, a good lives/self-regulation plan envisions positive movement forward toward achieving goals and obtaining important things in life, as well as self managing one's life and one's behavior. In addition to this orientation, the plan and its development reflect the entire GLM/SRM-R treatment approach—specifically, that treatment should help individuals to have as normal a level of functioning in life as possible in which restrictions are only placed where required on specific activities that are strongly related to problematic behavior (Ward, 2007; Ward et al., 2006). For example, a client who has offended against unrelated children outside his family unit should be able to have contact with his own children, perhaps under certain conditions such as supervision, if there is no evidence to suggest that being with his children poses a risk. Simply having offended against children is insufficient to make a determination that the man must avoid all children. Similarly, a rapist may need to avoid certain situations that pose a risk, but the expectation should not be that he abandons the possibility of attaining an adult relationship or that he must avoid all single women or men in the future.

Although developed throughout the entire course of treatment, the good lives/self-regulation plan is essentially an end product of treatment in that it is the integration of all facets of treatment. It has two unique but related goals: (a) the development and implementation of a comprehensive "map for living" that includes all the ingredients of a good life; and (b) the identification of strategies needed to respond to problematic situations that may disrupt or threaten the client's functioning in other areas of his life. The latter refers to the emergence of self-regulation problems and possibly also acute risk factors (Hanson et al., 2007), such as relationship conflict, emotional distress, or a significant stressful life event. In addition to indicating a potential change in risk, such factors may also be indicative of problems the client is having in living a good life and in implementing his good life plan.

It is essential that the good lives/self-regulation plan is comprehensive and includes all relevant elements related to self-regulation, risk, and the internal and external conditions necessary to attaining a good life. The plan also forms the basis for maintenance treatment and supervision in the community, where supervising agents ensure that clients are implementing the plan effectively (see chapter 13). Thus, while a traditional relapse prevention plan might include, for example, "warning signs" that problems might be occurring or that risk might be increasing, the good lives/self-regulation plan goes beyond this analysis and includes identification of signs that the plan is being implemented and is on track. Thus, a necessary part of maintenance and supervision within the GLM/SRM approach is monitoring to ensure that the client is regulating behavior effectively and actively working toward living a satisfying, fulfilling life.

Ad hoc adjustments to the plan should be avoided, as they can restrict access to important goods and might negatively affect the plan and, ultimately, achieving a good or goods. If an individual is unable to use the means that he has developed to achieve a particular good, making changes could result in not acquiring the good, thus negatively affecting his good life plan. For example, a client who has decided to return to school, but who is having difficulty preparing applications or being accepted into school, may decide to apply for work instead, thus, in effect, abandoning the original goal. This change in means will not result in obtaining the good of knowledge (i.e., via education) and, thus, the client will not be accessing this good. Therefore, he will not be implementing this part of his plan, will not be able to acquire a primary good he defined as important to him, and he will then potentially be jeopardizing his established good life plan.

Constructing a Good Lives/Self-Regulation Plan

A number of elements need to be included in the post-treatment good lives/self-regulation plan. By this point in treatment, both the therapist and client should have a full understanding of the elements that make up a good life for a particular client and how he can best attain this life. Strategies for eliminating or managing flaws in the client's plan will have been developed, risk factors addressed, and plans for self-regulation established and at least partially entrenched through rehearsal and practice. All of these elements are amalgamated into a plan that includes

1. primary goods identified in assessment and treatment as important to the client and specific plans to attain them;

2. secondary goods that represent the ways primary goods will be attained;

3. specific indicators (to the client and to others) that goods are being acquired and his good life plan is being implemented effectively;

4. specific indicators (to the client and to others) when the good life plan may be threatened or in jeopardy, and plans assembled to address this issue;

5. similarly, specific indicators (to the client and to others) of flaws in the good life plan, and plans to address these, as well;

6. specific ways that self-regulation will be attained and maintained, including skills developed and rehearsed during treatment;

7. specific risk factors and plans to manage risk; and

8. specific indicators (to the client and others) that risk may be re-emerging or becoming acute (i.e., warning signs).

The template provided at the end of this chapter may be useful for summarizing these elements in the development of a plan, although practitioners should remember that developing such a plan is an ongoing clinical process throughout treatment. Thus, it is insufficient to simply provide worksheets to clients so that they can write down their elements of a good life. By the time of the preparation of the plan at the end of treatment, all areas should have been addressed in treatment, with this exercise representing only a summary and integration of plans, skills, and strategies developed in treatment. In addition, as indicated by the list above, the plan is meant to be explicit and specific and to include skills developed during treatment in each area of the plan. Each of these elements of the good lives/self-regulation plan is described below.

Primary Goods Identified as Important

As indicated in previous chapters, primary goods are those activities and states of being that, in and of themselves, an individual values. During assessment and treatment, a client will have identified these primary goods and may have completed some work on writing them down. He should also have developed, rehearsed, and started to put into place plans to attain goods. Although the good lives/self-regulation plan is finalized and articulated toward the end of treatment, clients should have been constructing and developing the plan throughout all of treatment, with the assistance of the therapist and other participants (when treatment is conducted in a group format). The aim in developing a final plan, which can be presented to the group when treatment is delivered in this format, is to ensure that all goods identified as important to each client, and attendant strategies to attain these, have been included.

As with all treatment activities, it is essential that the plan be personal to each client. It is also not necessary that each plan include all primary goods. Although it is ideal that all goods be represented in the client's life to some extent, little is to be gained from developing plans to seek out primary goods that a particular client does not value and in which he would invest little energy to obtain. For example, for some individuals, having an intimate relationship may be important (the good of relatedness), but spirituality may not. Thus, the latter would not be included in the plan. That said, the plan should be comprehensive enough that a sufficient number of goods are represented to ensure a balanced and satisfying life (i.e., the plan should have adequate scope).

An example of conducting this exercise is provided below. It should be noted that the examples provided are general and are for illustrative purposes only.

Example: Client Exercise

Therapist: *You have talked in treatment about what is important to you and how these fit into larger categories. Here, please indicate how important each element is to you by putting a checkmark by the ones that are most important. Then list specific things you want in <u>all</u> of the categories:*

WHAT IS IMPORTANT TO ME	WHAT I WANT IN THIS AREA
✓ Life	I want to find a place to live.
	I want to have enough money to be able to survive and take care of my family.
	I want to be able to control my blood pressure.
	I want to go back to exercising like I used to when I was healthy.
✓ Knowledge	I want to go back to school to earn my degree.
	I want to learn to be a better parent.
	I want to be able to explain to my wife what happened when I offended.
Excellence in Play and Work	I want to go back to my job with my brother.
	I want to be able to relax on the weekends instead of working all the time.
✓ Excellence in Agency	I want to be in control in my relationships and not feel bullied anymore.
	I want to find a place to live and be independent.
✓ Inner Peace	I don't want to be depressed any more.
	I want to feel calm.
	I want to feel good about my life and who I am.
	I want to be able to relax more.
Relatedness	I want to contact my other brothers and my sister.
	I want to improve my relationship with my wife.

Community	I want to be able to go back to my church.
	I want to attend a support group.
Spirituality	I want to be able to go back to my church.
✓ Happiness	I want to live a "normal" life.
	I want to have a sex life that I can feel good about and that I don't have to worry about.
Creativity	I want life to be interesting.
	I want to get my certificate in woodworking.

Some of the statements in the above example are somewhat general, such as "I want my life to be interesting." In treatment, the client should be able to specify what it is, for him, that makes life "interesting." For example, does he need to have some excitement in his life, or does this represent having an array of relationships and activities? Such a statement may be provided by the client earlier in treatment, but by the conclusion of treatment when the plan is being developed, the client should be able to be more specific.

Specific details to obtain identified goods are also delineated in the plan. The primary goods can overlap with secondary goods, which represent the specific means, activities, and circumstances that will result in achieving primary goods. This process is described below.

SECONDARY GOODS

Secondary goods represent the means by which primary goods will be acquired. As with indicators of primary goods, clients should be specific as to what they will do to attain goods and achieve goals. The therapist must be alert to whether clients possess the capacity (i.e., internal skills) and external opportunities, in their own environments and circumstances, to be able to successfully meet these goals. For example, a client who indicates that he wants to re-establish his relationship with his partner—a partner who has filed for divorce—has established a secondary good that is unattainable (and is also demonstrating flawed means by which to attain the primary good of relatedness). Throughout treatment, this good must be deconstructed and the client assisted to delineate alternative methods to attain intimacy in his life and to develop the skills to attain it.

Building on the previous exercise, clients can describe the means (i.e., secondary goods), as well as the specific plans they will implement, to achieve specific goods. It is recommended that clients establish several routes or means to attain each primary good, and that they not rely on a single course of action.

As in all other aspects of GLM/SRM-R assessment and treatment, it is vital that the therapist elicit the client's thoughts, ideas, and solutions and guide the process into a comprehensive plan rather than prescribing a plan for the client. After all, this plan is the client's, and unless he has a stake in its development as well as its outcome, it will be far less personally relevant or meaningful. The exercises below are not intended to be a checklist of items that a client should complete. Rather, each area should first represent a client's initial thoughts. The client then brings the plan to the treatment group, collects feedback, alters the plan, and brings it back to the group prepared to discuss how he incorporated the feedback, and if he didn't incorporate the feedback, his rationale for not doing so. The final result should be easy to read, but in all likelihood difficult to arrive at.

> ***Therapist:*** *Here's the plan. You've had the chance to put down your thoughts about a good life plan. You've also worked very hard to build the best rapport possible with your peers in treatment. Today is your opportunity to present your plan to others. Obviously, this step is an important one in the process, as a good life plan is like the stars that one would sail a ship by when no compass is available. Before we go forward, may I ask: on a scale of zero to ten, how confident are you in this plan?*
>
> ***Murray:*** *I believe I'm at a seven.*
>
> ***Therapist:*** *Okay. Tell me about seven.*
>
> ***Murray:*** *Well, I'm not a six because I've put a lot of work into this and I'm confident it can work. I'm not an eight because I don't know what I'm missing.*
>
> ***Therapist:*** *You're looking forward to hearing from the others in the group.*
>
> ***Murray:*** *I'm a little nervous, but yes, I want to know what they think.*
>
> ***Therapist:*** *You're invested in this. Why didn't you choose a six?*
>
> ***Murray:*** *Because this is really important. My life is in the balance, and I never want to hurt anyone ever again.*
>
> ***Therapist:*** *Safety and a good life are really important to you.*
>
> ***Murray:*** *Absolutely.*
>
> ***Therapist:*** *And what would it take to get you to a nine?*
>
> ***Murray:*** *I need to hear what you and the others have to say. Then I can incorporate it into my plan. I know I need to add to it, and that's okay. It will only make it better. Then I need to practice it in real life.*

Example: Client Exercise

Therapist: Murray, you have talked in treatment about what is important to you and what you want in each area. Here, please expand on this by indicating how you will meet these goals. Please be specific.

WHAT IS IMPORTANT TO ME	WHAT I WANT IN THIS AREA	HOW I WILL GET WHAT IS IMPORTANT TO ME
Life	I want the life of a man in his 40s. I want to join a fitness club and exercise. I want to settle down with my girlfriend, Deborah, and have the patterns of daily life that other intimate partners have. I want to get a job with a company that publishes books or magazines.	I will spend my free time reading books, following the news, and keeping myself in good physical shape exercising (e.g., jogging, weightlifting). I will refrain from sports activities that are more popular with young people, such as Little League. I will practice meditation to maintain my focus on my good life plan. I will look for jobs in the publishing industry.
Knowledge	I want to learn about publishing, including editing, layouts, and how the printing process itself works. I want to continue in therapy to learn more about myself. I want to learn more about healthy living as I get older.	I will search for adult education programs that will help me learn about publishing. I will take any job I can get at a publishing company to learn more about how they work. I will work with my supervising agent and therapist in the community to ensure that I can stay in treatment.

Excellence in Play and Work	I will make publishing one of my missions, and learn about it both at work and at school. If no school is available, I will buy books on the topic. I want to make physical fitness a major hobby.	I will look for any job I can get in the publishing industry. I will seek out adult education programs in my city and identify bookstores where I can order books related to publishing. I will work out at the fitness club as a hobby, knowing that some days are more enjoyable than others.
Excellence in Agency	I want the autonomy that most men in their 40s have. I understand that I will have restrictions on my actions due to my legal status. I want to live independently within these restrictions.	I will use the decision-making and problem-solving skills that I have learned in treatment to cope with all the stresses of daily life. I will constantly remind myself that the restrictions I live under help me stay out of trouble. I will always be aware that I have choices in just about everything I do, and that autonomy involves making my own decisions. I will remind myself regularly that I am independent and will do self-monitoring to make sure I am not thinking the way I used to.
Inner Peace	I want to be as free from inner turmoil as I can be within the framework of my life.	I will continue to meditate for 20 minutes twice a day. I will reflect on my progress in attaining the other primary goods in my life. I will spend quiet time with Deborah. I will keep with my exercise program to relax.

Relatedness	I will maintain my relationship with Deborah. I will develop a small group of friends with whom I can talk openly and share quiet activities.	I will communicate openly with Deborah at all times. When we disagree, I will remind myself that at least half, and probably more, of everything she says is probably right. I will ask myself at the middle of each day how I can be more empathic. I will make sure that we do one activity each week that she enjoys and that I can enjoy, too. I will join a health club and attend at hours when young people are not there. I will make conversation with others there only to the point where I am not irritating to them. I will keep in touch with other guys in the treatment program, including those with whom I've been mutually supportive.
Community	I want to feel like I belong in my community.	Deborah and I will take walks around our neighborhood. I will spend extra time studying the history of my community. I will follow local elections and make sure that I vote in each one.

Spirituality	I want a sense of meaning and purpose in my life. I want the opportunity to reflect on my place in the universe.	At the end of each day, I will reflect for ten minutes on my accomplishments in these goods and ask myself how I can be a better partner and man. I will attend church with Deborah at least every two weeks.
Happiness	I want to experience happiness and pleasure. For me this means playing guitar, keeping fit, and having a good intimate and sexual relationship with Deborah and enjoying things together.	I will write letters to people who have been helpful to me, to thank them. As part of my end-of-day reflection, I will ask myself to list three things I did to lead a good life that day. I will work with Deborah to develop a list of pleasurable activities that we can do together in our spare time. These things can include hobbies that we share as well as ways to make routine activities more enjoyable together. I will initiate conversations with her to ensure that our sex life is satisfactory to her.
Creativity	I want to create a healthy and appropriate middle-aged life. This includes my work and my relationships with others. I want nothing to do with people, places, and things that contain childish themes.	I will gather feedback from others on how I can improve my work performance and relationships. I will sell my electric guitar (too childish) and buy an acoustic guitar that I can play by myself in whatever free time I might have.

INDICATORS THAT GOODS ARE BEING ACQUIRED

When developing relapse prevention plans, treatment typically includes indicators that risk has escalated (i.e., warning signs), in treatment and supervision and this model has not traditionally focused on indicators of strengths or progress. This deficit is likely the result of the predominantly negative, avoidance-based orientation that sexual offender intervention based on RP has taken in its approach. While identifying warning signs can be essential and should be included in treatment (see below), the GLM/SRM-R approach also includes indicators that clients are being successful in implementing their good lives plans, utilizing effective self-regulation, and making progress in managing risk. It is insufficient to include only indicators of risks or problems, however, just as it is insufficient to establish goals in treatment for which no follow-up is provided. Thus, an essential part of treatment and supervision is ensuring that clients are attaining those goods identified as important to them, that they are doing so via realistic and acceptable means, and that they are utilizing effective self-regulation to attain those goods as well as to manage risk.

Building on the previous exercise, clients can specify indicators of progress that will be obvious to both themselves and to service providers.

Example: Client Exercise

Therapist: OK, Murray, now that you have talked in treatment about what is important to you and how you will meet these goals, please expand on those conversations by indicating how you and others will know that you are meeting these goals. Please be specific.

WHAT IS IMPORTANT TO ME	HOW I WILL KNOW I AM ACHIEVING MY GOALS	HOW OTHERS WILL KNOW
Life	I will have found a job with a publisher. I will exercise four mornings a week at a fitness club. I will maintain a routine schedule with Deborah, including reasonable timeframes for sleep and awakening.	I will tell stories from my job to others that I enjoy telling (as opposed to focusing on the negative, like "I hate my boss"). I will be slim and in good shape. Deborah will report that we are keeping a reasonable schedule and not staying out late.

Knowledge	I will be satisfied with what I am learning and always curious to know a little more. I will have collected a number of resources for studying publishing. I will also possess a number of men's health books and/or magazines.	I will be able to describe how publishing works, and what some of the recent trends in books and/or magazines are. I will be able to disclose my progress in individual therapy. I will be able to describe what I am learning about men's health and how I am applying it to my daily life.
Excellence in Play and Work	I will experience overall satisfaction with my job. I will always be aware that, even if I don't have the job that I want, I am learning and practicing so that one day I can have an even more rewarding job. I will enjoy my good physical health.	I will be expressing overall satisfaction with my work. I will not be complaining or talking negatively about my job and others. I will appear healthy and robust to others. I will not be attending young persons' sports events.
Excellence in Agency	I will keep track of how I manage challenging situations by keeping a journal. I will write about difficult situations and how I coped and responded.	I will be able to describe to others at least three situations each week in which I have made good decisions or tackled challenging situations in ways that I could not have done have prior to my offense. I will bring my journal to my supervision meetings and will be willing to share it.
Inner Peace	I will be better able to focus on things that are happening in my life. I will be able to develop solutions to problems as they arise, or I will take time to develop them. I will ask for help if I need it.	I will appear calmer and have no explosive outbursts. I will not be irritable with others. I will not isolate myself. People will know when I am having a hard time because I will tell them and will include what I am doing to get through it.

Relatedness	I will be able to speak about my concerns openly and also be able to have fun with Deborah. We will have a small group of friends in our age range.	Deborah will self-report that she is happy, and be willing to do so when I am not present. She and I will be able to describe recent happy times that we have spent with others.
Community	I will be well versed in local events and will vote in each election. I will recognize the faces of others in the neighborhood and maintain an acquaintance connection with them.	If my supervising agent asks my neighbors, they will describe me as polite and helpful. Deborah will be able to describe the walks that we take together in the neighborhood and the interactions we have with others along the way.
Spirituality	I will have a strong sense of my own accomplishments. I will know from conversations with Deborah that I am contributing to her life and the lives of those around me. I will find myself enjoying church services.	When asked privately, Deborah will describe me as having a sense of purpose that I am always working toward. She will report that I am attending church services with her without complaining.
Happiness	At any time, I will be aware of three things that I am grateful for. I will consistently list three things I did well or things that made me happy at the end of the day. My list will be available to anyone who wants or needs to see it.	Deborah will report that we are engaged in enjoyable activities that are appropriate for people in their 40s. Friends and others will report that I appear to be happy and content.

Creativity	I will be able to find the time to play my guitar by myself in quiet hours before or after work. I will be satisfied with my new relationships and abilities to get along with others.	Deborah will describe how I spend private time playing guitar. She will also describe how I have considered her feedback about how I can improve my relationships with others and act upon it. That does not mean that I will always follow her advice, but she will be able to describe how I have used her feedback.

INDICATORS THAT THE GOOD LIVES PLAN MAY BE THREATENED

Despite well-established plans, some life circumstances will prevent clients from obtaining certain goods. This situation is unavoidable. When a client realizes that he has failed to obtain some of his primary goods, he needs to ensure that he is prepared for the situation and keep in mind the importance of those goals to himself and to his life. This process should also assist him in avoiding cognitive deconstruction and abandoning his higher level goals if the life circumstances present a risk to re-offend. In some cases, the plan may be jeopardized because unforeseen barriers arise, while in other cases, pre-established means to achieve goals may not work out as initially planned. For example, a client might have planned to attain the good of knowledge by pursuing education, but then found out that he had not been successful at being accepted into school. In such a situation, it would be important for him to utilize his self-regulation skills to cope with this rejection and with the threat to his good lives plan, and to accept that he must pursue, at least temporarily, other avenues to continue his education, such as correspondence courses. In addition, it would be important for him to include other activities that would lead to gaining knowledge, such as self study, part-time school courses, or on-the-job training. The good lives plan may require adjustment if the good is unattainable at this point in the client's life. Such adjustments should be related to the means to achieve the good, however, and not to the abandonment of the good or the goal of attaining it. It is important that any changes be made by the client in conjunction with the case management team (e.g., the maintenance therapist, community supervisor, and others involved in the client's case), and that any adjustments to the client's good live plan have the potential to meet the primary good. Thus, for example, had the client not included alternate activities to pursue the good of knowledge, adjustments to the plan would include the development of these alternative means.

Regardless of any advance planning accomplished, in the implementation of the good lives/self-regulation plan, it is equally as important that the client be able to identify and verbalize (e.g., in supervision) the status of these plans and, in particular, that he be able to self-monitor the status of his plans and the attainment of goods. In addition, it is also important that the client be able to indicate when self-regulation may be jeopardized by real or perceived threats to the plan. For example, a client who highly values relatedness via intimacy with his partner may perceive the plan to be threatened when an argument occurs. In such a case, threats to his good life plan may be linked to risk and/or to self-regulation failure in addition to the threat of not attaining the good of relatedness/intimacy. Thus, the client's responses to situations that could jeopardize the plan should also be included in the exercise and its discussion.

Building on the previous exercise, clients can specify indicators of good lives plan threats and links to risk (both for self-regulation failure and re-offending) that will be obvious to both the clients and the service providers.

Example: Client Exercise

Therapist: Murray, you have talked in treatment about what is important to you and what you want in each area. Here, please explain how you and others will know that you not able to meet some of your goals and describe what you will do in those situations. Also, indicate how those inabilities to accomplish your goals are linked to your risk factors. Please be specific.

WHAT IS IMPORTANT TO ME	SIGNS THAT I MAY NOT BE GETTING WHAT IS IMPORTANT TO ME	WHAT I WILL DO	LINK TO RISK
Life	Reducing my exercise Engaging in activities with childish themes (e.g., video games) Problems at work Problems with Deborah	Speak immediately with Deborah, a supportive peer, or supervising agent.	Not taking care of myself and my healthy functioning may mean that I am abandoning goals or becoming isolated. These are risk factors for me, and may also signal that I'm abandoning my goals.

Knowledge	Dropping out of therapy Slowing down or stopping my efforts at education, particularly informal education	Speak to my supervising agent and to Deborah. Ensure that I am considering all feedback from my therapist.	Dropping out of treatment or slowing the pace of my learning could signal a sense of entitlement to pursue one goal at the expense of others. It might also mean I am focusing my attentions in unsafe directions.
Excellence in Play and Work	Loss of job or conflicts at work Hobbies gravitate toward childish themes	Use skills learned in treatment to address conflicts directly and assertively. Work immediately to re-engage in healthy hobbies and activities.	Activities with childish themes could signal a return to emotional congruence with children or social isolation. Conflicts at work would signal the re-emergence of problems with regulating my emotions and other risk factors.
Excellence in Agency	Poor decision-making Not seeing my role accurately in situations Becoming impulsive Making statements that I don't have any choice in things	Review trends in decision-making with therapist, supervisor, and Deborah; not doing so would be another sign of things going wrong.	My offending was based on poor decision-making and not seeing my responsibility or options in my life.
Inner Peace	Persistent inner turmoil Trouble sleeping Appearance of irritability to others Complaining about my job or other people	Meditation Discussions with therapist and Deborah Will seek out their feedback	Part of my offending was about trying to feel better about things and about using the offense to cope with my emotions.

Relatedness	Relationship problems No friends	Call support persons and ask advice from supervising agent, peers from group, and Deborah. Remind myself that these are important people to me. Start spending more time with people who are important to me.	Problems with adult relationships might signal a return to seeking intimacy with young people. This is unacceptably close to offending.
Community	Staying at home constantly Lack of concern for others in my neighborhood	Enlist others to go out for walks or community activities. Develop plan with therapist to engage in a pre-determined number of activities each week and return to treatment to discuss how they went.	Staying home constantly or being unconcerned about others would signal that the balance of my good life plan is becoming distorted. Also, social isolation is a risk factor for me.
Spirituality	Not going to church Not taking the time to reflect on my place in the universe	I will talk to others and go back to church. I will talk to my pastor. Church is an important part of my life.	Not attending to spirituality might mean that I'm returning to a sense of selfishness and entitlement. I am at my safest when I am connected to my spirituality.

Happiness	Not reflecting on my accomplishments Being unable to name three things for which I am grateful or only doing so cynically Not engaging in pleasurable adult activities by myself or with others	I will seek out help from my peers, Deborah, and therapist. It is important that I pursue happiness (including joy and gratitude) actively. Immediately plan for pleasurable activities with others	Offending has been a poorly thought-out way of seeking pleasure for me in the past.
Creativity	Not playing guitar Not working at publishing Not being curious about other things I can do with my life and with others	Discuss with peers, therapist, and Deborah An absence of creativity may be a function of overemphasis in other areas.	This is not my most valued primary good, but it is important for maintaining the overall balance of my good life plan.

INDICATORS OF FLAWS IN THE GOOD LIVES PLAN

As described previously, four flaws can interfere with implementing the good lives plan and with clients' ability to achieve goods: means, conflict, internal and external capacity, and lack of scope. By this stage in treatment, these flaws should have been resolved via: (1) the establishment of appropriate means to achieve goods and manage oneself; (2) the resolution of conflict (e.g., by determining which of the conflicting goods is more important to the client); (3) the development of internal skills to ensure that access to goods is realistically possible in the client's own circumstances and environment; and, (4) the expansion of the scope of the client's good life plan.

As with plans to obtain goods, some circumstances can arise in implementing the good lives/self-regulation plan that result in the re-emergence of problems. This situation can also signal an increase in risk or a re-emergence of risk factors and/or a potential self-regulation failure. As such, it is important that clients be able to articulate past and potential future flaws or problems that could occur when implementing the plan, that they are able to recognize these when they occur, and that they are able to implement strategies to re-establish their good lives plans. These flaws are also linked to attaining and maintaining self-regulation, which is described in the following example.

Example: Client Exercise

Therapist: *You have talked in treatment about what is important to you and what you want in each area, as well as how things can sometimes go wrong. Here, please explain how you and others will know that specific problems are occurring and what you will do in these situations. Also, indicate whether these are linked to your risk factors. Please be specific.*

PAST AND FUTURE POSSIBLE FLAWS	SIGNS THAT THIS MAY BE HAPPENING	WHAT I WILL DO	LINK TO RISK
Means: **How I am Meeting My Goals**	I am persistently not meeting the basic aspects (for example, no job; conflict in relationship; conflicts with others, inner turmoil). I am disappointed with the outcomes of my efforts. I am not attending to my health or happiness. I am becoming too focused on myself and not enough on others or my place in the universe. I am not recognizing my capabilities or contributions to situations (agency). I am not attending to my less valued primary goods, such as creativity. I am seeking goods inappropriately, including watching children, using sex to cope with stress, and engaging in activities with childish themes such as video games.	Return to treatment to explore limits on means. If possible, bring Deborah in for a private session. Return to my good life plan, examine where limitations on means are having the greatest effect, and make interim adjustments until I can consult with others. Contact my supervising agent or therapist to develop an immediate strategy for returning to full adherence to my plan. Deborah will contact my therapist or supervising agent.	Not making progress attaining primary goods will suggest that I am reverting to historic attitudes, beliefs, and schemas. It may also suggest that I am abandoning my goals or that I feel entitled to do so. All of these may indicate some imminent risk.

Conflict: **When My Goals Are Not Aligned with Each Other**	Failure to properly balance my time with my work and with Deborah Pursuing pleasurable activities without reflecting on how they fit into the rest of my good life plan Failure to balance relatedness and autonomy Pursuing knowledge at the expense of happiness and pleasure, or vice versa Problems at work or conflicts with others could signal conflicts between goals.	Speak to work supervisor and Deborah independently and establish short-term plans for managing these competing needs. Ensure proper time for meditation and reflection twice a day, even when engaged in pleasurable activities. Discuss balance of autonomy and relatedness with others affected. Develop time for solitude as needed. Work with job supervisor, agent, therapist, and Deborah to resolve problems as needed. Deborah will contact my therapist or supervising agent.	Avoiding conflicts was a factor in my offending; it is vital that I address conflicts directly, assertively, and respectfully. If I don't address conflicts, I could be at risk to not be able to manage my emotional states and to not attain other goods.

Capacity: **When I Don't Use My Skills**	I will not have a positive attitude toward my work or may not meet my supervisor's expectations. I will not be continuing to read books on publishing. I will stop meditating or making time to reflect on my life. I will not be able to list my accomplishments for each day. I will not relate empathically with Deborah. I will not see myself as having control over my circumstances.	Bring these signs to the attention of Deborah, therapist, and supervising agent. Develop an interim plan for returning to my good life plan. Explore whether there are conflicts between my individual goals or a lack of means in my plan. Deborah will contact my therapist or supervising agent.	The signs such as not having a positive attitude may signal that I'm about to abandon my goals. It might also mean that I am isolating myself from others (risk factor) or that I am feeling entitled to stop following my plan.

Capacity: **When Problems in My Environment Interfere in My Goals**	Problems at work or with Deborah Problems with community or peers If people in my neighborhood react negatively to me because they know I have committed a sexual offense If I am unable to get a job in publishing	Call in the support of others to examine the situation and develop interim plan. Consult with my therapist and supervising agent. Deborah will contact my therapist or supervising agent.	These factors could jeopardize the balance of my good life plan, or make it seem okay to abandon my goals and revert to historical behaviors that have been precursors to my offending. My good life plan might be at risk if I feel justified in making an exception to my plan by engaging in self-centered behavior, or if I don't cope with stress and simply give up my plan. I could become irritable and start isolating myself if I feel like people are treating me poorly. Lack of employment was part of my previous offending, so not getting employment in my field could be a risk for me.

| Lack of Scope:

When I Am Focusing Too Much on One or Only a Few Goals | Calling in sick to work unnecessarily

Not taking the time needed to maintain my relationships

Not going to the gym per my schedule

Not keeping my schedule with Deborah

This lack of scope will appear similar to conflict among goals. | Find out what I am focusing on the most and why I am ignoring other things.

Call in supports (Deborah, therapist, supervising agent) for ideas and feedback.

Examine issues and develop interim plan.

Deborah will contact my therapist or supervising agent. | Focusing too much in one area could mean losing balance within my plan and could signal that pursuing some primary goods is becoming less valuable to me. This imbalance could result in a return to risk factors such as poor self-regulation, entitlement, or social isolation. |

ATTAINING AND MAINTAINING SELF-REGULATION

The above treatment activities and exercises focus on the parts of the good lives/self-regulation plan that are predominantly related to attaining primary goods and achieving goals in clients' lives. As is evident from the above exercises, however, as well as in the integrated GLM/SRM-R approach overall, primary goods and problems implementing the good lives plan are influential in the offending process and related to risk to re-offend (Yates and Ward, 2008; see chapter 3). Thus, in addition to addressing good lives elements, the plan also includes specific strategies to address self-regulation, particularly as related to the offense pathway(s) the individual has followed in offending.

Much of the above relies heavily on meta-cognition and self-monitoring; clients must be able to reflect on their circumstances and be aware of both progress and problems implementing their plans to achieve goals and manage risk and self-regulation. By this stage in treatment, clients should be able to link their good lives plans to their offending behavior and risk factors (see chapter 10), and they should have developed and rehearsed required skills during treatment.

In this part of the good lives/self-regulation plan, the focus is specifically on self-regulation and the implementation, both of strategies to achieve goals and those to prevent re-offending. As described in chapters 10 and 11, achieving goals and preventing re-offense is, in part, based on the offense pathway associated with offending and also with self-regulation of cognition, affect, and behavior in more general terms. Clients should be helped to be aware of their self-regulation styles and tendencies and should have rehearsed strategies to maintain self-regulation, again both globally and specifically with respect to their offense progression. For example, an individual following an avoidant pathway should be knowledgeable about his tendency to abandon his higher level goals and to cognitively deconstruct when risk and opportunities to meet goals via offending present themselves. An individual following an approach-automatic pathway should be aware of, and have changed, his cognitive schemas and implicit theories that support offending, and should have well-entrenched skills to regulate offense-related cognition.

Although implementing a comprehensive good lives plan should ameliorate much of the need to attain goods via offending, it is essential to include risk management—of which self-regulation is an integral part—in the good lives/self-regulation plan.

One method for developing a risk management plan can include some *in vivo* exercises. In one set of exercises, the therapist can prepare an extensive list of situations on a set of flash cards. These situations can include risk situations, flaws in implementing the client's good life plan, or offense-related behavior. The therapist can then read the cards to the client, whose task will be to provide a real-time response as to how he will manage that situation. For example, in the case described earlier in this chapter, situations might include the following.

- You've just been fired from your job. What is the first thing you do and why?

- You and your partner are having an argument over money. She makes an insulting remark about your offense history. What goes through your mind? What do you do? How do you manage this situation?

- You have just heard a child's voice on the radio and find it arousing. What do you do? Then what do you do next to cope with this?

- You are walking in the community and a neighbor gives you a dirty look and makes reference to your offense history. What goes through your mind? What do you do? How do you not let this situation bother you?

- Deborah is away and a child comes to your door trying to sell raffle tickets. The child asks about your guitar. What do you do?

- You find that this child is attractive and is now in your apartment. You are becoming aroused. What is going through the child's mind? What do you do? How do you stay safe?

- You have just put your hand on the child's back without any negative response. What is going through the child's mind? What do you do? How do you not offend in this situation?

The therapist should base such situational examples on the client's own offense history, dynamic risk factors, primary goods, and possible good life plan flaws. It can be helpful to think of this exercise as resembling combat training for pilots. In many cases, pilots are tested by being given dangerous scenarios and then are assessed by the accuracy and timeliness of their responses. The purpose is not to catch anyone unaware, but to assess their overall preparedness and to assist them to practice and rehearse self-regulation and risk-management strategies.

Another variation on this exercise is to have the client present his good life plan in a group therapy session and to have other clients ask him similar questions. Then the therapist and the group provide feedback regarding the client's responses. Again, the purpose is not to badger or harass the client, but to approximate real-life situations, in which things can happen quickly. It is very often the case that the client's peers will make astute and helpful observations, including things the therapist might not have considered. Further, due to the nature of group treatment, it often happens that the group's feedback is of particular relevance to the client.

It is impossible to prepare for every risky situation. These exercises, however, can quickly point out areas that require further work as well as identify strengths. The client can use the information generated in these sessions to prepare additional risk management plans and strategies. His plan can include a rank ordering of relevant dynamic risk factors, primary goods that would be implicated in subsequent re-offending, ways he might appear to others prior to re-offending, and steps he and others can take to intervene in the process.

Knowledge of Risk Factors, Plans to Manage Risk, and Indicators of Acute Risk

It is important to recall that, within the GLM, risk factors represent omissions or distortions in the internal and external conditions required to implement a good lives plan in a specific set of environments. Installing the internal conditions (i.e., skills, values, and beliefs) and the external conditions (resources, social supports, and opportunities) is likely to reduce or eliminate each individual's set of criminogenic needs.

An acceptable plan for risk management takes into account both warning signs and dynamic risk factors identified in research. Victim access, emotional collapse, social support collapse, hostility, substance abuse, sexual preoccupation, and rejection of supervision represent acute risk factors and are all essential for consideration. Likewise, it is important to examine factors that are unique to individual clients, such as medication compliance and complaints about supervision. Such indicators are important, as these may indicate an escalating sense of entitlement to abandon one's good life plan. Specifically, in such cases, the client may be experiencing increased self-efficacy with respect to managing risk and implementing his good life plan, and may be feeling as though he has reduced risk to a low level. Ultimately, the client himself and those around him can be excellent sources of information for warning signs of increasing risk or imminent re-offense. Questions such as, "What would you look like?" or "How would others know?" can yield excellent information for clients who have followed any pathways to offending. The client can discuss this information in therapy, and assemble a list of warning signs. The client can then assemble a list of instructions for others should he fail to intervene on his own behalf.

Summary

To this point, therapy has focused on altering risk factors, acquiring primary goods, developing skills and strategies to both manage risk and achieve goals in life, and other relevant factors. Near the end of treatment, the client and therapist typically bring these relevant factors and skills together in a plan. In this process, the client prepares a risk management plan (e.g., delineating those situations that pose a risk and the actions the client will take to reduce or eliminate risk in those circumstances). It is crucial, however, that this plan goes beyond risk management to actively work toward achieving goals in life. It is also essential that this approach not become negative and avoidance-based in orientation, focusing solely on risk and problem areas. Although the client and therapist develop the plan throughout treatment, the good life/self-regulation plan is essentially a final product integrating all facets of treatment. It has two unique but related goals, including the development and implementation of a comprehensive "map for living," and the identification of strategies needed to respond to problematic situations that may disrupt or threaten the client's functioning in other areas of his life. The plan also forms the basis for maintenance treatment and supervision in the community, which is the next and final topic in this book.

Good Lives/Self-Regulation Plan Template

GOODS DESIRED	WAYS TO OBTAIN GOODS (MEANS)	HOW I WILL KNOW I AM GETTING THESE	PROBLEMS I WILL NEED TO MANAGE	RISK FACTORS	WARNING SIGNS FOR RISK	SELF-REGULATION STYLE
Life						
Knowledge						
Excellence in Play and Work						
Agency						
Inner Peace						
Relatedness						
Community						
Spirituality						
Happiness						
Creativity						
Other						

PART IV

Post-Treatment Follow-Up and Community Reintegration

CHAPTER 13

Post-Treatment Maintenance and Supervision

Post-treatment maintenance and supervision are essential parts of the treatment of sexual offenders. Research suggests that these two elements of treatment in combination are more effective in reducing recidivism than either intervention alone (Gordon and Packard, 1998; McGrath, Cumming, Burchard, Zeoli, and Ellerby, 2009; McGrath, Cumming, Livingston, and Hoke, 2003). As with treatment in general, in order to be effective, community supervision requires that interventions be matched to clients' risk, need, and responsivity factors, that clients are active participants in the process, and that the therapist develop a strong working alliance and collaborative relationships with clients (Cumming and McGrath, 2005; McGrath et al., 2009; Yates et al., 2000). A comprehensive case plan is essential to effective supervision (Cumming and McGrath, 2005). An effective case plan should be based on all available information, risk assessment, and the case formulation that has been developed (see chapter 7). Lastly, the principles and techniques of motivational interviewing and effective therapeutic methods are as important for community maintenance programs and supervision as they are for treatment.

While historically most maintenance and supervision activities have been based on the Relapse Prevention Model (Cumming and McGrath, 2005), the approach presented in this chapter is based on the integrated Good Lives/Self-Regulation-Revised Model. Thus, as with treatment, the focus is on building upon clients' values, interests, and primary goods in addition to addressing and monitoring risk. While solely or predominantly establishing avoidance goals is unlikely to engage and motivate clients in the difficult process of change, the same is true of maintaining treatment gains and undergoing supervision. As with formal treatment, *one size does not fit all*, and the maintenance and supervision plan must be unique to each individual.

In addition to building in the integrated GLM/SRM-R approach, research has demonstrated that some individuals simply desist from, or cease, offending, and are able to reintegrate into the community successfully (Maruna, 2001). This evolution appears to be a dynamic process that involves change, setbacks, and, finally, complete cessation from crime. Desistance from crime is associated with various maturational, social, and cognitive variables. These factors include education, employment, marriage, positive public attitudes, a more constructive self-concept, strong relationships and social supports, and spirituality (Laub and Sampson, 2003; Maruna, 2001; McNeill, 2006; McNeill, Batchelor, Burnett, and Knox, 2005; Sampson and Laub, 1993; see Laws and Ward, in press for a review*). Supervision within the integrated GLM/SRM-R approach builds on this process.

Elements of Effective Supervision

Various well-defined elements of effective supervision (Cumming and McGrath, 2005), include

- varying the level of supervision to match risk and needs of each client;
- planning for transition and effective re-entry into the community from institutional settings, where applicable;
- developing a comprehensive case plan;
- establishing an integrated case management team that communicates and collaborates regularly;
- establishing treatment in the community;
- linking clients to required resources in the community (e.g., employment, mental health services, etc.);
- developing and providing training to a community support network; and
- ongoing risk assessment and risk management and appropriate intervention as required.

Traditionally, community maintenance programming and community supervision focus on ongoing evaluation of risk and intervention when clients experience difficulty managing risk or coping with life problems as they arise. Such risk management is an essential part of intervention with sexual offenders. Unfortunately, many jurisdictions pursue a dichotomous view of community supervision, which often means that supervising agents are expected both to carry out the orders of the court and to try to support efforts at rehabilitation at the same time. Many agents perceive these missions as separate, while agency policies can seem heavily slanted in the direction of invoking

---

*Note: Much of this research is general and not specific to sexual offenders.

sanctions rather than providing assistance. In some jurisdictions, offenders leaving prison are not permitted to begin researching programs and networks that may be available in the communities where they will reside. Their case managers often have large caseloads and few resources to help the offender make any sort of meaningful plan. The offender then re-enters society at the same time as he is seeking to locate the resources that will help him prevent re-offense and live out his good life plan.

Release planning and community supervision should involve both carrying out court orders and supporting efforts at rehabilitation simultaneously and in equal measure. In addition, there should be continuity between the releasing program and follow-up maintenance programming and supervision in order to maximize successful reintegration and enhance community safety. Consider the following example:

Case Example: Raman

Raman was released from incarceration to his community upon reaching his release date. His caseworker in prison was responsible for 150 clients, and was able only to provide some basic information on available services in the community. The local corrections department had a contract with one community provider, but that agency had a waiting list. Among Raman's conditions of release were that he would get a job and an apartment within the first month of his release.

Raman's community had residence restrictions setting clear guidelines regarding where he could live. Although he was able to stay with his brother for a few days, this arrangement was not a long-term option. Because of his status as a sexual offender, it was nearly impossible for him to gain employment because of this particular jurisdiction's local laws. By the time he had spent 30 days in the community, Raman's supervising agent found that he was not in compliance with his release plan because he had not been able to find acceptable living accommodations or employment within this timeframe, nor was he able to enroll in a treatment program due to waitlists. The court swiftly returned him to prison.

In this situation, Raman could not help but fail, but not as a result of his own efforts. With access to neither treatment nor any sort of assistance, Raman could not comply with the rules of his release. Although the supervising agent was carrying out the orders of the court, the agent provided no meaningful support for Raman's rehabilitation. This case is an example of the unfortunate reality in some jurisdictions. Had Raman had access to even a minimal number of services, the outcome might have been quite different for him and less costly to the public. Furthermore, his chances of rehabilitation would likely have been greater.

It is very often the case, however, that the best way for supervision officers to carry out the orders of the court is to provide active support for rehabilitative efforts. Effective community supervision and risk management can inform treatment and vice versa. Ultimately, the "dual roles" of community supervisors needn't clash in the vast majority of circumstances.

Beyond what more traditional measures can provide, the integrated GLM/SRM-R approach to community treatment and supervision involves monitoring the effective implementation of each client's good lives/self-regulation plan. Under GLM/SRM-R, monitoring each client's risk and personal functioning is tailored to the specific offense pathway(s) the client has followed in offending. For example, if a client has followed an avoidant pathway to offending and tends to respond to challenging situations and problems in an avoidant, passive manner, this information is important to the supervision of the client, in that the agent working with the client can then be alert to such responses when the client is faced with risk situations or particular problems. The supervising agent, based on this information, will be able to detect such problems as the loss of control or the cognitive deconstruction, which characterize this pathway. This approach will not only ensure effective monitoring of risk and changes in risk, but will also allow community service providers and case managers to monitor whether clients are implementing effective self-regulation strategies and actively working toward implementing their good lives plans, allowing clients to adjust plans and strategies as required.

The Good Lives/Self-Regulation Plan in the Community

As described previously, the good lives/self-regulation plan that is developed during treatment should contain all elements of attaining a good life, regulating cognition, emotion, and behavior, and managing risk (see chapter 12). By the time clients begin post-treatment maintenance and supervision, this plan should reflect an adequate scope of primary goods that are important to the clients, appropriate means to attain these goods, the internal capabilities and external opportunities required to assist the clients to put their plans for a better life into action, self-regulation strategies, and risk management plans. Once established, the challenge is to translate these plans into the clients' actual lives in the community. This process requires not only that clients develop the skills to manage risk and the ability to implement the good lives plan, but also that they have the opportunities to implement these plans and that supervising agents also have the capacity to assist the clients to implement their good lives/self-regulation plans. For example, while treatment may assist those clients who so desire to develop skills to attain and maintain relationships and intimacy, it is essential that they also have access to opportunities to meet appropriate partners. Such a relationship focus has not traditionally been the approach to supervision, which has focused predominantly on risks that such relationships may pose or, in some jurisdictions, on actually forbidding such relationships. Although it is recognized that some relationships may pose a risk, such restrictions should be minimal. Within the GLM/SRM-R approach, the opportunity to access as many interpersonal relationships as possible is explicitly pursued in the community. Similarly, in order to obtain the primary good of mastery at work, clients must be able to work at jobs they find challenging and worthwhile (a secondary good), must work for an employer who is willing to take them on (external opportunity), and must acquire the knowledge and skills required to perform the job (internal capacity). Thus, community intervention involves verifying the type of work a client finds satisfying and actively assisting him to achieve this through the development of both skills and opportunities. The supervising agent assists with this process. Community support persons can also be enlisted to help clients.

At the point of completing a treatment program guided by the GLM/SRM-R approach, clients will have a good lives/self-regulation plan formulated in collaboration with therapists and will have a detailed understanding of how the pursuit of primary goods was implicated in their offending and in their life problems. In addition, clients should possess a good grasp of the capabilities they require to be able to attain a good life, self-regulate effectively, and manage risk factors, although it is the role of community service providers and the case management team to assist in continuing the development and entrenchment of these capabilities. For example, clients should have an understanding of the manner in which goods such as intimacy and agency are important in their lives and so should have developed self-regulation strategies and other skills needed to achieve this those goods in personally satisfying, meaningful, and socially acceptable ways. Community treatment and supervision personnel assist in the implementation of these skills and strategies in addition to monitoring clients' risk. Thus, one goal of post-treatment maintenance and supervision within the GLM/SRM-R approach is to ensure monitoring of clients' implementation of their good lives plans and ensuring the clients are meeting important goals in addition to managing risk.

Irrespective of any skill deficits exhibited by offenders, the ultimate goal is to help clients to re-enter and reintegrate into the community in ways that promote their well-being and in ways that reduce their risk to re-offend. Because desistance from offending revolves around the availability of such factors as employment, education, friendships, romantic relationships, family, leisure, and health (Laws and Ward, in press), it is essential that therapists and supervisors assist the client to establish as many opportunities as possible to attain these goods. Again, this approach is in contrast to traditional methods that focus on assessing and monitoring the risk that could be posed by such activities and simply informing community support persons of clients' risk factors and supervision/treatment plans. Put another way, the involvement of others (including supportive peers, therapists, and supervising agents) in clients' lives goes beyond solely enlisting their assistance in managing offenders. The involvement extends to the active participation of offenders' case management teams and support persons to assist clients to attain a good life.

Case Example: Louis

Let's compare two approaches toward a case. Louis is on community supervision. He has been observed trying to spend an inordinate amount of time with a younger co-worker. She has told him that she is not interested in him, but he has continued to make advances toward her.

Scenario #1

Agent: Louis, tell me what's going on.

Louis: I just thought we might hit it off. I wanted to show her I was interested. I never imagined that it would come to this. If she's not interested, then neither am I.

Agent: Here are my concerns. I think you're sexually preoccupied and that she is too close to your victim age range. Furthermore, I did not give you permission to date. This is the sort of thing you need to check with me on.

Louis: I didn't think I needed your permission to at least talk to her to see if she was interested. We haven't even gone out on a date.

Agent: Those are the rules. You need to follow them. If you don't manage your own risk, others are going to manage it for you. This is between you and your future.

Scenario #2

Agent: Hi, Louis, can we talk about the concern raised by your employer?

Louis: Yes, I suppose we should.

Agent: Thanks. Tell me about that.

Louis: I just thought we might hit it off. I wanted to show her I was interested. I never imagined that it would come to this. If she's not interested, then neither am I.

Agent: So it's important to you to make some connections with others, which we know is part of your plan for living, and if she was available that would be nice and if she wasn't you weren't going to sweat it.

Louis: That's right. With my record, it's really hard to meet anyone. My boss was *concerned that she was young looking and said something about that. I noticed that, too, but she isn't as young as the girl I abused.*

Agent: *It's important to you to find happiness and relationships, and your options are limited.*

Louis: *Yeah.*

Agent: *And at the same time, your job is important to you.*

Louis: *Yeah.*

Agent: *So just this conversation with her got a lot of people concerned. Where does that leave you?*

Louis: *Well it doesn't seem fair, but I'm trying to look at things differently.*

Agent: *Are there other perspectives to consider?*

Louis: *Maybe, I guess so. Maybe I need to keep these things separate. My job is about autonomy, life, knowledge, and creativity. Meeting women is about happiness and pleasure. If I try to do them both at the same time, maybe there's going to be a conflict.*

Agent: *Kind of like if you try to do both, you'll actually do worse.*

Louis: *Yeah, and I don't want that.*

Agent: *It's important to you that you keep your life balanced and your goals simple so you can attain them.*

Louis: *Exactly. I need to work on this. But I still want to be able to date.*

Agent: *Can I make a suggestion?*

Louis: *Sure.*

Agent: *People are going to get concerned if you're trying too hard or you're asking people out in the wrong places. How about we make some guidelines that you won't ask people out that you work with, and that when you ask other people out, if they say "No," you don't keep asking. How does that sound?*

Louis: *Okay, I guess.*

Agent: *And to make sure that everything is okay, how about when you're about to ask someone out or if you do ask someone out, talk to me about it so that you're not out there alone with this. The more you're bringing it to your therapist and me, the less likely it is to raise eyebrows. Can you live with that?*

Louis: *I sure can.*

Agent: *You know, if you are going to date, you should also go back to your plan and work with your therapist about what kinds of resources are out there, like social clubs and things like that.*

Louis: *That's what I'll do.*

Agent: *I'll give your therapist a call in case there is anything you need to talk about*

> with her about that age difference. Sounds like that's the best place to have that conversation, but please do it next session and come back and tell me about it.
>
> **Louis:** I will.
>
> **Agent:** Okay, well good luck with those goals! I know you can do anything you set your mind to.
>
> **Louis:** Thanks.

In the first scenario, the supervising agent was clearly more concerned with whether Louis was complying with the conditions of his supervision. He did not pursue a collaborative approach and appeared uninterested in doing so and, in fact, was actually acting in a threatening manner toward the client. By not demonstrating any interest or providing any opportunities for Louis to make decisions for himself, it is unlikely that Louis will be motivated to be entirely forthcoming with his supervising agent in the future.

In the second scenario, Louis was clearly more invested in the process and will return to his next meeting with his agent more ready, willing, and able to discuss his private life with his agent. Some jurisdictions place restrictions on the ability of offenders to date. However, this issue needn't become a power struggle. After all, it is natural and healthy that someone would want to pursue the primary good of relatedness by dating. By maintaining a collaborative approach and guiding Louis in the direction of being more open and forthcoming, the supervisor is better placed to support efforts at rehabilitation and remain vigilant about indicators of imminent risk. As mentioned above, Louis' interest in dating is not in itself a concern and, in fact, reflects movement toward the primary good of relatedness (and possibly other goods). His interest in dating is worthy of affirmation. Whether Louis is pursuing this good with limited or inappropriate means can be the subject of further exploration in conversation. The supervising agent can also remain vigilant for signs that this pursuit is limiting the scope of Louis' good life plan or creating conflicts elsewhere within the plan. Furthermore, these pursuits can help provide information regarding Louis' overall self-regulation, which in turn can yield important information about Louis' current status in the community.

Given the above, it is essential that maintenance and supervision focus on assisting clients to implement their good lives plans and develop positive approach goals in addition to manage risk. Criminogenic needs are most effectively modified, eliminated, or managed by building clients' capabilities in a constructive, personal, goal-driven way in addition to specific strategies to manage risk factors.

SUPPORT IN SUPERVISION

Because clients need a broad range of needs, goals, risk factors, and self-regulation skills, some aspects of their functioning are best addressed by services and workers outside the immediate therapy team. Such additional personnel may include teachers, chaplains, employers, social workers, and/or recreation instructors, to name a few. This broader base of support is consistent with the standard approach to supervision that builds an integrated, collaborative case-management team to assist clients (Cumming and McGrath, 2005). The difference is, however, that within the GLM/SRM-R approach, this team is not exclusively focused on risk management. The larger team also actively assists clients to attain important goods and goals. Furthermore, while such individuals are typically enlisted to support community supervisors in monitoring risk and facilitating clients' implementation of risk-management plans, within the GLM/SRM-R approach, these individuals are also enlisted to help the offender attain important goals in life.

Concerning the extension of clients' good lives/self-regulation plans into the future, it is advisable for case managers and therapists to anticipate the social and personal environments into which clients will most probably be released so as to best prepare for their transition into the community. This process may entail the creation of social supports systems such as Circles of Support (Wilson, 2007) or employment or education opportunities. The good lives/self-regulation plan is not etched in stone, however, without opportunities to be modified. In fact, it makes sense to fill in the details gradually as the offender progresses through the various phases of treatment and supervision. Naturally, therapists and supervisors should ensure that clients' good lives/self-regulation plans are made available to all the relevant team members and support people within the community.

RISK AND SELF-REGULATION: WHEN THINGS GO WRONG

Despite the most thorough and well-conceived good lives/self-regulation plans, and the best intentions of clients and their various support people, sometimes things will go wrong, creating the danger of further offending. Therefore, it is important that the plan contain emergency instructions and well-rehearsed strategies that are designed to help clients react quickly and adaptively to threats to their own self-regulation and to good lives plans that could result in new offenses. Thus, internal and external threats and their manifestation (i.e., warning signs) in specific situations—such as thoughts, feelings and behavior—should be included and monitored in plans (see chapter 12). While the monitoring of warning signs is a standard component of supervision and post-treatment community maintenance, the difference here is that these warning signs and strategies are not restricted solely to risk, but also address circumstances that threaten the client's good lives plan and its implementation. This monitoring also includes evaluating the re-emergence of flaws in the good lives plan. Consider the following example:

Case Example: Murray

Let's return to the example in chapter 12. Murray has been in the community for six months, and has lived with Deborah, his girlfriend of many years. During the past six months, Murray has worked diligently to put his good life plan into place. His housing arrangements appear stable, and his relationship with Deborah has been stable and pleasurable. With his supervising agent's collaboration, he has taken an on-line class that provides an overview of publishing. Murray has taken good care of his health generally. He jogs six hours per week and lifts weights at a nearby fitness club early in the morning. He goes for walks with Deborah, and in his free time, he plays acoustic guitar and reads the news.

The current problem is that Murray had a promising lead at a small publishing company in the city. He was offered a position, but the offer was withdrawn due to unforeseen economic conditions. Murray was intensely disappointed. His agent is concerned that, unless Murray returns to school or finds another job, he may be out of compliance with his release rules. However, an unusual event has also occurred. Deborah came home and found Murray outside smoking a cigarette. This is unusual, as Murray had quit smoking many years earlier. Believing this to be a warning sign (and, for Murray, an inappropriate instrumental good toward the goal of happiness), Deborah has insisted that Murray meet with his therapist and supervising agent for a consultation. Her concern is that Murray's good life plan has encountered a flaw of means and that his goal of happiness is coming into conflict with his goal of a healthy life. Furthermore, his goals of knowledge and agency are going unmet due to the loss of his job.

Agent: *Deborah, thank-you so much for being the driving force in our meeting today; we all appreciate it. It shows tremendous dedication to Murray and to the community. Murray, my background is all about studying risk. I'm not as familiar with the good lives and self-regulation pathways, although I do know what you are working toward in your life and I do recognize when my clients are having a hard time. Losing a job and changing your behavior—with even just a cigarette—has concerned your girlfriend. Tell us what's going on.*

Murray: I really wanted that job. It broke my heart not to get it. And—I'll say it—I'm really worried you're going to take me back to court.

Agent: What I want is community safety <u>and</u> your success. I think they can both go together. Just the same, you know my obligations to the court. Tell me more.

Murray: Okay. I didn't get the job. That got me upset. I said to myself that I would take a couple of days before sounding the alarm on my good life plan. I made a commitment that I would talk to others and listen to their ideas under these circumstances. In this case, I just wanted a couple of days. I figured I would take some time to myself and put my head back on. I gave myself permission to smoke a cigarette, figuring it wasn't going to harm anyone else.

Therapist: How does that fit into your good life plan?

Murray: It really doesn't. My idea was that my coping skills were bearing the strain, and that a few smokes while I reflected on my circumstances wouldn't be so bad, but I guess it was if it made Deborah upset.

Therapist: Murray, it might help if you were to explain a bit more to your agent about your plan in your own words.

Murray: You've got the plan, and we've talked about it. You've got the basic ideas that the best way I can manage risk is to approach the healthiest and best life I can live. What we haven't talked about as much is how the pieces fit together. That job might be just another job to others, but it's about my independence and autonomy. It's about being good at my work and learning about something that I'm really interested in. It's also about my learning how to be a new person in this world. Part of the appeal of publishing is that it's not a place of employment where it's likely I'd see lots of kids or get caught up in flashy childish activities. And it interests me a lot. It's about my good life goal of knowledge: learning a new life and participating in other peoples' learning by being a part of publishing things. What happened in this case is that I didn't properly use all the coping skills that I learned in treatment.

What Deborah picked up on was that I was relying on that work, and when I didn't get the job I started going back to old behaviors. In the past, I could be really self-centered. I'd smoke because it tasted good, even though I knew it was compromising my goal of a healthy life. In the past I was self-centered enough that I abused kids. My intent here was to just take a couple of days and have a few relaxing smokes, but now I see that this is one inch closer to abandoning my goals, and I need to watch out when I do that. It would not be good if I quit my plans now.

So what I've been up against is worrying that I may not have the means to reach my goals of knowledge and agency. That makes me worry that I don't have the means to hang on to others, like Deborah. That's my relatedness goal. Smoking cigarettes is really a bad idea because now that's a conflict between goals. Sure, it's happiness and pleasure, but it's not health, and I don't exercise all those hours every week just to go and smoke.

My risk factors involved in this situation are entitlement (if I think I deserve something, I'm more likely just to take it), self-regulation problems, emotional collapse, and for me a cigarette might as well be substance abuse. I'm willing to do whatever it takes to make this better.

Agent: So you almost lost some things that are really important to you.

Murray: Yes, and I don't want to go near that. I want to do whatever I need to do to stay in the community, get a job, and enjoy my life with Deborah.

Agent: On the one hand, you really want to stay out and be independent and, on the other hand, you and other people have good reason to be concerned.

Murray: Yes.

Agent: What does your therapist think?

Therapist: What we know is that true change and true progress isn't always a straight line. People go backward and forward a bit. It's to be expected. However, this is something to take seriously, and the most important thing is that we're here. I am interested to hear from Murray what he feels we need to do next.

Murray: I'm willing to do whatever it takes to keep going. If it were up to me, I would start looking for other jobs until that company can hire me again. They liked me before, and they were ready to hire me except for the economic problems. I can tell them I'll stay available. I definitely need to work in treatment to figure out what went wrong. I think that my wanting to take a couple of days to myself to think about it was a not-so-good attempt at autonomy. After all, my autonomy was threatened. I need to go back to my good life plan and work out some better methods for when my autonomy is threatened.

Deborah: And you need to understand that including me in your thinking about these things doesn't mean you don't have autonomy. If you really want to be self-directed, you can be strong and include me!

Murray: Yeah, you're right..

Agent: All right, here's what I'm going to do. I'm satisfied that everyone is working hard at this situation and that you can keep yourself on track with the help of these people. However, the employment business is something that the court takes seriously, so let's really work at that. Murray, I want you to come back here next week to give me an update. I might make an unscheduled visit to your place to see how you are doing, or I might not. You and I are going to meet regularly, each week. I know your therapist will call if anything goes wrong. Work with these people and

come up with a plan like you were saying. Let's all get together for an hour in one month. We'll review the plan at that time. How does that sound?
Murray: *That sounds okay.*
Agent: *Murray, in the meantime, come back next week with a complete timeline of everything you've done to look for a job. Keep a journal of it, with names, addresses, phone numbers of places and people you've spoken with seriously, and we will take it from there. I want to support your efforts, and you know I have to carry out the orders of the court. Okay? In the meantime I'm going to follow your advice and consider anything that's not healthy and goal-directed to be a warning sign.*
Murray: *That works for me. Thank-you.*

The key factor in this example is an agent who is willing to hear about and support efforts toward change. He does not need to be a therapist to understand that people who are working on building a satisfying and fulfilling life are less likely to re-offend, particularly when they are compliant with supervision, and that clients will sometimes experience difficulty following through on or achieving their plans. The agent has actively assisted Murray to re-focus on his good life plan, to develop strategies for addressing flaws, and to utilize his self-regulation skills. Likewise, the therapist understands Murray's good life plan and is willing to work in close contact with the supervising agent. All parties have effectively motivated Murray to continue to follow his plan and to implement risk management strategies. The supervising agent has also re-evaluated risk factors, has put a plan into place to manage these factors, and has done so in a manner that is helpful and that explains his requirements under court orders without threatening the client with consequences for non-compliance. Ultimately, it is the willingness of all parties to come together and their understanding of Murray's goals that has made the difference.

GOOD LIVES AND SELF-REGULATION: WHEN THINGS GO RIGHT

Traditional approaches to community supervision typically do not monitor and reinforce clients' progress and success, as they are preoccupied with risk assessment, risk management, and compliance with court, probation, and other official orders. However, as has been illustrated throughout this book, the integrated good lives/self-regulation approach is explicitly strengths-based, forward-looking, and approach-oriented. This approach means that the emphasis in supervision must be placed on monitoring and reinforcing clients' progress and the implementation of effective self-regulation skills and good lives plans, along with providing assistance to clients to actively achieve their goals and manage risk. Thus, the supervision plan should also include indicators of successful implementation of clients' plans (see chapter 12) that are regularly monitored. Furthermore, the role of community supervisors and support persons within the GLM/SRM-R approach is to assist clients to adjust their good lives plan, should fine-tuning become necessary. For example, a client who highly values the primary good of excellence in work—but who is unable to find satisfying employment—may need to adjust his good life plan by including alternative, secondary goods designed to work toward achieving a job. As this situation may also threaten other aspects of the client's plan, such as life or agency, attention is paid to attainment of those goods as well.

Consider the following example:

Case Example: Murray

Agent: Hi, Murray. It's good to see you again. Tell me about your week.

Murray: Well, I've looked for work at about 15 places, and I think I might have found something. They'll let me know on Monday. The local newspaper needs help with preparation and printing. The only problem is that it's the second shift.

Agent: That's the time you'd usually be spending with Deborah.

Murray: True, but I think she and I can manage this conflict. I've spoken to her about it and it is okay, at least for now.

Agent: What kinds of complications does this present to your plan?

Murray: It means we will spend less time together and so we will need to make the best use of our time together and readjust our schedules. I can move my time with my guitar and the news to the early morning when she's at work. I can sleep then, too. That way, we'll spend our important time together.

Agent: You're really giving this some thought. This is really important to you.

Murray: Yes. This will build means with excellence at play and work, autonomy, and knowledge. It may also help a bit with risk because I'll be out when everyone else is asleep.

Agent: How is Deborah with this?

Murray: So far, so good. It's a change, so how about if I bring her in next time and we talk together?

Agent: That sounds like a good idea.

Murray: My main hope is to increase the means in my plan, as we discussed, without creating a conflict between my goals. My relatedness is still one of the most important goals. Working late keeps me away from the community a little bit, but it's a *community newspaper, so that has value, too, and maybe it's a way to be even more involved in my community.*

Agent: *So you're working hard to adjust your plan just a bit without upsetting the balance of your plan.*

Murray: *Exactly, and I hope it works.*

Agent: *And you're trying not to go too fast.*

Murray: *Well, I definitely need to bring this to my therapist and my treatment group, too.*

Agent: *Let me know how it goes.*

In this example, Murray is openly exploring the impact of a change to the implementation of his good life plan. He is reporting on the primary goods involved (which include relatedness, agency, excellence at work and play, knowledge, and other primary goods in lesser measure). He is also exploring what flaws might occur should things begin to go wrong (for example, if changing means creates conflicts in his good life plan). By attending to these areas and creating plans for preventing flaws, Murray is establishing a clearer plan for self-regulation and preventing the misregulation that might have occurred otherwise.

SUMMARY

This chapter proposes an alternative approach to community supervision and support that includes, but goes beyond, standard risk monitoring and management approaches typically used in supervision. Within the integrated good lives/self-regulation approach, an important role of supervision is to actively assist clients to reinforce and entrench self-regulation skills and strategies not only to manage risk, but in the service of implementing their good lives plans. Supervision builds on clients' values, goals, and needs that assist in the attainment of well-being and a satisfying life. One important role of the community supervision agent, case management team, and support persons is to explicitly create opportunities for clients to attain important primary goods in their lives and to apply their self-regulation skills to attaining these.

About the Authors

Pamela M. Yates, Ph.D., R.D. Psych has worked as a clinician and researcher in various capacities with adults and youth, including sexual offenders, violent offenders, individuals with substance abuse problems, and victims of violence, and has developed accredited offender treatment programs. Her research and publications include offender rehabilitation, assessment and treatment of sexual offenders, program evaluation, risk assessment, treatment effectiveness, psychopathy, and sexual sadism. She has written extensively on the Self-Regulation and Good Lives models of sexual offender intervention and their application in practice.

David Prescott, LICSW, is currently clinical director of the Becket Programs of Maine. He previously served as clinical director of the Minnesota Sex Offender Program in Moose Lake and as treatment assessment director of the Sand Ridge Secure Treatment Center in Wisconsin. Mr. Prescott is the author and editor of seven books about working with sexual offenders of all ages, and is a past president of the Association for the Treatment of Sexual Abusers. His clinical and training interests include motivational enhancement, developing and maintaining therapeutic relationships, and assessing treatment progress.

Tony Ward, Ph.D., DipClinPsyc, is currently professor of clinical psychology and head of department at Victoria University of New Zealand. His research interests include offender cognition, reintegration and desistance, ethical issues in forensic psychology, and evolutionary approaches to understanding human behavior. He has authored over 280 academic publications and his latest book (coauthored with Richard Laws) is *Desisting from Sex Offending: Alternatives to Throwing Away the Keys* (Guilford, October 2010).

References

Abel, G. G., J. V. Becker, and J. Cunningham-Rathner. 1984. Complications, consent, and cognitions in sex between children and adults. *International Journal of Law and Psychiatry* 7:89–103.

Abel, G. G., and J. L. Rouleau. 1986. Sexual disorders. In *The Medical Basis of Psychiatry*, ed. G. Winokur and P. Clayton, 246–67. Philadelphia: W. B. Saunders.

Andrews, D. A., and J. Bonta. 2007. *The Psychology of Criminal Conduct*. 4th ed. Cincinnati, OH: Anderson.

Aspinwall, L. G., and U. M. Staudinger, eds. 2003. *A Psychology of Human Strengths: Fundamental Questions and Future Directions for a Positive Psychology*. Washington, DC: American Psychological Association.

Augoustinos, M., and I. Walker. 1995. *Social Cognition: An Integrated Introduction*. London: Sage.

Austin, J. T., and J. B. Vancouver. 1996. Goal constructs in psychology: Structure, process, and content. *Psychological Bulletin* 120:338–75.

Bandura, A. 1986. *Social Foundations of Thought and Action: A Social Cognitive Theory*. Englewood Cliffs, NJ: Prentice-Hall.

Barbaree, H. E. 1991. Denial and minimization among sex offenders: Assessment and treatment outcome. *Forum on Corrections Research* 3:30–33.

Barbaree, H. E., and W. L. Marshall. 1991. The role of male sexual arousal in rape: Six models. *Journal of Consulting and Clinical Psychology* 59:621–30.

Barbaree, H. E., W. L. Marshall, E. Yates, and L. O. Lightfoot. 1983. Alcohol intoxication and deviant sexual arousal in male social drinkers. *Behaviour Research and Therapy* 21:365–73.

Barber, P. J. 1988. *Applied Cognitive Psychology*. London: Metheun & Co.

Baumeister, R. F., and T. F. Heatherton. 1996. Self-regulation failure: An overview. *Psychological Inquiry* 7:1–15.

Baumeister, R. F., and K. D. Vohs. 2004. *Handbook of Self-Regulation: Research, Theory, and Applications*. New York, NY: Guilford.

Beauchamp, T. L., and J. F. Childress. 2009. *Principles of Biomedical Ethics*. 6th ed. New York, NY: Oxford University Press.

Beck, A. T. 1964. Thinking and depression: 2. Theory and therapy. *Archives of General Psychiatry* 9:324–33.

———.1967. *Depression: Causes and Treatment.* Philadelphia, PA: University of Pennsylvania Press.

———. 1976. *Cognitive Therapy and the Emotional Disorders.* New York, NY: International Universities Press.

———. 1999. *Prisoners of Hate: The Cognitive Basis of Anger, Hostility, and Violence.* New York, NY: Harper-Collins.

Beck, A. T., A. Freeman, and D. D. Davis. 2004. *Cognitive Therapy of Personality Disorders.* New York, NY: Guilford.

Beech, A., and A. S. Fordham. 1997. Therapeutic climate of sexual offender treatment programs. *Sexual Abuse: A Journal of Research and Treatment* 9:219–37.

Beech, A. R., and T. Ward. 2004. The integration of etiology and risk in sexual offenders: A theoretical framework. *Aggression and Violent Behavior* 10:31–63.

Bem, D. J. 1972. Self-perception theory. In *Advances in Experimental Social Psychology,* ed. L. Berkowitz, 6:2–62. New York: Academic Press.

Binder, J., and H. Strupp. 1997. "Negative process": A recurrently discovered and underestimated facet of therapeutic process and outcome in the individual psychotherapy of adults. *Clinical Psychology: Science and Practice* 4:121–39.

Blader, J. C., and W. L. Marshall. 1989. Is assessment of sexual arousal in rapists worthwhile? A critique of response compatibility approach. *Clinical Psychological Review* 9:569–87.

Blanchard, G. T. 1995. *The Difficult Connection: The Therapeutic Relationship in Sex Offender Treatment.* Brandon, Vermont: Safer Society Press.

Bumby, K., and D. J. Hansen. 1997. Intimacy deficits, fear of intimacy, and loneliness among sex offenders. *Criminal Justice and Behaviour* 24:315–31.

Carver, C. S., and M. F. Scheier. 1981. *Attention and self-regulation: A Control-Theory Approach to Human Behavior.* New York, NY: Springer-Verlag.

———. 1998. *On the Self-Regulation of Behavior.* New York, NY: Cambridge University Press.

———. 1990. Principles of self-regulation: Action and emotion. In *Handbook of Motivation and Social Behavior,* ed. E. T. Higgins and R. M. Sorrentino, 3–52. New York, NY: Guilford.

Cochran, W., and A. Tesser. 1996. The "What the hell" effect: Some effects of goal proximity and goal framing on performance. In *Striving and Feeling: Interactions Among Goals, Affect, and Self-Regulation,* ed. L. L. Martin and A. Tesser, 99–120. New York, NY: Lawrence Erlbaum.

Correctional Service Canada. 2009. *Evaluation Report: Correctional Service Canada's Correctional Programs.* Ottawa, ON: Author. http://www.csc-scc.gc.ca/text/pa/cop-prog/cp-eval-eng.shtml

Cullen, M., and R. J. Wilson. 2003. *TRY—Treatment Readiness for You: A Workbook for Sexual Offenders.* Lanham, MD: American Corrections Association.

Cumming, G. F., and R. J. McGrath. 2000. External Supervision. In *Remaking Relapse Prevention with Sex Offenders: A Sourcebook,* ed. D. R. Laws, S. M. Hudson, and T. Ward. Thousand Oaks, CA: Sage.

———. 2005. *Supervision of the Sex Offender: Community Management, Risk Assessment, and Treatment.* Brandon, VT: Safer Society Press.

Cummins, R. A. 1996. The domains of life satisfaction: An attempt to order chaos. *Social Indicators Research* 38:303–28.

Deci, E. L., and R. M. Ryan. 2000. The "what" and "why" of goal pursuits: Human needs and the self-determination of behavior. *Psychological Inquiry* 11:227–68.

DiClemente, C. C. 1991. Motivational Interviewing and the Stages of Change. In *Motivational Interviewing: Preparing People to Change Addictive Behavior*, ed. W. R. Miller and S. Rollnick, 191–202. New York: The Guilford Press.

Dowden, C., and D. A. Andrews. 2000. Effective correctional treatment and violent offending: A meta-analysis. *Canadian Journal of Criminology and Criminal Justice* 42:449–67.

Drapeau, M., A. Körner, L. Granger, L. Brunet, and F. Caspar. 2005. A plan analysis of pedophile sexual abusers' motivations for treatment: A qualitative pilot study. *International Journal of Offender Therapy and Comparative Criminology* 49:308–24.

Duncan, B., S. Miller, B. Wampold, and M. A. Hubble. 2009. *The Heart and Soul of Change: Delivering What Works in Therapy*. Washington, DC: American Psychological Association.

Emmons, R. A. 1999. *The Psychology of Ultimate Concerns*. New York: Guilford.

Endler, N. S., and D. A. Parker. 1990. Multidimensional assessment of coping: A critical evaluation. *Journal of Personality and Social Psychology* 58(5):844–54.

Fernandez, Y. M., W. L. Marshall, S. Lightbody, and C. O'Sullivan. 1999. The Child Molester Empathy Measure: Description and examination of its reliability and validity. *Sexual Abuse: A Journal of Research and Treatment* 11:17–31.

Finkelhor, D. 1984. *Child Sexual Abuse: New Theory and Research*. New York, NY: Free Press.

———. 1986. *A Sourcebook on Child Sexual Abuse*. Beverly Hills, CA: Sage.

Fiske, S. T., and S. E. Taylor. 1991. *Social Cognition*. 2nd ed. New York, NY: McGraw Hill.

Freeman-Longo, R. E., S. L. Bird, W. F. Stevenson, and J. A. Fiske. 1994. *1994 Nationwide Survey of Sexual Offender Treatment and Models*. Brandon, VT: Safer Society Press.

Gannon, T. A. 2009. Social cognition in violent and sexual offending: An overview. *Psychology, Crime, and Law* 15:97–118.

Gannon, T. A., and D. L. L. Polaschek. 2006. Cognitive distortions in child molesters: A re-examination of key theories and research. *Clinical Psychology Review* 26:1000–19.

Gannon, T. A., T. Ward, A. R. Beech, and D. Fisher. 2007. *Aggressive Offenders' Cognition: Theory, Research, and Practice*. Hoboken, NJ: Wiley.

Garland, R., and M. Dougher. 1991. Motivational intervention in the treatment of sexual offenders. In *Motivational Interviewing—Preparing People to Change Addictive Behavior*, ed. W. R. Miller and S. Rollnick, 303–13. New York: Guilford Press.

Garlick, Y., W. L. Marshall, and P. Thornton. 1996. Intimacy deficits and attribution of blame among sexual offenders. *Legal and Criminological Psychology* 1(2):251–58.

Gendreau, P., and C. Goggin. 1996. Principles of effective correctional programming. *Forum on Corrections Research* 8:38–41.

———. 1997. Correctional treatment: Accomplishments and realities. In *Correctional Counseling and Rehabilitation*, ed. P. Van Voorhis et al., 271–79. Cincinnati, OH: Anderson.

Gendreau, P., T. Little, and C. Goggin. 1996. A meta-analysis of the predictors of adult offender recidivism: What works! *Criminology* 34:3–17.

Gordon, A., and G. Hover. 1998. The twin rivers sex offender treatment program. In *Sourcebook of Treatment Programs for Sexual Offenders,* ed. W. L. Marshall, Y. M. Fernandez, S. M. Hudson, and T. Ward, 3–15. New York: Plenum Press.

Gordon, A., and T. Nicholaichuk. 1996. Applying the risk principle to sex offender treatment. *Forum on Corrections Research* 8:36–38.

Gordon, A., and R. Packard. October 1998. *The Impact of Community Maintenance Treatment on Sex Offender Recidivism.* Paper presented at the Association for the Treatment of Sexual Abusers 17th Annual Research and Treatment Conference, Vancouver, BC.

Grant, D. A., and E. A. Berg. 2003. *The Wisconsin Card Sort Task Version 4 (WCST).* Lutz, FL: Psychological Assessment Resources.

Groth, A. N. 1979. Sexual trauma in the life histories of rapists and child molesters. *Victimology* 4:10–16.

Haaven, J. 2006. Evolution of old/new me model. In *Practical Treatment Strategies for Forensic Clients with Severe and Sexual Behavior Problems among Persons with Developmental Disabilities,* ed. G. Blasingame. Oklahoma City, OK: Wood'N'Barnes Publishing.

Hall, G. C. N., and R. Hirschman. 1991. Toward a theory of sexual aggression: A quadripartite model. *Journal of Consulting and Clinical Psychology* 59(5):662–69.

Hanson, R. K. 1996. Evaluating the contribution of relapse prevention theory to the treatment of sexual offenders. *Sexual Abuse: A Journal of Research and Treatment* 8:201–08.

———. 1997. How to know what works with sexual offenders. *Sexual Abuse: A Journal of Research and Treatment* 9:129–45.

———. 1999. Working with sex offenders: A personal view. *Journal of Sexual Aggression* 4:81–93.

———. 2000. What is so special about relapse prevention? In *Relapse Prevention with Sex Offenders,* ed. D. R. Laws, 1–31. New York: Guilford.

———. 2006, September. *What Works: The Principles of Effective Interventions with Offenders.* Presented at the 25th Annual Convention of the Association for the Treatment of Sexual Abusers, Chicago, Ill.

Hanson, R. K., G. Bourgon, L. Helmus, and S. Hodgson. 2009. The principles of effective correctional treatment also apply to sexual offenders: A meta-analysis. *Criminal Justice and Behavior* 36:865–91.

Hanson, R. K., M. T. Bussière. 1998. Predicting relapse: A meta-analysis of sexual offender recidivism studies. *Journal of Consulting and Clinical Psychology* 66(2):348–62.

Hanson, R. K., R. Gizzarelli, and H. Scott. 1994. The attitudes of incest offenders: Sexual entitlement and acceptance of sex with children. *Criminal Justice and Behavior* 21:187–202.

Hanson, R. K., A. Gordon, A. J. R. Harris, J. K. Marques, W. Murphy, V. L. Quinsey, et al. 2002. First report of the collaborative outcome data project on the effectiveness of treatment for sex offenders. *Sexual Abuse: A Journal of Research and Treatment* 14:169–94.

Hanson, R. K., and A. J. R. Harris. 2000. Where should we intervene? Dynamic predictors of sexual offence recidivism. *Criminal Justice and Behaviour* 27:6–35.

———. (2001). A structured approach to evaluating change among sexual offenders. *Sexual Abuse: A Journal of Research and Treatment* 13:105–22.

Hanson, R. K., A. J. R. Harris, T. Scott, and L. Helmus. 2007. *Assessing the Risk of Sexual Offenders on Community Supervision: The Dynamic Supervision Project*. User Report No. 2007–05. Ottawa: Public Safety Canada.

Hanson, R. K., and K. Morton-Bourgon. 2004. *Predictors of Sexual Recidivism: An Updated Meta-Analysis*. Ottawa: Public Safety and Emergency Preparedness Canada.

———. 2005. The characteristics of persistent sexual offenders: A meta-analysis of recidivism studies. *Journal of Consulting and Clinical Psychology* 73:1154–63.

Hanson, R. K., and H. Scott. 1995. Assessing perspective taking among sexual offenders, non-sexual criminals and non-offenders. *Sexual Abuse: A Journal of Research and Treatment* 7:259–77.

Hanson, R. K., and D. Thornton. 1999. *Static-99: Improving Actuarial Risk Assessment for Sex Offenders*. Ottawa: Department of the Solicitor General of Canada.

Hanson, R. K., and P. M. Yates. 2004. Sexual violence: Risk factors and treatment. In *Anthology on Interventions Against Violent Men*, ed. M. Eliasson. Uppsala, Sweden: Department of Industrial Relations.

Hare, R. D. 2003. *The Hare Psychopathy Checklist–Revised*. 2nd ed. Toronto: Multi-Health Systems.

Harris, M. J. 1991. Controversy and culmination: Meta-analysis and research on interpersonal expectancy effects. *Personality and Social Psychology Bulletin* 17:316–22.

Heidt, J. M., and B. P. Marx. 2003. Self-monitoring as a treatment vehicle. In *Cognitive Behavior Therapy: Applying Empirically Supported Techniques in Your Practice*, ed. W. O'Donohue, J. E. Fisher, and S. C. Hayes, 361–67. Hoboken, NJ: Wiley.

Hildebran, D., and W. D. Pithers. 1989. Enhancing offender empathy for sexual-abuse victims. In *Relapse Prevention with Sex Offenders*, ed. D. R. Laws, 236–43. New York: Guilford Press.

Hudson, S. M., W. L. Marshall, D. S. Wales, E. McDonald, L. W. Bakker, and A. McLean. 1993. Emotional recognition skills in sex offenders. *Annals of Sex Research* 6:199–211.

Hudson, S. M., D. S. Wales, and T. Ward. 1998. Kia Marama: A treatment program for child molesters in New Zealand. In *Sourcebook of Treatment Programs for Sexual Offenders*, ed. W. L. Marshall, Y. M. Fernandez, S. M. Hudson, and T. Ward. New York: Plenum Press.

Huesmann, L. R. 1988. An information-processing model for the development of aggression. *Aggressive Behavior* 14:12–24.

Jenkins, A. 1990. *Invitations to Responsibility: The Therapeutic Engagement of Men Who Are Violent and Abusive*. Adelaide, Australia: Dulwich Centre Publications.

Jenkins-Hall, K. 1994. Outpatient treatment of child molesters: Motivational factors and outcome. *Journal of Offender Rehabilitation* 21:139–50.

Jennings, J. L., and S. Sawyer. 2003. Principles and techniques for maximizing the effectiveness of group therapy with sex offenders. *Sexual Abuse: A Journal of Research and Treatment* 15:251–68.

Johnston, L., S. M. Hudson, and T. Ward. 1997. The suppression of sexual thoughts by child molesters: A preliminary investigation. *Sexual Abuse: A Journal of Research and Treatment* 34:303–19.

Johnston, L., and T. Ward. 1996. Social cognition and sexual offending: A theoretical framework. *Sexual Abuse: Journal of Research and Treatment* 8:55–80.

Karoly, P. 1993. Mechanisms of self-regulation: A systems view. *Annual Review of Psychology* 44:23–52.

Kear-Colwell, J., and P. Pollack. 1997. Motivation and confrontation: Which approach to the child sex offender? *Criminal Justice and Behaviour* 24:20–33.

Keenan, T., and T. Ward. 2000. A theory of mind perspective on cognitive, affective, and intimacy deficits in child sexual offenders. *Sexual Abuse: A Journal of Research and Treatment* 12:49–58.

———. 2003. Developmental antecedents of sexual offending. In *Sexual Deviance: Issues and Controversies*, ed. T. Ward, D. R. Laws, and S. M. Hudson, 119–34. Thousand Oaks, CA: Sage Publications.

Kekes, J. 1989. *Moral Tradition and Individuality*. Princeton, New Jersey: Princeton University Press.

Knight, R. A., and D. T. Thornton. 2007. *Evaluating and Improving Risk Assessment Schemes for Sexual Recidivism: A Long-Term Follow-Up of Convicted Sexual Offenders*. Final report for NIJ grant 2003-WG-BX-1002. Retrieved August 19, 2010, from http://www.ncjrs.gov/pdffiles1/nij/grants/217618.pdf

Langevin, R., M. A. Wright, and L. Handy. 1988. Empathy, assertiveness, aggressiveness, and defensiveness among sex offenders. *Annals of Sex Research* 1:533–47.

Laws, D. R., ed. 1989. *Relapse Prevention with Sex Offenders*. New York: The Guilford Press.

———. (2003). The rise and fall of relapse prevention. *Australian Psychologist* 38(1):22–30.

Laws, D. R., S. M. Hudson, and T. Ward, 2000. The original model of relapse prevention with sex offenders: Promises unfulfilled. In *Remaking Relapse Prevention with Sex Offenders: A Sourcebook*, ed. D. R. Laws, S. M. Hudson, and T. Ward, 3–24. Newbury Park: CA: Sage.

Laws, D. R., and W. L. Marshall. 1990. A Conditioning Theory of the Etiology and Maintenance of Deviant Sexual Preference and Behaviour. In *Handbook of Sexual Assault: Issues, Theories, and Treatment of Offenders*, ed. W. L. Marshall and H. E. Barbaree, 103–13. NY: Plenum.

Laws, D. R., and T. Ward. 2006. When one size doesn't fit all: The reformulation of relapse prevention. In *Sexual Offender Treatment: Controversial Issues*, ed. W. L. Marshall, Y. M. Fernandez, L. E. Marshall, and G. A. Serran, 241–54. New Jersey, NY: John Wiley & Sons.

———. In press. *Desistance from sexual offending: Alternatives to throwing away the keys*. New York, NY: Guilford Press.

Leahy, R. L. 2001. *Overcoming Resistance in Cognitive Therapy*. New York, NY: Guilford.

Linley, P. A., and S. Joseph. 2004. Applied positive psychology: A new perspective for professional practice. In *Positive Psychology in Practice*, ed. P. A. Linley and S. Joseph, 3–12. New Jersey, NY: John Wiley & Sons.

Lockhart, L. L., B. E. Saunders, and P. Cleveland. 1988. Adult male sexual offenders: An overview of treatment techniques. In *Journal of Social Work and Human Sexuality* 7: 1–32.

Lösel, F., and M. Schmucker. 2005. The effectiveness of treatment for sexual offenders: A comprehensive meta-analysis. *Journal of Experimental Criminology* 1:117–46.

Malamuth, N. M., and L. M. Brown. 1994. Sexually aggressive men's perceptions of women's communications: Testing three explanations. *Journal of Personality and Social Psychology* 67:699–712.

Malamuth, N. M., C. L. Heavey, and D. Linz. 1993. Predicting men's antisocial behavior against women: The interaction model of sexual aggression. *Sexual Agression: Issues in Etiology,*

Assesments, and Treatment, ed. G.C.N. Hall, R. Hirschman, J.R. Graham, and M.s. Zaragoza, 63–97. Washington, DC: Taylor and Francis.

Mann, R. E. 1998. *Relapse prevention? Is That the Bit Where They Told Me All of the Things That I Couldn't Do Anymore?* Paper presented at the 17th annual Research and Treatment Conference of the Association for the Treatment of Sexual Abusers, Vancouver, BC, October 2003.

———. 2009. Getting the context right for sexual offender treatment. In *Building Motivation to Change in Sexual Offenders,* ed. D.S. Prescott. Brandon, VT: Safer Society Press.

Mann, R. E., and A. R. Beech. 2003. Cognitive distortions, schemas, and implicit theories. In *Sexual Deviance: Issues and Controversies,* ed. T. Ward, D. R. Laws, and S. M. Hudson. Thousand Oaks, CA: Sage.

Mann, R. E., and C. R. Hollin. 2001, November. *Schemas: A Model for Understanding Cognition in Sexual Offending.* Paper presented at the 20th Annual Research and Treatment conference of the Association for the Treatment of Sexual Abusers, San Antonio, TX.

Mann, R. E., and J. Shingler. 2006. Schema-driven cognitions in sexual offenders: Theory, Assessment, and Treatment. In *Sexual Offender Treatment: Controversial Issues,* ed. W. L. Marshall, Y. M. Fernandez, L. E. Marshall, and G. A. Serran, 173–85. Hoboken, NJ: Wiley.

Mann, R. E., S. D. Webster, C. Schofield, and W. L. Marshall. 2004. Approach versus avoidance goals in relapse prevention with sexual offenders. *Sexual Abuse: A Journal of Research and Treatment* 16:65–75.

Marlatt, G. A. 1982. Relapse prevention: a self-control program for the treatment of addictive behaviors. In *Adherence, Compliance, and Generalization in Behavioral Medicine,* ed. R. B. Stuart, 329–78. New York: Brunner/Mazel.

Marques, J. K., D. M. Day, and C. Nelson. 1992. *Findings and Recommendations from California's Experimental Treatment Program.* Unpublished manuscript, Sex Offender Treatment and evaluation Project, Atascadero State Hospital, California.

Marshall, W. L. 1996. The sexual offender: Monster, victim or everyman? *Sexual Abuse: A Journal of Research and Treatment* 8:317–35.

———. 1997. The relationship between self-esteem and deviant sexual arousal in nonfamilial child molesters. *Behavior Modification* 21:86–96.

———. 2005. Therapist style in sexual offender treatment: Influence on indices of change. *Sexual Abuse: A Journal of Research and Treatment* 17(2):109–16.

Marshall, W. L., D. Anderson, and Y. M. Fernandez. 1999. *Cognitive Behavioral Treatment of Sexual Offenders.* Chichester, UK: Wiley.

Marshall, W. L., and H. E. Barbaree. 1988. The long-term evaluation of a behavioral treatment program for child molesters. *Behaviour Research and Therapy* 26:499–511.

———. 1990. Outcome of comprehensive cognitive behavioural treatment programs. In *Handbook of Sexual Assault: Issues, Theories, and Treatment of the Offender,* ed. W. L. Marshall, D. R. Laws, and H. E. Barbaree. NewYork: Plemum, pp. 363-385.

Marshall, W. L., P. Bryce, S. M. Hudson, T. Ward, and B. Moth. 1996. The enhancement of intimacy and the reduction of loneliness among child molesters. *Journal of Family Violence* 11:219–35.

Marshall, W. L., F. Champagne, C. Brown, and S. Miller. 1997. Empathy, intimacy, loneliness, and self-esteem in non-familial child molesters. *Journal of Child Sexual Abuse* 6:87–97.

Marshall, W. L., and J. Darke. 1982. Inferring humiliation as motivation in sexual offenses. *Treatment for Sexual Aggressiveness* 5:1–3.

Marshall, W. L., Y. M. Fernandez, G. A. Serran, R. Mulloy, D. Thornton, R. E. Mann, and D. Anderson. 2003. Process variables in the treatment of sexual offenders: A review of the relevant literature. *Aggression and Violent Behavior* 8:205–34.

Marshall, W. L., and L. S. Hambley. 1996. Intimacy and loneliness, and their relationship to rape myth acceptance and hostility toward women among rapists. *Journal of Interpersonal Violence* 11:586–92.

Marshall, W. L., S. N. Hudson, and S. Hodkinson. 1993. The importance of attachment bonds and the development of juvenile sex offending. In *The Juvenile Sex Offender*, ed. H. E. Barbaree, W. L. Marshall, and S. M. Hudson, 164–81. New York: Guilford.

Marshall, W. L., S. M. Hudson, R. Jones, and Y. M. Fernandez. 1995. Empathy in sex offenders. *Clinical Psychology Review* 15:99–113.

Marshall, W. L., and A. Mazzucco. 1995. Self-esteem and parental attachments in child molesters. *Sexual Abuse: Journal of Research and Treatment* 7(4):279–85.

Marshall, W. L., C. O'Sullivan, and Y. M. Fernandez. 1996. The enhancement of victim empathy among incarcerated child molesters. *Legal and Criminological Psychology* 1:95–102.

Marshall, W. L., and W. D. Pithers. 1994. A reconsideration of treatment outcome with sex offenders. *Criminal Justice and Behavior* 21:10–27.

Marshall, W. L., G. Serran, H. Moulden, R. Mulloy, Y. M. Fernandez, R. E. Mann, and D. Thornton. 2002. Therapist features in sexual offender treatment: Their reliable identification and influence on behaviour change. *Clinical Psychology and Psychotherapy* 9:395–405.

Marshall, W. L., D. Thornton, L. E. Marshall, Y. M. Fernandez, and R. E. Mann. 2001. Treatment of sexual offenders who are in categorical denial: A pilot project. *Sexual Abuse: Journal of Research and Treatment* 13:205–15.

Maruna, S. 2001. *Making Good: How Ex-Convicts Reform and Rebuild their Lives*. Washington, DC: American Psychological Association Books.

McFall, R. M. 1990. The enhancement of social skills: An information processing analysis. In *Handbook of Sexual Assault: Issues, Theories, and the Treatment of the Offender*, ed. W. L. Marshall, D. R. Laws, and H. E. Barbaree. New York, NY: Plenum.

McGrath, R. J., G. F. Cumming, B. L. Burchard, S. Zeoli, and L. Ellerby. 2009. *Current Practices and Emerging Trends in Sexual Abuser Management: The Safer Society 2009 North American Survey*. Brandon, VT: Safer Society Press.

McGrath, R. J., G. Cumming, J. A. Livingston, and S. E. Hoke. 2003. Outcome of a Treatment Program for Adult Sex Offenders: From Prison to Community. *Journal of Interpersonal Violence* 18:3–17.

McKibben, A., J. Proulx, and R. Lusignan. 1994. Relationships between conflict, affect, and deviant sexual behaviours in rapists and paedophiles. *Behavior Research and Therapy* 32:571–75.

McMurran, M., and T. Ward. 2004. Motivating offenders to change in therapy: An organizing framework. *Legal and Criminological Psychology* 9:295–311.

Miller, P. A., and N. Eisenberg. 1988. The relationship of empathy to aggressive and externalizing/antisocial behaviour. *Psychological Bulletin* 103:234–344.

Miller, S., M. Hubble, and B. Duncan. 2007. Supershrinks: Who are they? What can we learn from them? *Psychotherapy Networker* 27–56.

———. 2008. Supershrinks: What's the secret of their success? *Psychotherapy in Australia* 14:14–22.

Miller W. R., and S. Rollnick. 2002. *Motivational Interviewing: Preparing People for Change*. 2nd ed. New York, NY: Guilford.

Millon, T., C. Millon, R. Davis, and S. Grossman. 2009. *The Millon Clinical Multiaxial Inventory-III*. San Antonio, TX: Pearson Assessments.

Miner, M. H., D. M. Day, and M. K. Nafpaktitis. 1989. Assessment of coping skills: Development of a situational competency test. In *Relapse Prevention with Sex Offenders*, ed. D. R. Laws, 127–36. New York: Guilford.

Moore, B. S. 1990. The origins and development of empathy. *Motivation and Emotion* 14:75–80.

Moulden, H. M., and W. L. Marshall. 2009. A hopeful approach to motivating sexual offenders for change. In *Building Motivation for Change in Sexual Offenders*, ed. D. S. Prescott. Brandon, VT: Safer Society Press.

Mulloy, R., W. C. Smiley, and D. L. Mawson. 1997, June. *Empathy and the Successful Treatment of Psychopaths*. Poster presented at the Annual Meeting of the Canadian Psychological Association, Toronto, ON.

Murphy, M. C. 2001. *Natural Law and Practical Rationality*. New York, NY: Cambridge University Press.

Murphy, W. D. 1990. Assessment and modification of cognitive distortions in sex offenders. In *Handbook of Sexual Assault: Issues, Theories, and Treatment of the Offender*, ed. W. L. Marshall, D. R. Laws, and H. E. Barbaree, 331–42. New York, NY: Plenum.

Neidigh, L., and H. Krop. 1992. Cognitive distortions among child sexual offenders. *Journal of Sex Education and Therapy* 18:208–15.

Nicholaichuk, T. P. 1996. Sex offender treatment priority: An illustration of the risk/need principle. *Forum on Corrections Research* 8:30–32.

Nussbaum, M. C. 2000. *Women and Human Development: The Capabilities Approach*. New York, NY: Cambridge University Press.

O'Brien, M.D., L. E. Marshall, and W. L. Marshall. 2009. The Rockwood Preparatory Program for sexual offenders: Goals and the methods employed to achieve them. In *Building Motivation for Change in Sexual Offenders*, ed. D. S. Prescott. Brandon, VT: Safer Society Press.

Pavlov, I. P. 1927. *Conditioned Reflexes*. (Translated by G.V. Aurep). London: Oxford.

Pithers, W. D. 1990. Relapse prevention with sexual aggressors: A method for maintaining therapeutic gain and enhancing external supervision. In *Handbook of Sexual Assault: Issues, Theories, and Treatment of the Offender*, ed. W. L. Marshall, 343–61. New York: Plenum Press.

———. 1991. Relapse prevention with sexual aggressors. *Forum on Corrections Research* 3:20–23.

Pithers, W. D. 1993. Treatment of rapists: Reinterpretation of early outcome data and exploratory constructs to enhance therapeutic efficacy. In *Sexual Aggression: Issues in Etiology, Assessment, and Treatment. Series in Applied Psychology: Social Issues and Questions*, ed. G. C. Nagayama Hall & R. Hirschman et al., 167–96. Washington, DC: Taylor and Francis Group.

———. 1994. Process evaluation of a group therapy component designed to enhance sex offenders' empathy for sexual abuse survivors. *Behaviour Research and Therapy* 32:565–70.

Pithers, W. D., L. S. Beal, J. Armstrong, and J. Petty. 1989. Identification of risk factors through clinical interviews and analysis of records. In *Relapse Prevention with Sex Offenders*, ed. R. D. Laws, 77–87. New York, NY: Guilford Press.

Plaud, J. J., and D. E. Newberry. 1996. Rule-governed behaviour and pedophilia. *Sexual Abuse: A Journal of Research and Treatment* 8:143–59.

Polaschek, D. L. L. 2003. Relapse prevention, offence process models, and the treatment of sexual offenders. *Professional Psychology: Research and Practice* 34:361–67.

Polaschek, D. L. L., and T. A. Gannon. 2004. The implicit theories of rapists: What convicted offenders tell us. *Sexual Abuse: A Journal of Research and Treatment* 16:299–314.

Polaschek, D. L. L., and T. Ward. 2002. The implicit theories of potential rapists: What our questionnaires tell us. *Aggression and Violent Behavior* 7:385–406.

Prescott, D. S. 2009. Motivational interviewing in the treatment of sexual abusers. In *Building Motivation for Change in Sexual Offenders*, ed. D. S. Prescott. Brandon, VT: Safer Society Press.

Prentky, R. A. 1995. A rationale for the treatment of sex offenders: Pro bono publico. In *What Works: Reducing Re-Offending—Guidelines from Research and Practice*, ed. J. McGuire, 155–72. New York: Wiley.

Prentky, R. A., and A. W. Burgess. 1990. Rehabilitation of child molesters: A cost-benefit analysis. *American Journal of Orthopsychiatry* 60:108–17.

Prochaska, J. O., and C. C. DiClemente. 1992. *Stages of Change in the Modification of Problem Behaviors*. Newbury Park, CA, Sage.

Proulx, J., A. McKibben, and R. Lusignan. 1996. Relationships between affective components and sexual behaviors in sexual aggressors. *Sexual Abuse: A Journal of Research and Treatment* 8:279–89.

Quinsey, V. L., G. T. Harris, M. E. Rice, and C. Cormier. 2005. *Violent Offenders: Managing and Appraising Risk*. 2nd ed. Washington, DC: American Psychological Association.

Rice, M. E., T. C. Chaplin, G. T. Harris, and J. Coutts. 1994. Empathy for the victim and sexual arousal among rapists and nonrapists. *Journal of Interpersonal Violence* 9:435–49.

Ryan, R. M., and E. L. Deci. 2000. Self-determination and the facilitation of intrinsic motivation, social development, and well-being. *American Psychologist* 55:68–78.

Salter, A. 1988. *Treating Child Sex Offenders and Victims: A Practical Guide*. Thousand Oaks, CA: Sage.

Schwartz, B. K. 1992. Effective treatment techniques for sex offenders. *Psychiatric Annals* 22:315–19.

Scully, D. 1988. Convicted rapists' perceptions of self and victim: Role taking and emotions. *Gender and Society* 20:200–213.

Seidman, B. T., W. L. Marshall, S. M. Hudson, and P. J. Robertson. 1994. An examination of intimacy and loneliness in sex offenders. *Journal of Interpersonal Violence* 9:518–34.

Serran, G. A., Y. M. Fernandez, W. L. Marshall, and R. E. Mann. 2003. Process issues in treatment: Application to sexual offender programs. *Professional Psychology: Research and Practice* 4:368–74.

Skinner, B. F. 1938. *The Behavior of Organisms*. New York, NY: Appleton-Century-Crofts.

Smallbone, S. W., and M. R. Dadds. 2000. Attachment and coercive sexual behaviour. *Sexual Abuse: Journal of Research and Treatment* 12(1):3–15.

Snyder, C. R., S. T. Michael, and J. S. Cheavens. 1999. Hope as a psychotherapeutic foundation of common factors, placebos, and expectancies. In *The Heart and Soul of Change: What Works in Therapy*, ed. M. A. Hubble, B. L. Duncan, and S. D. Miller, 179–200. Washington, DC: American Psychological Association.

Stangor, C., and T. E. Ford. 1992. Accuracy and expectancy-confirming processing orientations and the development of stereotypes and prejudice. *European Review of Social Psychology* 3:57–89.

Stermac, L., and Z. Segal. 1989. Adult sexual contact with children: An examination of cognitive factors. *Behaviour Therapy* 20:573–84.

Teyber, E., and F. McClure. 2000. Therapist variables. In *Handbook of Psychological Change: Psychotherapy Process and Practices for the 21st Century*, ed. C. Snyder, and R. Ingram, 62–87. New York: Wiley.

Thornton, D. T. 2002. Constructing and testing a framework for dynamic risk assessment. *Sexual Abuse: A Journal of Research and Treatment* 14:139–53.

Wampold, B. E. 2001. *The Great Psychotherapy Debate: Models, Methods, and Findings*. New York: Routledge.

Ward, T. 2000. Sexual offenders' cognitive distortions as implicit theories. *Aggression and Violent Behavior* 5:491–507.

Ward, T., J. Bickley, S. D. Webster, D. Fisher, A. Beech, and H. Eldridge. 2004. *The Self-Regulation Model of the Offence and Relapse Process: A Manual: Volume I: Assessment*. Victoria, BC: Pacific Psychological Assessment Corporation. Available at www.pacific-psych.com.

Ward, T., and A. Beech. 2006. An integrated theory of sexual offending. *Aggression and Violent Behavior* 11:44–63.

Ward, T., and T. Gannon. 2006. Rehabilitation, etiology, and self-regulation: The Good Lives Model of sexual offender treatment. *Aggression and Violent Behavior* 11:77–94.

Ward, T., T. Gannon, and P. M. Yates. 2008. What works in forensic psychology. *Victimology* 15:183–208.

Ward, T., and S. M. Hudson. 1998. A model of the relapse process in sexual offenders. *Journal of Interpersonal Violence* 13:700–725.

———. 2000. A self-regulation model of relapse prevention. In *Remaking Relapse Prevention with Sex Offenders: A Sourcebook*, ed. D. R. Laws, S. M. Hudson, and T. Ward, 79–101. New York: Sage Publications.

Ward, T., S. Hudson, and K. France. 1993. Self-reported reasons for offending behaviour in child molesters. *Annals of Sex Research* 6:139–48.

Ward, T., S. M. Hudson, L. Johnston, and W. L. Marshall. 1997. Cognitive distortions in sexual offenders: An integrative review. *Clinical Psychology Review* 17:1–29.

Ward, T., S. M. Hudson, and T. Keenan. 1998. A self-regulation model of the offense process. *Sexual Abuse: A Journal of Research and Treatment* 10:141–57.

Ward, T., S. Hudson, and W. Marshall. 1995. Cognitive distortions and affective deficits in sex offenders: A cognitive deconstructionist approach. *Sexual Abuse: A Journal of Research and Treatment* 7:67–83.

Ward, T., S. Hudson, W. L. Marshall, and R. Siegert. 1995. Attachment style and intimacy deficits in sex offenders. *Sexual Abuse: A Journal of Research and Treatment* 7:317–33.

Ward, T., and T. Keenan. 1999. Child molesters' implicit theories. *Journal of Interpersonal Violence* 14:821–38.

Ward, T., K. Louden, S. M. Hudson, and W. L. Marshall. 1995. A descriptive model of the offence process. *Journal of Interpersonal Violence* 10:453-473.

Ward, T., R. Mann, and T. Gannon. 2007. The Good Lives Model of offender rehabilitation: Clinical Implications. *Aggression and Violent Behavior* 12:87–107.

Ward, T., and W. L. Marshall. 2004. Good lives, etiology, and the rehabilitation of sex offenders: A bridging theory. *Journal of Sexual Aggression* 10:153–69.

———. 2007. Narrative identity and offender rehabilitation. *International Journal of Offender Therapy and Comparative Criminology* 51:279–97.

Ward, T., and S. Maruna. 2007. Rehabilitation: Beyond the risk-paradigm. *Key Ideas in Criminology Series* (Tim Newburn, Series Ed.). London: Routledge.

Ward, T., J. Melser, and P. M. Yates. 2007. Reconstructing the Risk Need Responsivity Model: A theoretical elaboration and evaluation. *Aggression and Violent Behavior* 12:208–28.

Ward, T., and C. Nees. 2009. Surfaces and depths: Evaluating the theoretical assumptions of cognitive skills programmes. *Psychology, Crime, Law* 15:165–82.

Ward, T., D. L. L. Polaschek, and A. R. Beech. 2006. *Theories of Sexual Offending*. New Jersey: John Wiley & Sons.

———. In press. The ethics of care and the treatment of sex offenders. *Sexual Abuse: A Journal of Research and Treatment*.

Ward, T., and C. A. Stewart. 2003. The treatment of sex offenders: Risk management and good lives. *Professional Psychology: Research and Practice* 34:353–60.

Ward, T., J. Vess, R. M. Collie, and T. A. Gannon. 2006. Risk management or goods promotion: The relationship between approach and avoidance goals in treatment for sex offenders. *Aggression and Violent Behavior: A Review Journal* 11:378–393.

Ward, T., P. M. Yates, and C. A. Long. 2006. *The Self-Regulation Model of the Offence and Relapse Process, Volume II: Treatment*. Victoria, BC: Pacific Psychological Assessment Corporation. Available at www.pacific-psych.com.

Wegner, D. M. 1994. Ironic processes of mental control. *Psychological Bulletin* 101:34–52.

Welford, A. T. 1960. The measurement of sensory-motor performance: Survey and reappraisal of twelve years' progress. *Ergonomics* 3:189–230.

Wells, A. 2000. *Emotional Disorders and Metacognition: Innovative Cognitive Therapy*. Chichester, UK: Wiley.

Wells, A., and G. Matthews. 1994. *Attention and Emotion: A Clinical Perspective*. Hove, UK: Erlbaum.

———. 1996. Modelling cognition in emotional disorders: The S-REF model. *Behavior Research and Therapy* 34:881–88.

Williams, S. M., and A. Khanna. 1990, June. *Empathy Training for Sex Offenders*. Paper presented at the Third Symposium on Violence and Aggression, Saskatoon, SK.

Williams, J. M. G., F. N. Watts, C. Macleod, and A. Mathews. 1997. *Cognitive Psychology and Emotional Disorders*. 2nd ed. Chichester: Wiley.

Willis, G., J. Levenson, and T. Ward. In press. Desistance and attitudes towards sex offenders: Facilitation or hindrance? *Journal of Family Violence*.

Wilson, R. J. 2007. Circles of support and accountability: Empowering communities. In *Knowledge and practice: Challlenges in the treatment and supervision of sexual abusers*, ed. D.S. Prescott, 280–309. Oklahoma City, OK: Wood'n'Barnes.

——. 2009. Treatment readiness and comprehensive treatment programming. In *Building Motivation for Change in Sexual Offenders*, ed. D. S. Prescott. Brandon, VT: Safer Society Press.

Wilson, R. J., L. Stewart, T. Stirpe, M. Barrett, and J. E. Cripps. 2000. Community-based sexual offender management: Combining parole supervision and treatment to reduce recidivism. *Canadian Journal of Criminology* 42:177–88.

Wilson, R. J., and P. M. Yates. 2005. Sex offender risk management: Assessment, treatment, and supervision. In *Encyclopedia of Prisons and Correctional Facilities*, ed. M. Bosworth, 2:891–95. Thousand Oaks, CA: Sage Publications Inc.

Winn, M. E. 1996. The strategic and systemic management of denial in the cognitive/behavioral treatment of sexual offenders. *Sexual Abuse: A Journal of Research and Treatment* 8(1):25–36.

Wong, S., T. Witte, and T. P. Nicholaichuk. 2002. *Working Alliance: Utility in Forensic Treatment Programs*. Ottawa, ON: National Health Services Conference.

Wormith, J. S., and R. K. Hanson. 1991. The treatment of sexual offenders in Canada: An update. *Canadian Psychology* 33:180–97.

Yates, P. M. 1996. *An Investigation of Factors Associated with Definitions and Perceptions of Rape, Propensity to Commit Rape, and Rape Prevention*. Ottawa, ON: Carleton University, Unpublished doctoral dissertation.

——. 2002. What works: Effective intervention with sex offenders. In *What Works: Risk Reduction: Interventions for Special Needs Offenders*, ed. H. E. Allen. Lanham, MD: American Correctional Association.

——. 2003. Treatment of adult sexual offenders: A therapeutic cognitive-behavioral model of intervention. *Journal of Child Sexual Abuse* 12:195–232.

——. 2005. Pathways to the treatment of sexual offenders: Rethinking intervention. *Forum, Summer*: 1–9. Beaverton OR: Association for the Treatment of Sexual Abusers.

——. 2007. Taking the leap: Abandoning relapse prevention and applying the self-regulation model to the treatment of sexual offenders. In *Applying knowledge to practice: The treatment and supervision of sexual abusers*, ed. D. Prescott, 143–74. Oklahoma City, OK: Wood'n'Barnes.

——. 2009a. Using the good lives model to motivate sexual offenders to participate in treatment. In *Building Motivation to Change in Sexual Offenders*, ed. D. S. Prescott. Brandon, VT: Safer Society Press.

——. 2009b. Is sexual offender denial related to sex offence risk and recidivism? A review and treatment implications. *Psychology Crime and Law Special Issue: Cognition and Emotion* 15:183–99.

——. In press. Models of sexual offender treatment. In *Sexual Offenders: Classification, Assessment, and Management*, ed. A. Phenix and H. Hoberman. New York: Springer.

Yates, P. M., B. C. Goguen, T. P. Nicholaichuk, S. M. Williams, C. A. Long, E. Jeglic, and G. Martin, G. 2000. *National sex offender programs*. Ottawa, ON: Correctional Service of Canada.

Yates, P. M., and D. A. Kingston. 2005. Pathways to sexual offending. In *The Sex Offender*, ed. B. K. Schwartz and H. R. Cellini, 3:1–15. Kingston, NJ: Civic Research Institute.

Yates, P. M., and D. A. Kingston. 2007. *A companion text to the Casebook of Sexual Offending for use in scoring the Risk for Sexual Violence Protocol (RSVP)*. Victoria, BC: Pacific Psychological Assessment Corporation. www.pacific-psych.com.

Yates, P. M., S. Hucker, and D. A. Kingston. 2007. Sexual sadism: Psychopathology and treatment. In *Sexual Deviance: Theory, Assessment, and Treatment, (2nd ed)*, ed. D. R. Laws and W. O'Donahue. New York: Guilford Press.

Yates, P. M., D. A. Kingston, and T. Ward. 2009. *The Self-Regulation Model of the Offence and Re-offence Process: Volume III: A Guide to Assessment and Treatment Planning Using the Integrated Good Lives/Self-Regulation Model of Sexual Offending*. Victoria, BC: Pacific Psychological Assessment Corporation. Available at www.pacific-psych.com.

Yates, P. M., and T. Ward. 2007. Treatment of sexual offenders: Relapse prevention and beyond. In *Therapists' Guide to Evidence-Based Relapse Prevention*, ed. K. Witkiewitz and G. A. Marlatt, 215–34. Burlington, MA: Elsevier Press.

———. 2008. Good lives, self-regulation, and risk management: An integrated model of sexual offender assessment and treatment. *Sexual Abuse in Australia and New Zealand: An Interdisciplinary Journal* 1:3–20.

Young, J. E. 1999. *Cognitive Therapy for Personality Disorders: A Schema-Focused Approach*. Sarasota, FL: Professional Resource Press.